Gawin Douglas

The poetical works of Gawin Douglas, Bishop of Dunkeld

Vol. I

Gawin Douglas

The poetical works of Gawin Douglas, Bishop of Dunkeld
Vol. I

ISBN/EAN: 9783743373518

Manufactured in Europe, USA, Canada, Australia, Japa

Cover: Foto ©Lupo / pixelio.de

Manufactured and distributed by brebook publishing software (www.brebook.com)

Gawin Douglas

The poetical works of Gawin Douglas, Bishop of Dunkeld

THE POETICAL

WORKS OF GAVIN DOUGLAS,

BISHOP OF DUNKELD,

WITH MEMOIR, NOTES, AND GLOSSARY

BY JOHN SMALL, M.A., F.S.A.SCOT.

VOLUME FIRST.

EDINBURGH. WILLIAM PATERSON.
LONDON: H. SOTHERAN & CO.
MDCCCLXXIV.

TO

DAVID LAING,

LL.D., ETC.,

IN RECOGNITION OF HIS LABOURS IN THE VARIOUS

DEPARTMENTS OF SCOTTISH LITERATURE

AND ANTIQUITIES,

THIS EDITION

OF

THE WORKS OF GAVIN DOUGLAS,

BISHOP OF DUNKELD,

IS RESPECTFULLY DEDICATED.

PREFACE.

IT is a circumstance somewhat surprising that the long period of three centuries and a half should have elapsed between the death of the celebrated poet, GAVIN DOUGLAS, Bishop of Dunkeld, and the publication of this the first collected edition of his works. While the separate poems of the Bishop, which have been printed at intervals between 1553 and 1830, are fully described in the following Biographical Introduction, a few notes as to editions of his works formerly projected may not be uninteresting in this place. So far back as the year 1786, the indefatigable Scottish Antiquary, John Pinkerton, in his "List of all the Scottish Poets, with brief Remarks," (*Ancient Scot. Poems*, i. p. cxxv.) intimated his intention of editing the works of such as might be deemed *classic*, and, whose works would "be reprinted to the end of the English language." These he considered to be "Barbour; King James I.; Henry the Minstrel; Dunbar; Gavin Douglas; Sir David Lindsay; Drummond; in number seven." Pinkerton's multifarious labours no doubt prevented the fulfilment of this promise to the literary public. His intention, however, in regard to Douglas was "to reprint only the Palice of Honour, King Hart, and Prologs, &c., to Virgil," thus omitting the principal work of the distinguished author.

In 1806, however, there appeared an announcement by the well-known Edinburgh publishers, Messrs Constable, that the works of the Bishop were forthwith to appear in four octavo volumes, under the editorial superintendence of Sylvester Douglas, Lord Glenbervie. His Lordship was a lineal descendant of that branch of the great family of Douglas to which the Bishop belonged, and he made extensive preparations for the proposed work. Writing to Mr Constable on 20th June 1806, he says: "I should suppose the translation of Virgil would, printed in the manner of Sir W. Forbes' Life, &c., of Dr Beattie, make alone a larger quarto than either of his volumes, and the other poems, together with a life, historical and critical, a preface, and Ruddiman's Glossary *enlarged* (though our friend Chalmers' severity on poor Sibbald in his dissertation in the third volume of his new publication is enough to terrify one from that part of the undertaking) would make another—or perhaps the whole might be printed in four volumes of the size nearly of Tyrrwhit's

Chaucer. In the meantime I will immediately set about collecting materials. One MS. Mr Thomson will tell you I have heard of in England. Ruddiman appears to have used one which belonged to the College Library. Is that still forthcoming, and will the College allow me the use of it? Is there any MS. in the Advocates' Library or elsewhere in Scotland that you know of? Pray shew this letter to Mr Thomson, and procure and take the trouble to send me what information you can. Enquire if there exists anywhere any picture or print of Gawin Douglas."

The Records of the University of Edinburgh bear that on the 18th February 1807, permission was given to Lord Glenbervie, to borrow the two MSS. of the Translation of Virgil, preserved in its Library, and from various letters from his Lordship to Mr Constable, now in the possession of his son, Mr Thomas Constable, it would appear that Mr Henry Weber, the Editor of "Early English Romances" and other works (the amanuensis also of Sir Walter Scott), was employed to make the necessary collations.*

Referring to Mr Weber's connection with the proposed work, Mr George Chalmers, who had in 1806

* In 1809 Lord Glenbervie states, in a letter to Mr Constable, that he paid Triphook £23 for the four large interleaved volumes, to which two copies of the Virgil had been sacrificed, and which he had done by the advice of Mr Todd, the well-known editor of Milton's Works, &c.

published his well-known edition of the poems of Sir David Lindsay, writing to Mr Constable in August 1809 states, "I am glad that Mr Weber undertakes to relieve Lord Glenbervie from his distress. I presume that my Lord has agreed upon the plan which Mr Todd, you and I thought the only one: taking Ruddiman's copy as *the text* to be collated. A fictitious text like Tyrrwhitt's Chaucer will never do; but, taking the matter up on the other plan, Mr W. may get through in a month or two. It will give me pleasure to be kind to Mr Weber, and to give him every assistance in my power. I shall be glad to hear from you on your ultimate plan of Gavin Douglas, and I shall be the better enabled to help you forward."

In November of the same year, Mr Chalmers in another letter to Mr Constable remarks, "Weber will tell you better than I can write, in what a state of mind he left Lord Glenbervie on the subject of Gavin Douglas. My belief is that you will never see Gavin Douglas from his Lordship's hand. He seems to me to sink under the work, which was and is too heavy for his anvil. He feels this, yet is ashamed to confess that he is unequal to the task, and he is too high-minded to be advised. His dissertations on the Douglases, which might be spared, he finds a *bore*, now that a friend of yours has cut short the line of that assuming family. He grumbles in the gizzard when he thinks of this, and, like his great progenitor, Bell-the-Cat, he carries about a concealed dagger,—'Willing to wound, yet afraid to strike.' All this while your friend has been trying, as you may have heard from your H. and W. to help him in every possible way. But help and instruction are alike unwelcome to him. He has not yet made up his mind whether the language of Gavin Douglas be from the Anglo-Saxon or the Gothic of Scandinavia, and we tried in vain to convince him. He will make a new Glossary, without any previous preparation, instead of taking Ruddiman's or allowing W. to make him one. If he worked as hard, morning, noon, and night as your friend, he could not make such a Glossary in less than seven years. But considering his avocations I believe his task is hopeless. In saying all this, I endeavour to act with a proper regard to him and my usual kindness to you."

After the lapse of several years Lord Glenbervie, writing from New Park, Lyndhurst, on 25th April 1814, after stating that he had "entirely finished the first eleven Books of Gavin Douglas' Virgil, having transcribed every word with my own hand, and personally collated the two MSS. of the Edinburgh College Library," goes on to say:—

"I am therefore prepared to send you the Manuscript of any number of the Books already transcribed, which it may be convenient for you or the printer to have, but I must first enquire, whether he can answer for preserving the MS. entire and unsullied, and also a great number of short notes and memorandums written in pencil on the blank side of the leaves, and which, though not to be printed, contain material hints for notes. I must also add that, as there are to be at the bottom of each page of the general Prologue and First Book three series of notes, with literal and numerical references, one explanatory of the versification; the second containing the various readings, and the third the varieties of orthography, all of which will require the same minute accuracy which we expect to find in correct editions of the Greek or Latin Classics, a great number of revises will probably be necessary, and therefore it seems to me hardly practicable to print the book at Edinburgh within any reasonable time; I, who must be the ultimate corrector of the press, residing in London; it is therefore extremely to be wished that some printer resident here could be employed."

After an interval of more than two years, Lord Glenbervie, writing from Pheasantry, Tedding, on 25th November 1816, after stating that he had finished his collations of the MSS. and Editions of Virgil, says that he was "almost in a state to begin printing it, but as my plan is to give all Gavin Douglas' extant works, I have still to collate his poem called the Palace of Honour, and that ascribed to him also, called King

Hart, and also to write out the introductory historical and critical discourse on his life and writings which I mean to prefix, and considerably to enlarge Ruddiman's glossary to his edition. Till this is done therefore I should be unwilling that the printing of the text of his Virgil should be begun."

Thus, after ten years labour, it may be said that the projected edition fell to the ground, although much had been done by Lord Glenbervie to ensure the greatest possible accuracy in his text, while his account of the family of Douglas, which he proposed to prefix, would no doubt have been in the highest degree valuable.

In reference to the present Edition it may be proper to state that it was undertaken to form one of a series of the works of the early Scottish Poets in course of issue by the present Publisher; and it follows the works of Dunbar, Henryson, and Lyndsay, edited by Mr David Laing.

In Volume I.—which contains the minor works of the author, viz.: The Palace of Honour, King Hart, and Conscience—the first of these, The Palace of Honour has been reprinted from the Edinburgh Edition of 1559, carefully collated with the First edition, printed at London in 1553. The other poems, King Hart and Conscience, have been carefully collated with the originals preserved in the Lauderdale MS. in the Pepysian Library, Cambridge, and the Editor's thanks are due to the Fellows of Magdalen College for the facilities they afforded for this purpose.

In Volumes II.-IV.—which contain the author's best known work, the translation of the Æneid of Virgil—the text has been derived from the Elphynstoun MS. in the Library of the University of Edinburgh. This valuable MS. so nearly resembles the MS. belonging to the Library of Trinity College, Cambridge, (which was edited by Mr George Dundas, afterwards Lord Manor, for the Bannatyne Club), that it was thought desirable to use it for the text rather than to reprint the Cambridge MS. In this way some advantage has been gained; a new MS. has been printed, and various readings have been given of passages which are difficult to follow.

In the Biographical sketch of Bishop Douglas, use has been made of information derived from Canon Myln's 'Vitæ Episcoporum Dunkeldensium,' the life by Bishop Sage prefixed to Ruddiman's well-known edition of the Translation of Virgil, and the elegant life and criticisms on the works of Douglas by the late Dr Irving. Many letters and papers, however, have been inserted which are printed from transcripts of the originals preserved in the British Museum, the Rolls House, London, and the General Register House, Edinburgh. Of these one or two are given in the original Latin, as they are printed for the first time, others, which are accessible in the "Epistolæ Regum Scotorum" and Theiner's "Vetera Monumenta," have been translated.

The Glossary has been prepared with care, and besides older authorities, the chief sources of information have been Dr Jamieson's well known Scottish Dictionary, the excellent works by Halliwell and Wright on English Archaic words, various Glossaries of the Dialects of the North of England, and the most recent French, Anglo-Saxon, Danish and Icelandic Dictionaries. As the Glossary has been made very comprehensive, comparatively few explanations of difficult words or passages are given in the Notes appended to each volume.

In conclusion, the Editor has to offer his warmest acknowledgements to Dr Charles Wilson, James Richardson, Esq., Advocate, and the late Professor William Stevenson, D.D., by whose encouragement the work now finished was undertaken, and who throughout have taken the greatest interest in its progress. To the Rev. Walter W. Skeat, he is much indebted for a thorough revisal of the text of King Hart, at the Pepysian Library, Magdalen College, Cambridge, and for several valuable notes on the Palace of Honour, and on the greater part of the Glossary, which he carefully read.

To the following gentlemen, who have furnished the Editor with valuable assistance—David Laing,

Esq., LL.D., John Stuart, Esq., LL.D., the Rev. R. Demaus, London, the Rev. Professor Dickson, Glasgow, the Rev. Thomas Dickson, General Register House, Edinburgh, the Rev. Professor Mitchell, St Andrews, Andrew Gillman, Esq., London, and Mr James Gordon, of the University Library, his best acknowledgements are also due.

UNIVERSITY OF EDINBURGH,
1st January 1874.

CONTENTS.

LIST OF ILLUSTRATIONS.

VOL. I.

VOL. II.

VOL. III.

ERRATA IN VOL. I.

Page lxxxv. line 13, *for* Lege *read* Sege.
,, 136, ,, 28, *for* wo *read* no.

BIOGRAPHICAL INTRODUCTION.

THE family of Douglas produced so many men connected with the leading events in the history of Scotland that there was a popular rhyme :—

> " So many, so good as of the Douglasses have been,
> Of one surname were ne'er in Scotland seen."

Like most of the old Scottish families, the origin of the Douglases has been carried back to very ancient, if not to fabulous times. Their chroniclers, however, agree that Sholto, chief of the Brigantes, was the first who took the name of Douglas, about the year A.D. 767. The legend is, that Solvathius, king of Scotland, having been attacked by Donald Bane, a bloody battle ensued. The king's army were beginning to give way, when Sholto with his son Hugh and followers arrived, and made such a furious onset upon the rebel army that Donald Bane was slain and his army scattered. Hume of Godscroft adds:—"The king being desirous to know of his Lieutenants the particulars of the fight, and inquiring for the author of so valiant an act, the nobleman being there in person, answer was made unto the king in the Irish tongue (which was then only in use) Sholto Du Glasse, that is to say, Behold yon black, gray man, pointing at him with the finger, and designing him by his colour and complexion, without more ceremony or addition of titles of honour. The king, considering his service and merit in preserving his crown, and delighted with that homely designation, rewarded him royally with many great lands, and imposed upon himself the name of Douglas, which hath continued with his posterity until this day."*

According to George Chalmers, this distinguished house, long the rival of royalty, dates from a period no further back than the year 1170. Arnold, who was Abbot of Kelso from 1147 to 1160, granted some lands on Duglas† Water in Lanarkshire, "Theobaldo Flamatico," to Theobald the Fleming, and his heirs. As this grant of Arnold to Theobald is the first link in the chain of title deeds to Douglasdale, this family, says Chalmers, must therefore relinquish their original domain, or acknowledge their Flemish origin.

The branch of the family from which Bishop Gavin Douglas was descended was that of William, first Earl of Douglas, whose son George (by Margaret Stewart, Countess of Angus and Mar) in 1389 had a grant of his mother's Earldom of Angus, and afterwards married the youngest daughter of King Robert

* History of House of Doug. p. 3. † Duglas means Black Water.

III. The fifth Earl in succession,* and the father of the Poet, was Archibald, surnamed from a well known incident in Scottish history "Bell the Cat," but generally styled the Great Earl of Angus. This Earl had four sons by his wife Elizabeth, daughter of Robert, Lord Boyd, Lord High Chamberlain of Scotland; viz., George, Master of Angus, Sir William Douglas of Glenbervie, Gavin, Bishop of Dunkeld, and Archibald Douglas of Kilspindy.

The place of Gavin's birth has not been ascertained. The powerful family to which he belonged had extensive estates in several of the counties of Scotland, and one of his biographers remarks that the place of his birth might have been the Castle of Douglas in Lanarkshire, Tantallon Castle in East Lothian, Dudhope in the district of Angus and neighbourhood of Dundee, or Abernethy in Strathearn, in all which places the Earls of Angus had residences. The date of his birth was the end of the year 1474, or the beginning of 1475.

Of his early years little is known. It has been stated that his father was very careful of his education, and caused him to be instructed at home in the liberal arts and sciences. But if it be true that old 'Bell-the-Cat' gave

> "Thanks to Saint Bothan, son of mine,
> Save Gawain, ne'er could pen a line—" †

then the progress of the youthful Gavin must have been due in a great measure to his own natural talent for acquiring knowledge. At that period it was not

* According to Hume of Godscroft, the sixth.

† Marmion, canto vi. 15.

unusual for the youth of the higher classes to be sent to monasteries to be instructed by learned monks, among whom, it may be mentioned, Ferrerius, who taught in the Abbey of Kinloss, was one of the most learned men of his time in Scotland.

The Universities of Glasgow and St Andrews were the only two then existing in Scotland, and the latter was the one selected for the completion of the education of the youthful Poet. In the Registers of the University of St Andrews his name occurs in the lists of *Incorporati*, or those who were matriculated in the year 1489. The usual course, then as now, extended over four years, and was devoted to the study of philosophy, including rhetoric, dialectics, ethics, and physics. In the middle of the third year students were allowed to present themselves as candidates for the Degree of Bachelor of Arts; and for this purpose those who had completed or determined their course of study during the course of the *trivium*, were called *Determinantes*, such as acquitted themselves satisfactorily being confirmed as Bachelors by the Dean of Faculty. The *Licentiati* were a class further advanced, and denoted that they were prepared to take their Master's Degree. For obtaining this a more extended examination took place before they were *laureated*, or received the title of Master of Arts, which qualified them to teach the seven liberal Arts.*

Douglas seems to have enjoyed the advantage of a full curriculum, as his name occurs among the Determinantes in 1492, and among the Licentiati or

* Knox's Works, by D. Laing, vol. i., p. 555.

Masters of Arts in 1494. This extended course of study, from 1489 to 1494, is perhaps to be explained by the circumstance that he was intended for the Church; and as, by a law of king James I., no one could become a Canon or Prebendary in any Cathedral or College Church unless he were a Bachelor in the Canon Law or had taken a Degree in Theology, he felt it necessary to improve himself in learning in order to obtain any preferment in his profession. Bishop Sage thinks it not improbable that he was encouraged and incited to a diligent pursuit of his studies by the example of his sovereign, James IV., who was only two years his senior; and that, after finishing his course of studies at home, he went abroad that he might further improve himself by conversation with great and learned men, and by observation of the laws and customs of other countries.*

Shortly after leaving the University he entered into priest's orders, and, with his high family connection, he did not wait long for preferment. In 1496 he had a grant of the teinds of Monymusk in Aberdeenshire. In the Record known as the Registrum Secreti Sigilli, the following entry occurs:—"Lettre for Master Gawane of Douglas.—A Lettre direct to Schireffis in that pairt to charge thaim to command in the Kingis naim the Lord Forbess, Duncan Forbess, and Duncanis wife to haf na intromitting with the teyndis of Monymusk perteyning to Master Gawane of Douglas, and to charge the parochinaris to obey to the said Master Gawane in the paying to him and

* Warton states that there is undoubted proof that his education was finished at the University of Paris.—*Hist. of Eng. Poet.*, vol. iii. p. iii.

his factouris of the samyn tendis according to the Priouris lettres, and to summond the said personis to the xij day of October next to cum, etc.

Ex deliberatione Dominorum Concilii."*

Two years later he obtained from the king a presentation to the parsonage of Glenquhom when it should become vacant by the resignation of Sir Alex. Symson. He also became Parson of Lynton and Rector of Hauch, now known as Prestonkirk, but at what date is uncertain.

This last preferment has been frequently misunderstood by his biographers. Canon Myln, in his "Vitæ Episcoporum Dunkeldensium" where he mentions Gavin Douglas, styles him Rector de Hawche. By misreading this word, Bishops Sage and Keith state that he was Rector of Heriot, a parish sixteen miles south of Edinburgh. Later writers supposed it to signify Hawick in Teviotdale. We are indebted, however, to Dr Laing for the true reading of the original MS. which is Hawche, an ancient synonym of Linton or Prestonhaugh, better known now as Prestonkirk, near Dunbar. This is borne out by the earliest MS., of his Translation of Virgil, where he is expressly styled, "Provest of Sanct Geylys Kyrk in Edinburgh, and Person of Lyntoun in Lothian." †

* Reg. Mag. Sig., vol. i., fol. 16.

† In 1342 the church of Linton or Prestonkirk was annexed to the collegiate church of Dunbar. In the subsequent appointment of Douglas by the Pope as Bishop of Dunkeld in 1516, he was formally allowed to retain his former promotions, "una cum retentione beneficiorum, viz., Prepositure de Edinburgh et Prebende de Dunbar," *see* post p. liii. In his will reference is made to teinds due to him from Aberlady and Preston, while there is no mention of Hawick. Sir John Ireland was Parson of Halch in 1423,

The present church of Prestonkirk is built on an obviously ancient site, slightly elevated above the alluvial haugh-land on the northern bank of the Tyne, and at a distance of half-a-mile from the linn or fall of the river where the modern village of Linton is situated. It is probable that at an early date there may have been a chapel at Linton as well as at the Haugh: hence the alternation of the names of Lyntoun and Haugh in ecclesiastical records may have had its origin in the different description of tithes payable from the two places to the pluralist incumbent.

The right of presentation to this church in ancient times was attached, as it is still, to the barony of Hailes, which, before 1451, belonged to the Earl of Douglas. It then passed into the hands of Hepburn, the first Lord Hailes, whose son was an adherent of the Boyds; and as a daughter of this house was mother of Gavin Douglas, his early presentation to the parsonage and rectory was not unnatural.

In the retour of the barony of Hailes in 1652 in favour of George, Earl of Winton, there is included "advocatioun of the Church of Hauche, called the Prebendarie of Linton." *

It was about the year 1501 that Douglas was appointed Dean or Provost of the Collegiate Church of St Giles in Edinburgh. This church, which was on a more extensive scale than any other of the kind in

when a suit was heard in Parliament regarding his right of Pasturage in the Moor of Preston.—*Charters of the Coll. Church of St. Giles*, p. xxxiii.

* Inquis. Ret. Haddington, No. 233. This interesting information with reference to Hawche has been supplied by the Rev. John Struthers, minister of Prestonpans.

the country except the Chapel-Royal at Stirling, supported a Provost, a Curate, sixteen Prebendaries, and seven other officers, on the original foundation, to which was superadded a vast number of altars and chaplainries, some of them richly endowed.* The appointment placed him in a situation of dignity and emolument, and he appears to have retained along with it his other benefice. While he filled these less elevated stations, he devoted himself to literature, and began to compose those works which have rendered his name famous. In his allegorical poem, The Palice of Honour, finished in 1501, he concludes with a poetical address to King James IV., in which, with what may be called false modesty, he refers to his own "vulgair ignorance," and says,—

> "Ressaue this roustic rurall rebaldrie
> Laikand cunning, fra thi puir leige vnleird." †

This, Dr Laing thinks with much probability, may have induced the king to bring the author from his rural occupations, when the opportunity presented itself, to the more congenial atmosphere of a city. The precise date of his appointment is uncertain; but in the Treasurer's accounts it appears that the sum of nine shillings was paid on the 11th of March 1502-3, to John Ireland, Vicar of Perth, "for writing off the citations and letters on Maister Gawin Douglas, Prowest of Sanct Gelis Kirk." ‡

Between the period when he received his preferment to St Giles', and 1513, when the disastrous battle of

* Lee's History of the Church of Scotland, vol. i. p. 47.
† See p. 81. ‡ Historical Notices of St Giles' Church, p. xxxiv

Flodden was fought, the notices of Douglas are very scanty. Several deeds signed by him as a witness while he was Provost have been discovered, and on one or two occasions the Provost of St Giles' Church is recorded as having been present at meetings of the Lords of Council.* We are, therefore, left to conjecture that he was either too busy with his literary labours to give much attention to public business; or that he was travelling abroad, and making interest for himself at the Court of Rome, which then interfered with the bestowal of all ecclesiastical dignities.

It seems probable that at this period he translated Ovid, a performance which is now lost, but which must have helped to render such work the more easy to him, for in January 1512, he began the translation of Virgil, and finished this, the best known of his writings, in July 1513.

* Whilst Provost of St. Giles, Gavin Douglas seems to have taken much interest in the due celebration of the religious services of that church, as we find that on the 17th of February 1511, he, along with the Prebendaries, having taken into consideration that the mass of the Most Holy Blood of our Lord Jesus Christ had been omitted to be solemnized on that day, bound themselves in order to guard against any such omission in future, to have that mass celebrated every fourth week day, under a penalty of 2d payable by each Prebendary failing to attend on a week day, and of 4d. for every such failure on a feast day, and in the event of the mass not being celebrated at all, they bound themselves to pay by way of fine, one merk to the common good of the fraternity of the Holy Blood.—*Charters of St. Giles, Edin.*, p. lxxx.

In September 1512 Master Gavane Douglas, Provost of Sanct Gelis Kirk, was one of a great Assize when an Act was passed anent "the resset of Rebellis, and Personis being at our souerane Lordis horne."

The first honour he received after this literary feat was the freedom of the City of Edinburgh, which was conferred upon him without charge. On the 30th of September, 1513, the Town Council records bear—"Ult° Sept. j^{m} v^{c} xiij° Archibald Dowglass, Erll of Anguis, Prouest; *ane Priest made Burgess.* Magister Gavinus Dowglass Prepositus Ecclesie Collegiate Beati Aegidii hujusmodi Burgi effectus est Burgensis pro communi bono ville, gratis."

This honour, it has been surmised, may have been conferred in compliment to his father, who was Provost of the City, but it may quite as probably have been due to his literary fame. It is well known that at a somewhat later period, the Town Council of Edinburgh not only gave the freedom of the City to Ben Jonson, when he came to visit Drummond of Hawthornden, but entertained him at a "banequett," which cost, according to the Treasurer's books, tua hundreth, tuenty-ane pund, sex schillings, and four pennyis.*

The year 1513, when the Battle of Flodden was fought, was an eventful one for Gavin Douglas. His father, the old Earl of Angus, had prudently advised King James IV. not to enter into battle with the English. He found, however, his counsels disregarded, and left the field. His eldest son, George, Master of Angus, and his second son, Sir Wm. Douglas of Glenbervie, were killed along with their Sovereign. The Earl, hearing of the fatal issue, retired to St Mains, a religious house in Galloway, where he died of grief in the beginning of 1514.

* Proceedings of Society of Antiquaries of Scotland, vol. iii. p. 206.

While Queen Margaret was in great distress after the loss of her husband, Gavin Douglas, as the Provost of St Giles' Kirk, was one of the Lords of Council appointed, with one or two others, to remain daily with her, for the purpose of giving her comfort and advice in the trying circumstances in which she was placed.

Archibald, son of George, Master of Angus, who now succeeded to the Earldom, was remarkable for his personal comeliness, and for his ambitious spirit. Although a youth he was already a widower, having been, according to the evil custom of the time, married in his childhood. This young nobleman attracted the attention of Queen Margaret, the youthful widow of James IV. and sister of Henry VIII. of England, who had been appointed Regent of Scotland during the minority of her son James V. The Queen encouraged his addresses, and was furnished by Lord Drummond with an excuse for following her inclination, on his representing how much she required the aid of the powerful Douglas clan and their allies to aid the English party in Scotland against the Duke of Albany and the French faction. Without waiting for the general consent of the nation, she was married to him on the 6th of August 1514 (hardly eleven months after the death of James IV.) at one of the altars in the church of Kinnoull, by the Earl's near relation, John Drummond, Parson of Kinnoull and Dean of Dunblane.*

* By this marriage she had a daughter, Lady Margaret Douglas, born in 1515, who married Matthew, fourth Earl of Lennox, whose son, Lord Darnley, husband of Queen Mary, was father of King James VI.; consequently the Royal Family of Great Britain derive their descent from this lady. Her tomb, near that of her daughter-

From the intimate connection which existed between the Queen and his family, Douglas now hoped for speedy preferment, and everything seemed to favour his views.

In the Battle of Flodden many warlike ecclesiastics were slain along with the King. Among them were the youthful Archbishop of St Andrews, Alexander Stewart,* the king's natural son, a man of very promising talents, who also held the Abbacies of Aberbrothock and Dunfermline, together with the Priory of Coldingham; George Hepburn, Bishop of the Isles; the Abbots of Kilwinning, Inchaffray, Cambuskenneth, Glenluce, with many others. While there were thus many rich benefices vacant, Douglas was, about June † 1514, appointed by the Queen, Abbot of Aberbrothock, and he aspired to still higher preferment.

Although the Scottish kings had maintained their prerogative of appointing persons chosen by themselves to vacant Sees and Abbacies, the consent of the Pope was an indispensable form to complete an election. With so many vacancies to be filled up, it is not surprising that warm contests and intrigues should have arisen concerning them, not only in Scotland, but at the Court of Rome.

The Queen wrote the following letter to the Pope, requesting the confirmation of her appointment of Douglas to the Abbacy:—

in-law, Mary, Queen of Scots, forms one of the most interesting monuments in Westminster Abbey.

* Educated under the celebrated Erasmus.

† His name as "Postulat of Arbroth" appears in the Sederunt of the Lords of Council of 2d June 1514.

To Leo X., the Supreme Pontiff.

Most holy Father, blessed governor of the Church. Among the benefices now vacant in this kingdom, which we have often recommended your Holiness to confer upon persons nominated by us according to the apostolic privileges conferred upon us to that effect, is the Abbey of St Thomas the Martyr of Aberbrothock, of the Benedictine order, in the diocese of St Andrews, which Abbey is designated for a man highly acceptable to us, Mr Gavin Douglas, foremost in rank among the nobles of this kingdom, second to none in literature and morals, who already presides over the Monastery by our ordinary authority as Oeconomus, [or administrator of its revenues] nor would his family permit him to be deprived of that office; in fact his extrusion could only be accomplished by superior force, or if accomplished at all, could only be so at no small risk. On that account, Holy Father, we again and again entreat that, shewing special favour to the man above mentioned, who is worthy not only of the Abbacy, but of the highest ecclesiastical authority, even the Primacy, you would favourably incline to our request and recommendation in his behalf, and grant to him the Monastery designed for him, and commit the same to his care and administration, until you have elevated him to higher ecclesiastical preferment. This we earnestly entreat, and have taken upon us to beg from the clemency of your Holiness. Holy Father, farewell, &c.*

On the 5th of August, the day before her marriage with the Earl of Angus, the Queen wrote, in the name of her infant son, James V., to the Pope, intimating the appointments necessary to be made to fill up the vacant Sees.

To Leo X. the Supreme Pontiff.

Most holy Father, blessed Governor of the Church: We have repeatedly, though in vain, written to you, that

* From orig. in Epist. Reg. Scot., vol. i., p. 183.

as the Roman Pontiffs in granting letters appointing to vacancies in Cathedrals and Abbeys have been accustomed to wait till they received the requests of other kings and princes, that persons suitable for the respective kingdoms and faithful to the sovereign might be selected, they granted not merely by verbal obligation, but by bulls, a delay of eight months to the kings of Scotland and their descendants, on account of the sentiments of sincere devotion and firm fidelity, which they, in critical emergencies, have shown to the Roman Church. By these obligations and bulls the pontiffs were to confer and promote to sees and benefices exceeding in value 200 ducats according to the royal request; as in former years the then Pontiff Julius did not appoint to sees even when vacant by death within the city of Rome, without consideration of the letters of the king our father; and for having received benefits from his son, our late dearest father, he conceded in return the royal privileges. And we having formerly written to your Holiness when our most serene deceased father, most dutiful to the holy See, was prematurely taken away from us, and we, whilst an infant of one year old—still, in fact, in our cradle,—being called to the crown by the nobles of the kingdom, then particularly needed your protection, that entering upon the government in our infancy we might the more peaceably and securely reign. This result would be greatly promoted by conferring the sees and benefices that may become vacant in this kingdom on persons selected by us. For the greater sees and benefices cannot, consistently with our own safety and that of our kingdom, be conferred on persons different from those nominated by our sovereign authority; because the ecclesiastical order, the first estate of the kingdom, is so superior to the others, that Prelates and Abbots, our chief counsellors, enjoy the highest offices of the government, and the greatest weight in the deliberations on affairs of state, and the custody of the royal person belongs to the

Archbishop of St Andrews by ancient custom, as the king our grandfather, when quite an infant, and in circumstances of much peril, having been intrusted to the charge of the then Archbishop of St Andrews, was thus enabled to enjoy a long and happy life and reign. From considerations of this kind it follows that not only the presence of an Archbishop, but even his zealous services are due and necessary alike to a youthful sovereign and to the kingdom. And since your Holiness had frankly declared in briefs delivered to us by your envoy Balthazar on 4th October 1513, that your Holiness would be wanting in no effort necessary to promote the quiet of the kingdom and the dignity and advantage of the Royal infant and the Queen his mother; therefore we implore you in the most urgent manner, by your paternal goodness to your son, for the sake of the quiet of the kingdom, and especially by your regard for our safety, that our foster father, the present bishop of Aberdeen,* a prelate distinguished for judgment and experience, be transferred to the Archbishopric of St Andrews; that George, Abbot of Holyrood, of the order of St Augustine, be appointed bishop of Aberdeen; that Patrick, Abbot of Cambuskenneth of the same order and diocese, be promoted to the Abbey of Holyrood; that the foresaid Abbacy of Cambuskenneth be given, *ad commendam*, for life, to the reverend father, Andrew, Bishop of Caithness; and that the other monasteries be given in terms of our letters, as follows, in this manner, Arbroath to Gavin Douglas, Dunfermline to James Hepburn, Inchaffrey to Alexander Stewart, Glenluce to the Bishopof Argyle, Coldingham to David Hume, who are among the chief nobility of the kingdom. If your Holiness do this, and preserve the privileges of our ancestors to us, still but a royal minor, you will not only lead us to consider that from our earliest infancy we have been under great obligations to the Holy See and your Holiness, but you will give consolation to the Kingdom now mourning the loss of

* William Elphinstone.

the late King, and will do much to restore it to a position that will enable it to acquire glory and reputation. For our Parliament lately came to a resolution that a contrary course could not be tolerated in an emergency like the present, when king, kingdom, and privileges were alike imperilled, and all here have come to the conclusion that we can as little dispense with our beloved Archbishop recommended by us, as consent to the dismemberment and partition of the kingdom. Wherefore we earnestly entreat that your Holiness will grant our prayer, and will favourably receive the letter of an infant king, and grant this favour, which at an advanced age we may the more amply repay in that deference to your See which has characterized the Kings of Scotland, and your Holiness will render us a most devoted son to you by your benefits conferred on us, who will endeavour to repay such personally, and by our influence with the kings our relatives. We bid your Holiness farewell. From our town of Perth the 5th of August 1514.*

Aberbrothock or Arbroath, the most valuable of the Scottish Abbeys, had been held *in commendam* by George Hepburn, Bishop of the Isles; but although Douglas was postulated to it, and signed letters and papers under this designation, his nomination, as will be seen by the sequel, was never completed.

With his nephew married to the Queen Regent, it might naturally be expected that Gavin would have thus met with little interruption in his advancement to the highest dignities of the Church. Far different, however, was the result. This precipitate match was the cause of troubles and vexations to him which were only terminated by his early death.

The Scottish nobility were filled with indignation

* From orig. in Epist. Reg. Scotorum, vol. i., p. 197.

at the prominence of the Earl of Angus, and broadly stated that the Earl, as the head of the house of Angus, was already great, that the Queen's marrying him had made him greater still, and that, if her authority as Regent were to be continued, her husband's power would be so excessive as to endanger the peace and safety of Scotland. An indication of the popular feeling is given in a contemporary Diary, where it is stated that "all the court was rewlit by the Erle of Angus, Mr Gawin Dowglass, and the Drummonds, but nocht weill."

On the 18th September 1514, about a month after the marriage, Gavin appeared at a meeting of the Lords of Council and gave in a commission in his favour from the Queen "to compear for her in Dunfermline, and except against the Lords of Council, and make protestations and appeal in her behalf, and do everything needful for her." And much she needed his assistance; for at the same meeting the Lords resolved that the Duke of Albany be sent for as Governor of Scotland, and declared that the Queen, by her marriage with the Earl of Angus, had "tynt the office of Tutrix to the King her son, and shall cease from using the same in time coming, and shall not intromit with any matters pertaining to the crown." The general dissatisfaction was so strong that the Lords of Council sent the Lord Lyon-king-at-arms to inform Angus, that he must forthwith appear before the Lords to answer for his boldness in marrying the Queen without their assent and recommendation.

When the Lord Lyon, Sir William Cumming, went

into the royal presence to deliver officially the summons, he found the Queen supported by her spouse and his maternal grandsire, Lord Drummond. He demanded to be admitted, not to the presence of the reigning sovereign, but simply to "my lady Queen, the mother of his Grace our King." This, says Miss Strickland, was a terrible dereliction, the fruits of her recent deposition by the Council. It produced great irritation among the Queen's partisans; so much so, that when the herald approached the Earl of Angus to announce that he was summoned before the National Council, Lord Drummond gave him a box on the ear.*

These proceedings indicate a condition of great anarchy in Scotland. The Queen retired to Stirling and Perth, while the Parliament ruled at Edinburgh. She trusted that her brother, Henry VIII. (who was quite complacent at his sister's marriage), would aid her in establishing her failing power; she was at the same time anxious for an opportunity of being revenged on the Lords of the Scottish Council, who had stopped her dower-rents, and almost went the length of treating her and her supporters as rebels.

An act was committed at this time, designed apparently with the twofold purpose of shewing contempt for the authority of the Lords of Council, and promoting the advancement of Gavin Douglas. James Beaton, Archbishop of Glasgow, and Lord Chancellor of the kingdom, had expressed his strong disapproval of the second marriage of the Queen. He was now summarily arrested at Perth by the

* Queens of Scotland, vol. i., p. 107.

Earl of Angus, and deprived of the Great Seal of Scotland, which was then handed over by the Earl to the keeping of his uncle Gavin Douglas.

On the 21st September the minutes of the Lords of Council bear—"The Lords ordains that a letter be written under the King's Signet requiring Gavin, Postulat of Arbroth, to deliver the keyis of the Grete Sele fra him to James, Archbishop of Glasgow, Chancellor;" and further, "The Lords decretis that the Clerk of Register sall deliuer fra him the Grete Sele to my Lord Archbishop of Glasgow, Chancellor, because the samyn was taken fra him vnorderlie."

Notwithstanding these minutes which, considering the circumstances, seem rather mildly worded, the "Postulat" retained the title of Chancellor for several months. On the 14th of November of the same year his name occurs appended to a state paper as "Gawinus *Cancellarius*."

To add to the confusion, Henry VIII. now claimed the office of Protector or Governor of Scotland, and on the 14th of November letters were sent by the Lords of Council to the Pope denying any right or title of the king of England to such an office.

The letters were to the effect that the Lords "are informed that the king of England makes his writing to the See of Rome, calling himself Protectour and Governour of Scotland, which are not founded on veritie; certifying to his Holiness and the College of Cardinals that the said king of England, nor none of his predecessors, was ever Protectour and Gouernour of Scotland, and they neuer consented thereto, nor will euer admit him to the same; and therefore beseech his Holiness and College of Cardinals that they give no faith thereto, for eschewing of great inconueniencies that may follow thereupon."

Henry, finding it impossible to arrange matters favourably for his sister's interest in Scotland, at last endeavoured to persuade her to convey herself and her young sons to England. He well knew how much Scotland would be injured by the detention of its sovereign in England, as had happened in the case of David II. and James I. This scheme was promoted by Adam Williamson, a Scottish ecclesiastic, in the employment of Lord Dacre, Warden of the English Marches, as a confidential envoy in the English interest at the Court of Henry. Williamson used all his endeavours to gain the Queen's consent, and also strove to obtain the co-operation of Gavin Douglas in the matter. To Margaret he held out the prospect that her son might be declared heir-apparent to the English throne; to Douglas was displayed the promise of whatever Scottish benefices he pleased through the influence of Henry at the Court of Rome.

Williamson's letters to Douglas and the Queen are as follow—

Adam Williamson to Gavin Douglas.

This is the fryst letter that I send in Scotland with Schir James Ynglis, Secretary to the Quene.

MY LORD,—efter all dew recommendacioun plesse yt you to vnderstand that sen the second day off Nouembre, on wiche I presentytt the Queneis lettre to the Kynggis Grace off Ynglond, hyre derest brother, I haffe sollicited the

Quenys materis with the Kyng and hys Lordys of Consell with the moost diligens that vas possible to me to do. I found euer his Grace and his Consell nerly inteirly sett to the synguler vell and deffens off his sister the Quene and his derest nevois the Kyng and the Prince of Scotland. The Kyng and his Consell persewitht by the Quenys lettris sent to hym that she and hir chyildryn and hir husbond the Earl of Angus beyn in gret danger and lyke to be lossyt by the in[im]es the rebell Lordis off Scotland withowt his help and succours wiche var to his gret dyshonour. My Lord, I ensur you the Kynggis Consell has settyn ofter to take good dyreccion for the well off the Quene and hyr childryn and husbond than for any other mater sen my fyrst comyng in to Ynglond. The Kyng and his Consell has sent now sens Cristmes an vysse clerk off his Consell, and me also to the Lord Dacre, and has chargytt the said Lord Dacre on his allegians to consell, succour, and helpe the Quene, hir childryn and husbond to the vttermest off his power, becawsse he is a notable vysse lord and nechtbour, and off kyn to my Lord of Angus. The Kynggis Consell and the said Lord Dacre also thynkis nessesary and expedient to the Quene to avoid all dangers off hir enimys to resort shortly to the marches of Ynglond with hir two sonys, the Kyng and the Prince off Scotland, and vytht hir husbond my Lord of Angus, othyr to Carloil or to Penrytht, the myd marchis, or the est marchis wher yt shall plesse my Lord of Angus, and ther to kep ther hussold with the Quene and hir sonys, the Kyng and the Prince; and the Kynggis Grace her off Ynglond to furnyshe my Lord of Angus all thynggis necessary, mony or men, Scottis or Yngles, or boytht, to subdeu the rebell Lordis of Scotland; for iff the Kyng shuld raysse his gret riall arme men vold thynk that he vold take the rewme off Scotland in his own handdis, wiche I knaw well he not entendytht, bot only that his newois be obeyyt, and that good justys be kepit in Scotland to ther profet [and] to the vell of the rewme of Scotland. Yff the Quene and hir chyldryn come in Ynglond for succour all Yngles men will ryse with hyr to the distruccioun off hir enimes, and the Kyng and his brother shall get the hartis off Yngles men, soo that if it happyn the Kyng to depart withowt yshew, his newoy the Kyng of Scotland shall succed to the crone off Ynglond, and off this shall come mor good and vell to bothe Ynglond and Scotland than tung can tell. Schir James can informe you in this mater to whome yee shall gyff credens; yff the Quene tack this vays and be rulyt be the consell of her derest brother off Ynglond, Scotland shall multiplie in grace and ryches, and iustys shall be kepyt; and Frans shall neuer defeytht vs more, wich vas the detht of the King and off the Lorddis. The Frens men now mokis and scowrnys Scottismen for ther labour. My Lord, wher can the Quene and hyr childryn be so sure as with the noble Kyng off Ynglond, hir brother and ther derest vnkyll; yff he shuld not entrett them vell all the world vold cry owt on hym, and also it war agens hym selff, wherfor lat not the Quene forsaik this gret and kynd offer off hyr derest brother the Kyng in no vysse, yff ye lowffe hir and your blood. And wher ye writ to me to haff a salff condyt, it nedis not, for yee or eny off youris may come and be welcome to the Kynggis grace of Ynglond as to the Castell off Dowglas; how be yt ye shall [haf] a salfe condyt shortly. My Lord, I beseche you gyff credens to my writtyng, for yff I shulde dysymull with the Quene my mastres and suffrane, or with the Kyng my nateff prince, or with my Lord of Angusse, to whom all my frenddis beyn servanttis, or with your Lordshipe my most synguler good Lord, it var vorthy that I war drawyn with vyld horss. I am come off a trew stok and shal be tren to al them that shall trust in me; and in especiall to my suffrein the Quene, to your blood with the grace off owr Lord, who euer preserue you; writtyn the xx day off Januarij.

Tuus obsequentissimus familiarius,

ADAM WILLIAMSON.

My Lord Dacre has delyueryt to Schir James iij letteris wiche var direct to fals Panter the Sacrittary, wherin yee may see that Murray has gettyn the gift off all the best benifices of Scotland. Yff the Quene folow the Kynggis consell, as I haff vrittyn, Murray shal be prevyt a tratour, and yee shall haue what benefices that yee desyre in Scotland.

My Lord ewyn now wils I vas vrittyng this copy, thynkkyng to haue vryttyn it ageyn *in mundo*, ther come a post to the Lord Dacre, and tuyk hym a letter from the Consell, wiche shewis that the Kyng of Frans is ded, and that the Duyk is on the see, wherfor it is nedful to mak hast iff ye thynk to saue the Quene and hir childryn, my Lord off Anguse, and your frenddis. *

Adam Williamson to Gavin Douglas.

This is the copy of the second lettre wryttyn to the said Postulat off Arbrotht delyuer this day to Scotland.

My Lord.—I haff raseyvyt a lettre from the Quenys Grace and iij other from your Lordshipe, with on masse off lettris dyrect to Master Ihon Berry in Flandres the xxvj day off Januarij, wryttyn in Sanct Ihonston the xxij day off the same monetht; And wher the Quenys Grace and yee wryttis that hyr Grace with hyr chyldryn and husbond cannot resort to the merchys off Ynglond acordyng to the desyre and consell off hyr derest brother the Kyng of Ynglond, and hys vyse Consell, wiche studys for the only vell and suite of hys sister the Quene and her chyldryn his derest nevoys, I am ryght sory and voo therfor. I dred soyr that and the Quene and yee doo not efter the avysse and consell

* *Indorsed.* 1515, 20 January, Adam Williamson. The K. of England's care of the K. of Scotts and the Q. his mother. My Lo. Dacres a notable wise man commanded to advise her. The K. of Scotts heire to the Crowne of England. MSS. Brit. Mus. Caligula. B. VI. fol. 113.

off the Kyng hyr derest brother it shall twrn hyr, hyr chyldryn, and husbond to ower gret danger and preiudice for euer; I know vell that the Quene has no sure frenddys in Scotland but only my Lord off Angus and hys familier seruants; as for the other Lorddis that takys hyr part now ther is no trust in them, bot to day a frend to morn a foo; gyff the Quene be in danger and haff the veyker part they wyll leyff hyr, and than is to layte to repent. My Lord, I beseyk you traist not to myche in your awn wytt, take the sure vay and leyff the vnsure. Yff the Quene, hyr chyldryn, and husbond com in Ynglond all the Lorddis off Scotland wilbe feyne to resort to hyr and to obey hyr, or ellys thei man nedis cheysse som other land to dwell in. The Kynggis entent is only, I knaw vell, that his sister and hyr husbond shalbe obeyyt in Scotland on to the tyme that his nevoys come to age, acordyng to ther faderis testament and will. For Goddis sack my Lord doo efter the Kynggis consell and yee canot doo amysse, I ensure you your own contremen wyll do with hym agens you. I knaw more than I dyd when Schir James vas heyr. Take good tent to my vorddis. I knaw well, it is trew that I say, thei labour agens you heyr; preveyn them or yee bee vndoyn; yff yee soo doo yee shall haff in Scotland what promocioun that it shall plesse you to haff, and Murray shall be a sclayff as he begane. Yee writ that I haff not spokyn agens hym heyr; yes, in good feytht I haffe put hym in such dysfavour her with the Kyng and hys Consell that, and he be gottyn in Ynglond, he shall neuer profett hys frenddis, nor hurt his foys. Remembyr my Lord that the Quene has put hyr and hyr chyldryn in your handdis; yff yee folow the consell and avysse off hyr brother the Kyng yee canott doo amysse, as I haue vryttyn afore, your blood is maid for euer. And yff yee doo the contrary she may cowrs the tyme that euer she mellyt with your blood. Yff the Quene and hyr chyldryn come in Inglond by gret possibilitie hys sonys salbe the grettest Scottis men that euer vas. I knaw mare than I will vritt in this mater. I knaw vell that hyr comyng in Ynglond shall be for the perpetuall vell off boytht the rewmys, and specially for the rewme off Scotland, for withowt this vays ther shall neuer justice be kepyt in Scotland, but it shal be a land off rubry, and come to fynall dystruccion. Yff the Quene forsayk this kynd offer off hyr derest brother I fer that she shall soyr repent heyrefffter. Remembyr that heyr is vysdom, strentht, honour, ryches to deffend hyr; in Scotland is pouerte, dysseyte, and vnsure frenddis not able to resyste. I ensure you the Kyng of Ynglond is belowyt and dred off his Lorddis and subiettis more than vas euer eny of hys predyssessurs in so short tyme; ther is no rewme able to vithstond hys malys at this tyme, and wher that yee writ that yee bee susspect that ye will come in Ynglond, me thynk that shuld gyff you the mor occasion to come; who that says agens you now wold say yff ye var in Ynglond that yee dyd vysly soo to doo. As for the devysse and maner off your comyng, yff the Quene, my Lord of Angus and yee specially agre therto, my Lord Dacres wyll take upon hym to bryng you all sayff to Carleyll, under the forme and maner as he has writtyn to you; gyff credens to hym for your awn vell, I counsell you; as for the masse of letteris directe to Master Ihon Berry in Flandres my Lord Dacres has send it vp by post with all dylygence to the Kyng, and the lettre that yee vrat to me with all for the better expedicion. I dowt not bot the Kynggis writtyng for your promocion shall be at Rome before the masse. As for the Kyng of Frans he is deid without eny dowt; it is comon her in euery mannys moutht; ther is a monk come hedyr that was in Frans when he deydt, wiche was on new yerris day; wherfor me thynk that yee shuld mak hast for your own surete *juxta illud Lucani—"Tolle moras, semper nocuit differre paratis."* Wher yee writ that ye ned not to fle the land, yee fle not the land but yee come for surte of the Kyng and his moder the Qwene, and off your self and frenddis, and for the vell off all Scotland. I dar on me vithowt dyssymulacion

[say] gretkynggis has doyn such lyk not beyng in such danger as yee bee in; blame not me thoucht I speke playn, for I haff beyn in the gretest danger that eny man mycht be in and schape with his lyff. I haffe lossyt my gooddis that I shuld haff leyff apon in my age for the Quenys sayk and yourris. I set not by all this a pont and the Quene and yee wilbe rulyt be cousell and doo vell. Sey not but I haff varnyt you off euery thyng efter my power, reson and vytt; gyff the Quene and yee doo not vell, as God forbed but yee shuld, my days wil be short in this vorld. My Lord I haffe teyn a letter that the Lord Flemyng send out off Frans in Scotland sen Schir James depart frome me; he can informe you of what he writtis. I vald haff send the lettre to you but I cannot haff it for certen cawsis. Schir James knawis the sentens theroff.

tuus ADAM WILLIAMSONE.*

Adam Williamson to the Queen.

This is the copy of the Quenis Lettre delyveryt this day to Scotland.

Madame. I beseche your Grace at the reuerens off God for your awn synguler vell, and for the promocion off your chyldryn my natyff Kyng and Prince to folow the avysse and consell of your derest brother the Kyng of Yngland, wiche entendytht only for your vell and the promocion off your sonys. Your enemys labours to mak pes with your brother the Kyng; I haff seyn their vrittynggis sen Schir James departytt fra me; what incoveniencssis may fall to your hwrt theroff your Grace may soyn vnderstond. Preveyn your enemys and doo after your brotheris consell, and yff yee soo doo I ensure you Madame by gret possibilite your sonnys shalbe the grettest Scottismen that euer vas. I haffe seyn a lettre off the Lord Flemyngis awn hand send owt off Frans. I haff writtyn to Schir James now at this

* Mus. Brit. MSS. Cotton. Caligula, B. II., fol. 303.

tyme the sentens theroff; he can informe your Grace off that mater; see hys lettre also, Madame; see the lettre that I haff writtyn to my Lord the Postulat of Arbrotht; in eny vysse merk euery vord well and doo therafter and yee cannott doo amysse; yff yee doo not after the Kyng your derest brotheris awysse and consell yee and all we that takys your part shalbe vndoyn; in whome shuld yee traist but in your brother, wiche is moost able to dyffend you agens your enemys. Madame, I ensure you he is the best belowyt prince and moost dred with lowff of his Lorddis and sugettis off eny prince [in] the vorld to my vnderstondyng. Perdon me Madame thoucht I writ playne to your Grace. I spek of trew hart, I haffe beyn in so gret danger and lossyt my gooddis also for your sack * and in your servys, that yff eny thyng shuld come to you but good, as God forbed, my days shuld be short in this vorld. Yff your Grace prospare and doo well, I car not for all my labour and losse; off on pont I am and shalbe trew and feythtfull to your Grace, with the help of God, who euer haff your Grace in his holy proteccion. That is and shalbe my dayly preyer, writtyn the xxvij day off Januarij.—Your humble Chaplen and Bedeman,

ADAM WILLIAMSONE.†

To the scheme proposed in these and other letters of Adam Williamson the Queen expressed herself well disposed, as may be gathered from the following letter to that ecclesiastic:—

To our traist Clerk Master Adam Williamson.

Traist Clerk, we grete you hartly wele, and we haf ressauit your cunsell with the instructions fra our familiar Clerk Schir James Ingliss, and considerit the samyn, quhilk

* The allusion here is to Williamson's having been shipwrecked when on some business of the Queen.

† *Indorsed*—Adam Williamson to the Q. of Scotts. Advising her to followe the direction of K. H. VIII. Mus. Brit. MSS. Cotton. Caligula, B. III., fol. 152.

was rycht plesant to ws yff it hald bene possible to doo efter the said counsell; bot as your self may wele consider the inoportunitie that was quhen you war here, and sethin fer mare, and that folk of this land ar sa inquisitife that sic thing may nocht be performit without grete knawledge to sindry folkis, and there is nane that I may trust bot my husband and his uncle quhilk ar rycht glad therto yf it mycht be—praying to be diligent in all matteris as you hafe bene in tyme past, in vther thingis gife credens to the Appostolate and Schir Jamys writingis. At Perth, the xxii day of Januarye.*

MARGARET R.

In the midst of these plots an opportunity occurred for the preferment of Gavin Douglas. William Elphinston, Bishop of Aberdeen, to whom the Archbishopric of St Andrews had, with general assent, been offered, died on the 25th October 1514, and it was commonly reported that his successor would be Andrew Forman, Bishop of Moray. The Queen, however, lost no time in recommending Douglas for this the highest dignity of the Church in Scotland.

She also obtained the assistance of her brother Henry, who wrote the following letter to the Pope on his behalf:—

Henry VIII. to Pope Leo X.

Most holy Father, after most humble commendation and devout kissing of your blessed feet: We have been informed that the Queen of Scotland, our dearest sister, has lately most urgently recommended to your Holiness a venerable man Mr Gavin Douglas and has entreated that you would be pleased to promote him to the Archbishopric of St Andrews, the Primacy and Metropolitan See of the Kingdom of Scotland, in accordance with the ancient privileges

* State Papers, Scotland, vol. i., No. 12.

granted to that Kingdom by the predecessors of your Holiness in regard to appointing only those persons who have been recommended to vacant benefices by the Sovereigns of Scotland for the time being. We well know that this Mr Gavin is distinguished by nobility not only of birth but of mind, evinced by his extraordinary learning conjoined with prudence, modesty, probity, and a great zeal for the public good: We therefore consider him worthy to be strongly recommended to your Holiness. Accordingly we most urgently entreat that you would find some way under divine providence by which the said Gavin may obtain the foresaid Metropolitan See and thereby your Holiness will confer honour on a most deserving man, will consult the advantage of the Primacy, and will place a great stone, in fact the corner stone in laying the foundation of peace and concord, and besides will do a most acceptable service to us. In regard to the Bishop of Moray, he not only is wholly unlike the said Gavin in nature and temperament, but we know for certain that he will never be admitted to the foresaid Archbishopric of St Andrews. Wherefore we think it most deeply concerns the inborn piety of your Holiness and your most excellent purpose for the promotion of universal concord not only to eliminate the seeds and causes of controversies which may occur between kingdoms and nations, but to prevent dissentions within the bounds of individual countries, and not permit the native vetch and tares to grow, but rather to eradicate them completely. No course could be more acceptable than this to God, more conducive to the highest interests of nations nor more glorious to your Holiness, to whom we wish long and ample prosperity. From our Palace at Greenwich the 28th of January 1514-15.

Your Holiness' most devoted and dutiful son, by the grace of God King of England and France and Lord of Ireland.* HENRY.

* Translated from the original in Theiner's Vet. Monumenta, p. 513.

Buchanan informs us that Douglas took possession of the Castle of St Andrews, relying on the splendour of his family, on his own virtue and learning, and on his having been nominated by the Queen.

The Queen, however, was unable to maintain him in possession of his new dignity. John Hepburn, Prior of the Regular Canons of St. Andrews—whom Buchanan describes as a powerful, factious, and cunning priest—had been Vicar-General of the Diocese, and manager of its revenues during the vacancy. He induced his own monks to elect him to the Archbishopric, under the pretext of an ancient right which the monastery, in conjunction with the Culdees, had once enjoyed. Hepburn then expelled the servants of Douglas from the castle, and fortified it with a strong garrison; nor did the Earl of Angus, with a party of his retainers, succeed in an attempt to recover the possession of the stronghold.

The affairs of Scotland were at this time closely watched by the Lords of Council of England; and Thomas, Lord Dacre of Gilsland, Warden of the English Marches, sent to them frequent reports of events that were passing in Scotland. In his letter of 27th November, addressed to the "Lords of the King's most Honorable Counsaile," Dacre says:—

My singuler good Lordis, in most humble wise I commende me vnto your good Lordships, pleas it the same to witt that on the xix day of this moneth at xi of the clok in the night I receyvid your full honorable lettres by post, togiddir with a pacquit of lettres to the Queen of Scottis, which I send hir be a seruant of mine, with deligence, which com to hir in Striveling on Wednisday the xxii day of the said moneth, and therupon she has made ansuer in writing as may appere in a pacquete of lettres which I send here enclosed (she durst not make superscription). Verely she has been evill intented, and was brought and convoyed from Striveling to Edinburghe be the Erl of Arane and the Chamberlain, and there receyvid by the Chancellor and the Lordis of Counsaill in hoppe of her hertis ease and fulfilling hir mynde. Albeit when as they had hir there, they yode there from hir waies, and soo she withdrew hirself be wisdome from Edinburghe to Striveling on the said Teuesday and Therle of Anguse with hir.

The Prior of Sanct Andrews, callit Hebburn, with all his perttakers has laid siege to the Castell of Saint Andris belonging to the Bisshop wherin hir seruantis lies. My said seruant sawe when as the lettres of the same newes were delivered to hir; Wherupon the erle of Anguse with all hir household servants to the nomber of 60 horses rode towardis the reskue and wairned all there perttakers to the same. . . . There was neuer soo mickill myschefe, robbry, spoiling and vengeance in Scotland then there is nowe, without hoppe of remedye, which I pray our Lord God to continewe, who preserve you my singuler good Lordis. At Kirkoswald the xxvii day of Nouember.

Yours with hyest seruise,

THOMAS L. DACRE.*

Although the Queen and the Earl of Angus were filled with indignation at these violent proceedings,

* Brit. Mus. MSS., Calig., B. i. 154. In the indorsation of the letter the number of the Earl of Angus' retainers is stated at 600. "The Q. of Scottes hardly used by the nobilitie of Scotland. She returned from Edinburgh back to Striveling with the Erle of Anguiss, who with her household seruantis to the number of 600 horses hasteth to releeve her seruantis lying in the castle of St Andrewes being ther besieged by the prior of St Andrewes."

they were powerless to assist Douglas against Hepburn, as the latter had the support of some of the principal nobility of the kingdom. Before, however, any further steps could be taken in favour of Douglas, a new and more formidable aspirant for the high appointment appeared in the person of Andrew Forman, Bishop of Moray, and Ambassador of Scotland at the French Court. Forman was descended from the family of the Formans of Hutton, in *vico de* Berwick. He was a man of versatile talents, long busied in the subtleties of negociation, and one who often pursued his own advancement at the expense of his country. "He blended," says Pinkerton, "his private avarice and ambition with every foreign negociation. His concessions to England procured for him the rich priory of Coldingham; his influence at the French Court the Archbishopric of Bourges; and by his interest at the Court of Rome, the influence of the King of France and the Duke of Albany, he now obtained a Bull from the Pope for the Archbishoprick of St. Andrews. He was at the same time invested by the Pope with the Abbeys of Dunfermline and Aberbrothock, and all the other benefices held by the late Archbishop."*

Forman was openly charged before the Scottish Lords of Council that he "had, against the privilege granted by the Pope to the King and his successors, purchased the maist part of all the benefices vaikand by thaim that deceisit in the feild in Northumberland be sinister information made to his Haliness contrar the commonweil of the realm; and he re-

* Hist. of Scot., vol. ii., p. 85.

quired the Lords to assist in defence of the King's privilege.

In answer to this, Mr Robert Forman, Dean of Glasgow, in name of his brother, the Archbishop of St Andrews, Primate and Legate of Scotland, protested and represented that the said Archbishop had purchased the said benefices for observing the privileges of the realm, so that he, as a Scotsman, should bruik them rather than Italians should impetrat the same." *

Forman, although so successful at the Court of Rome, was afraid to publish in Scotland the Papal Bulls, until he prevailed on Lord Home, Warden of the Scottish Marches, by bestowing on his brother the Priory of Coldingham, to undertake the support of his cause. This powerful nobleman enabled the Archbishop to appear at Edinburgh with 10,000 men-at-arms, where the requisite ceremony was performed. Forman, with his host, then hastened to St Andrews to take possession of his See, but found Hepburn, the Prior, sufficiently prepared for his reception. So considerable a garrison had been placed in the Castle and the Church, that Forman was unwilling to hazard an attack, and deemed it prudent to settle his claims by an amicable negociation. It was finally stipulated that he should be put in quiet possession of the Primacy, and that Hepburn should receive a yearly allowance from the Bishopric of Moray, and should retain such rents as he had already levied from the Archbishopric of St Andrews.

Thus, partly by violence, and partly by intrigue,

* Acta Dom: Concil. 25th January 1515.

Douglas was disappointed both of the Abbacy of Aberbrothock and the Primacy of Scotland.

In January 1515, however, by the death of George Brown, Bishop of Dunkeld, another opportunity occurred for the promotion of Gavin Douglas. The Queen was at the time at Perth, with such of the Lords of Council as were of her party, and being informed of the vacancy, she, with the advice of these Lords, presented him to the See of Dunkeld in the name of the King.* There was, however, already a powerful competitor for this See. The death of Bishop Brown, which happened at his castle of Cluny, had been reported at Dunkeld some time before it actually happened, and Andrew Stewart, Prebendary of Craig, and brother of John Earl of Athole, got himself postulated Bishop by such of the Chapter as were then present. Although he was not capable of being fully elected according to the canon law, as he had not arrived at the office of a sub-deacon, yet he was supported by all the enemies of the Queen and her husband. Canon Myln informs us that the Earl called the Canons together and requested them to make choice of his brother, and in the mean-time to put him in possession of the Episcopal palace. Some of the Canons being his relations, and others afraid, they agreed to do all that was desired. "This affair," says Myln, "went the more easily, because the Earl was very powerful, and could defend everybody belonging to the church from plunderers of every kind."

* For the names of the lords of her party, see p. lxiv.

On the 17th January the following letter was sent from the Queen to the Pope :—

Beatissime Pater, paucis supra diebus Reuerendo Patre Georgeo Dunkeldensi Episcopo viam vniverse carnis ingresso, illa Cathederalis ecclesia pastore, proch dolor, orbata est, verum nos ne tot presulum insperata et repentina morte hoc regnum vacillet, occurrere cupientes ad Sanctitatem vestram confugimus, virum sane omnium scientia et probitate insignem, illustrem Sacerdotem Magistrum Gawinum Douglas, de maiori regni comitali domo genitum, et nobis in primis charum, surrogandum et promouendum ad jam nuper defuncti Episcopi sedem commendamus. Obnixe rogantes ut hunc hominem, vita moribus et nostris litteris tociens ad altiora commendatum, tandem nostris multiplicatis precibus, si laudatissima viri merita non sufficiant, saltem ad hanc Cathedram sublimetis, vnde melius sedi quam viro prouisum fore speramus, neque vnquam existimare possimus Sanctitatem vestram ejus mentis fore ut nobis et hoc regno ab apostolica sede indulta priuilegia infringere velit, aut insueto ordine Scotum quemuis nostris absque commendaticiis assumere ad Prelaturam, cum per breve suum et oratorem qui hactenus apud nos degit pollicita sit se nobis et regno in nullo offuturam; quod firmissime credimus observari per Sanctitatem vestram, quam et optata concedere et felicissime valere cupimus. Ex oppido nostro de Perth decimo septimo Januarii.

E. V. S. Deuoti oratores Jacobus Scotorum Rex et einsdem Testamentaria Tutrix Gubernatrix Custos et Mater Regina.*

* Mus. Brit. MSS. Calig., B. ii., fol. 364.—It is followed by the copy of another letter in favour of Douglas : —" Vnde sanctissimo litteris nostris commendatum fecimus egregium illum et illustrem sacerdotem omnium scientia et virtute preditum, pacis cultorem, justicie apicem, et nobis charissimum Magistrum Gawinum Douglas."

On the 18th and 21st of January Douglas wrote the following letters to Adam Williamson and Lord Dacre, in which he mentions the steps that were being taken for his advancement.

In the second of these letters, dated the 21st of January, Douglas expresses his opinion of the danger and impropriety of the proposal of Henry VIII., made through Adam Williamson for the removal of the Queen and her young sons to England, for which he has been blamed. In fact, Douglas had views which were quite incompatible with such an arrangement. In a letter of Lord Dacre, afterwards introduced, we find that he was scheming to get himself made guardian to the young King James V. and his brother, in place of the Archbishop of St Andrews, who, both by ancient custom and by the will of James IV., was entrusted with this duty.

Gavin Douglas to Adam Williamson.

Brother Master Adam I commend me to yow in my harty wyss, and ye sall knaw that sen my last wrytyng of Perth the last day of December, quhilk I trust ye haf seyn, and hard forthar all thingis be Schir James, the Byschop of Dunkelden is decessyt this Monunday the xv day of January; and becaus yon euyll myndyt Byschop of Murray trublys all our promociones, and has sped Sanct Andris to hymself wyth Dunfermlyng, Arbroth, legacy and other faculteys, quhilkis ar nedfull and allways man be retretyt, yit nocht the less sen syk debatis and contrauersyes ar costly and doutuus, in all auentour the Quenys Grace, my self and frendis thinkis nedful I be promouit to that Seyt quhilk now is vacand and but pley, and an rycht gud Byschopry of rent and the thryd Seyt of the realm. And to that effect hes the Quenys Grace wryttyn for me to the

Papis Halynes, and Cardinalis, quharof ye sall wyth this ressave the copy to solyst syk lyke wrytingis fra the Kingis Grace hyr brother. And be nocht hyr lettyris obeyt in the curt of Rome ye solyst euyll your memoryall, less than the Kyng wyll do nocht for his systyr, as I knaw the contrary bayth in deyd and wryte, I dout nocht bot ye wyll solyst my materis als trewly as your awyn, thocht the Qwenys Grace had nocht wrytyn for me. And as I wrate to yow laytly the promotion of hyr seruandis and frendys is hyr weylfar and autorising, and hyndyryng of hyr aduersaryes, I pray yow at a word sped thir lettyris to Flandris as thai ar dyrectyt, and sped wyth thaim the Kingis wrytyngis. And gyf ye kowth do sa mekyll as causs the Kyng mak a post therfor, I war indyttyt to hys Grace and yow for euer—a wyse frend is soyn chargeyt.

Item ye sall knaw that mi Lord Erll of Huntlye was heyr at the Quenys Grace and wyll go hyr way, and bryng mony of the other Lordis to hyr opynion, and wyth hys avyss scho hes mayd proclame a Parlyament in this toun to be haldyn and begyn in this toun the xii day of March quhar we trast tyl haf all thyngis redressyt. I wald nocht ye leyt the Byschop of Murray nor yon Duk steyll hyddyr by yow as now latly his clerk Master John Sawquhy hes doyn, and landyt at Leyth furth of a Franch schyp, and brocht wyth hym the bullys of Sanctandris and publyst the samyn on hys maner in Edynburgh this last Twysday the xvi day of Januar, bot I beleve he sall nocht haf possessyon this yeyr. Nedfull it is, and that is a speciall punct of your memoryall to caus the Kyng writ to the Kyng of Frans heyrupon to the effect that by hys ways the Kyng, our souerane Lord, be nocht hurt in his priuylegis and faculteys, for that war to byreif hym hys croun. Nor that hys gud systyr the Quenys Grace [be] ocht therby mynyst in hyr autorite, bot raythar mantenyt and defendyt by hym in the samyn. And that hes beyn doyn by hys wrytyngis in the contrary other in fanouris of yon Byschop of Murray or ony otheris that the samyn be hys ways and solystation be reuersyt agan. that therby na preiudice may happyn to the Kyng nor this hys realm, now in tyme present nor yit in tyme cumyng by euyll exemple, so that syk doyng nor attemptatis be na preparatyve to otheris in tyme to cum. And kowth the Kyng solyst his brothyr of Frans to haf that Byschop rendyrryt to hym othyr be pollycy or otherways, that he mycht thereftyr be demanyt as efferis, all thir thre realmis I trast war brocht to grete rest, for he is and hes bene the instrument of mekyll harm, and I dreyd sall yit be of mayr and he be nocht suybbyt. Tent to hym and yon Duyk gif the Kyng thar luffis the weylfar of hys syster and mast tendyr nevois and als the quyet of hys awyn realm. Hast ansuer agayn and be solyst as ye haf beyn in tyme by passyt, and God keyp yow: of Perth the xviii day of January wyth the hand of

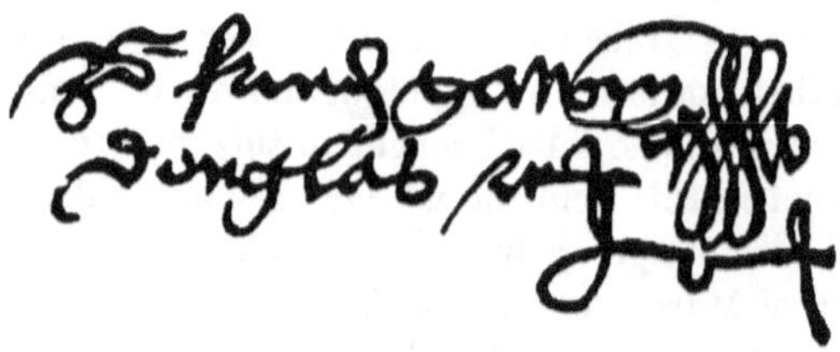

Postscript to the letter, written in a small hand.

The Queyn thynkis ye haf beyn ouer slewthfull, that sa lang tym ye beand in Ingland ther hes beyn nocht doyn nother in Rome nor the curt of Frans aganys yon wykkit Byschop of Murray and byddis yow mend that falt. Item at ye solyst the Kyng hyr brothyr that na lettres pass throu hys realm na fra that belangis ony Scottisman, less than he haf hyr speceall wrytyngis and request therfor, ffor syk lettres hes ellis doyn gret harm, and was the first caus of all the truble anent the promociones and is daly a preparative to solyst yon Duyk of Albany to cum hyddyr. Remembyr my salue conduct and sped the samyn to me as I wrat to yow latly. And gif ony of my wrytyngis concernyng the Queyn cum furth of Flandris or Rome to your handis, na fors bot the Kyng se or knaw the contentis ther-of, at thai may be the bettyr and mar hastyly sped to hyr Grace or me, for I wayt hys Henes wyll stop nain of hyr lettriz nor myne quhilk salbe cum to hys honor and avayll.*

Gavin Douglas to Adam Williamson.

Brothyr master Adam, I commend me hartly to yow, and hes ressauyt your layt wrytyng and credens fra your companzeon Schir James, and be ye suyr the Queyn and we all wald be glad to follow the Kyngis mynd thar, and thankis hys Henes als lawly as we may of the grete enteyr luf and kyndnes profyrryt and schawyn to vs, for the quhylkis we beyn addettyt to be hys trew seruandis, befor all otheris, our allyegans to our soueran Lord hys nevo only exceppyt. Ye may weyll considdyr it is nocht to us possybyll that ye devys, for albeyt my Lord and I wyth other frendis mycht cum to tha partis quhen we plesyt, it suld nocht be possybyll to carry the Kyng nor his brother thyddyr, thocht perauentour and that full hard wyth gret defyculte and nocht honestly we mycht bryng the Queyn thyddyr in habit onknawyn and dysagysyt, bot nayn other ways; And therfor ther man be thocht sum other remed, for my wyt kan nocht attayn quhow that may be at this tyme. And als we be in na syk danger at we neyd leyf the cuntre, I wrat to yow layt that the Kyngis wrytyngis wald stanch all this debayt, ffor I trast thai suld be als weyll obeyt heyr as in Lundon wyth the mast party of the Lordis. Lat nocht the Kyng spar thar feyr, that and he wald cum wyth hys army or send hys pyssans in this realm and declar to the pepyll hys actyon war to haf justyce and gud rewll, and to caus the Kyng hys nevo and the Queyn hys systyr be obeyt as thai aucht, bot cummand on this wyse and notyfyand the sammyn to our commonys be proclamation bot he suld fynd mony to tak his part, for I assur yow the pepyll of this

* Brit Mus. MSS. Cott. Calig., B. ii., fol. 357.

realm ar sa oppressyt for lak of justyce by thevys, rubry and other extortiones that thai wald be glayd to leyf ondyr the gret Turk to haf justyce. Ye wryte that the Kyngis Grace thar hes wrytyn twyse to Roym aganys Glasgw, bot I had leuer he had wrytyn aganys the Byschop of Murray, and yit nyedlyngis he man wryte aganyst him and [haif] all hys promotion reuersyt, lyk as at mayr lenth the Quenys Grace hes wrytyn to the Kyng hyr brother therapon. Master Adam, brother, forzet nocht to solyst and convoy weyll my promotyon to Dunkeldene, as ye luf me, for I haf gevyn the mony quhar ye bad me. Lat se quhou ye kan convoy syk a mater for your frend, and I sall do mekyll, bot I sall sp[eke] wyth yow in Lundon or Pasch, for I haf mony devyses that I wald fayn enclos to the Kyng thar, quhilkis I wyll nocht wryte. And gyf it be possybyll that ther may be fund ony tyme to perform the Kyngis plessour and desyr as ye haf wrytyn wyth Schir James, I sall do my devoir and full best to convoy that mater at all punctis; bot I kan nocht hastely beleyf as yit quhou it may be, les than the Kyng wald cum hymself in this realm, and than mycht he do quhat hym lykyt, for he wald fynd lytyll or na resystans; and be ye souer the grettest of our aduersareys crynys hym gretly at this hour, on syk wyse that thai wald geif mekyll of thair walzeand to haf hys fauouris. Gyf the Kyng of Frans be ded it is rycht euyll for bayth thir realmys. Bot heyr is arryvyt a Franch schyp the xv day of this moneth instant, quhilk proportis na thyng therof, and therfor I wondyr quha suld haf schawyn my Lordis of Consell thar syk tythyngis. Gyf we had money, I trast we suld debayt weyll enewch our aduersaris in thir partis quhyll the sommyr sesson, quhen the Kyng mycht moyf quhat army hym lykyt, and than I trast also we salbe mar pyssant than we ar now. I am surly informyt furth of Frans the Duyk dysponys hym nocht hydder quhyll this nyxt moyn, less than this decess of the Kyng of Frans caus hym preueyn the tyme, and yit I trast the Kyng thar and hys wyse Consell hes prouydyt mayr warly in all auentouris, so that the Dalphyn is als weyll bund to observe the pece and all punctis therof as was the Kyng, and I trast he dar nocht brek the trewys nor pace astablysyt, to send the ilk Duyk agayn hys oblysyng; And gyf he wald lat ilk frend mak pace wyth other quhyll we be all reuengyt on Frans for God knawys quhat thai haf doyn to vs. I haf gud hope and is in convoyng a mater of dyscord amang our party aduersary, on syk wyse that I trast ye sall heyr quhow this promotion now impetrat be yon dyssatfull Byschop of Murray sall turn to our weyll, and cause bayth hym and yon Duyk cum in euyll consayt ouer all this realm, quhilk man nedwayes redund to our profyt, and sall purches vs ma frendis, and I dred nocht bocht quha sa euer be Kyng in Frans he salbe mayr glad to haf pace and amite wyth the Kyng of Ingland than hys Grace sal be to except the samyn. I pray yow schaw this wrytyng to my Lord Dacre and the contentis therof to the Kyngis Grace. God keyp yow. Wyth my hand in hast at Perth, the xxi day of Januarii.

Tuus totus GAWING DOUGLAS, &c.*

Gavin Douglas to Lord Dacre.

My Lord I commend me to your L. in my mast hartly wyss, and as towart the Kyngis desyr and instructiones send to the Queuys Grace with Schir James Inglys hir Henes hes wrytyn heyr wyth ansuere to the Kyng hyr broder and to your Lo. and in sum hart as I kowth thynk eftyr my lytill wyt. I haf wrytyn tyll Master Adam to be schawyn to your L. and to the Kyngis Grace thar quhow soyn he sall cum to his presens and be ye suyr the Queuys Grace, my Lordis and we all wald be als glad to fulfill the Kyngis desyr gif it was to vs possibyll as wyth hand or mynd may be deuysit, and kan nocht sa mekyll as we beyn addettyt for

* Indorsed—"Gawen Douglashe to Adam Williamson" and addressed in Bishop Douglas' handwriting "To his trast frend Mast. Adam Wyllyamson."—Brit. Mus. MSS. Cott. Calig., B. ii., fol. 356.

our part rendyr thankis to his Heynes therof, and not the les of a thing he salbe suyr that our seruys salbe hys befor all othyr men leuyng, our allegens to our soueran lord hys nevo alanerly exceppit. My Lord ye sall knaw ther is an Byschop latly deid in this land callyt the Byschop of Dunkell, and for alsmekyll as thir othir benefyces be now in pley and debaitt be this Byschop of Muray, therfor the Quenys Grace my soueran lady has wrytyn for especiall writyngis to the Popis Halynes for my promotioun therto, and forther hes by thir hyr wrytyngis oblyst the Kyngis Grace hyr brothyr to wryte and lawbor effectuusly to the samyn effect. Quharfor I beseyk your L. that the sayd lettres mycht be convoyit wyth deligens and gyf your gud assistans and commendation to the Kyng for me, sen our houssys are of the auld allyat, and mekyll tendyr aquentans and kyndnes hes beyn betwyx tham of lang tym as approvyt weyll be my grandfather at the sege of Nawart, and I beleyf that ay mayr and mayr tendyrnes and amyte sall daly incres amongis thaim. Gud war ye suffyryt na other lettres to haf passag throw the realm but syk as salbe send fra the Queyn, the caus quhy I haf wrytyn to Mast. Adam, and gyf ther be ony sted, seruys, or plesour I may do to your Lo. I sal do at command, as knawys God, quha haf your L. in hys blyssyt kepyng. At Perth the xxi day of Januar wyth hand of your Cousyng, and at all his power your

GAWYN, Postulat of Arbroth, &c.*

To strengthen her authority in making this appointment, the Queen having thus applied for the assistance of her brother King Henry VIII., in response to their united application Pope Leo X. wrote the following apostolical letter in favour of Gavin Douglas on 18th February 1515; stipulating in it, however, for a ratification of the appointments which he had previously awarded to Forman.

* Brit. Mus. MSS. Calig., B. i., fol. 27.

Litere Pape.

Carissima in Cristo filia nostra, et dilecti filii, salutem et apostolicam benedictionem. Litteras vestras accepimus quibus dilectum filium Gavinum Douglace nobis plurimum commendastis, et inter alia vt eum ecclesie Dunkeldensi, nuper pastoris solatio destitute, in episcopum et pastorem preficeremus hortastis. Qua in re nos tam vestro intuitu quam virtutibus ipsius Gavini, quarum odorem ex locupleti testimonio et relatione venerabilis fratris Andree Archiepiscopi Sanctiandree nostri et apostolice sedis per vniuersum regnum Scotie Legati plene intelleximus, duximus maiestati et deuotioni vestris morem gerere. Verum cum optima ratione ducti decreuerimus nullam vel promotionem ad aliquam ecclesiam vel prouisionem de aliquo monasterio seu ecclesiastico beneficio istius regni vacanti vel deinceps vacaturo ullatenus facere, donec prefatus Andreas Archiepiscopus pacificam dicte ecclesie Sancti Andree, aliorumque monasteriorum et beneficiorum ecclesiasticorum in eodem regno consistentium que sibi in titulum vel commendam contulimus possessionem assequatur, Maiestatem et deuotionem vestras hortamur in Domino, et precipue requirimus vt pro dei et religionis honore nostroque, et huius sancte sedis apostolice reuerentia ac justitie cultu velitis mandare atque efficere vt prefatus Andreas Archiepiscopus, qui virtute, religione et integritate plurimum prestat, vestrique honoris atque amplitudinis dicti regni studiosissimus existit, quique toto huic regno apud nos et sedem apostolicam in Romana curia plurimum utilis, honorificus et fructuosus esse potest, possessionem ecclesie et monasteriorum ac beneficiorum huiusmodi omnino assequatur, nosque ac litere et mandata nostra in dicto regno pro tempore facta debite obediantur, que faciendo bone opinioni quam de deuotione et obseruantia vestra in nos et Romanam ecclesiam sanctamque sedem apostolicam concepimus plene respondebitis, honorique vestro et dicti regni vtilitati consuletis. Quippe ea adimplendo ac prefatum Andream Archiepiscopum tanquam Legatum et benemeritum vestrum in pace ac tranquillitate pertractando, id efficietis quod clarissime memorie Jacobus olim Rex Scotorum coniux tuus cui idem Andreas Archiepiscopus ut accepimus plurimum gratus et acceptus erat, aliique maiores cui semper facere sunt soliti scilicet ut prouisiones et decreta nostra et apostolice sedis, ac pro tempore existentis Romani Pontificis illic in ea obseruantia et reuerentia habeantur in qua a maioribus tuis aliisque Christi fidelibus, presertim ab hiis qui regnis et principatibus in terris presunt, haberį debent. Quod si premissa feceritis prout firmiter credimus, vos quod nos ad confirmationem priuilegiorum et indultorum regibus Scotie a Romanis Pontificibus pro tempore existentibus concessorum, ac ad prouisionem dicte ecclesie de persona ex dicto regno grata procedamus, aliisque in rebus illius regni commoda et ornamenta cure habeamus non indigne merebimini. Datum Rome apud Sanctum Petrum sub annulo piscatoris, die xviij Februarii M° D xv. Pont. nostri anno secundo.*

In May of the same year, however, John Stewart, Duke of Albany, grandson of King James II., and cousin of James IV., who had been declared Regent of Scotland after the marriage of the Queen with the Earl of Angus, arrived from France and assumed the reins of government. He summoned a Parliament to meet at Edinburgh in July, and at a meeting of the Lords of Council Gavin Douglas was elected a member.

At various times between 1471 and 1493 the Scottish Parliament had passed Acts to put down the negociation (or purchase) of benefices at the Court of Rome. An Act of James III. (Par. vi. cap. 43)

* Acta Dom. Conc., xxvii., fol. 26.

recites "the great damnage and skaith daylie done to all the realme be Clerkes, religious and seculares, quhilkis purchassis abbacies and uther benefices at the Court of Rome, quhilks were never thereat befoir." In particular, the Act Jas. IV., Par. i. c. 4, (1488), relates to "Clerkis that purchasis benefices contrair the Kingis presentation," and declares that they are to have "proscription, rebellion, and treason execute upon them—les nor they leave the said benefices, after they be required thereupon."

The intrigues which had been going on for the Scottish benefices naturally attracted the notice of the Regent and his first Parliament. Forman, afraid of these laws, which were now to be enforced, resigned into the hands of the Regent all the benefices he had obtained by purchase from the Pope. He was, however, allowed to retain the Archbishopric of St. Andrews and the Abbacy of Dunfermline; but the Abbacy of Aberbrothock was given to James Beaton, Archbishop of Glasgow and Chancellor of Scotland, who, after holding it for some years, resigned it in favour of his nephew, afterwards the famous Cardinal Beaton.

The proceedings of the Queen in promoting Gavin Douglas to the Bishopric of Dunkeld were narrowly watched by the Regent and the party opposed to the Earl of Angus, and it would appear from the following interesting letter of Lord Dacre that arrangements were made for intercepting the Papal Bulls when they should arrive at the Scottish Border:—

Lord Dacre to the Lords of Council of England.

My Lords, after mooste humble and due recomendation

unto your goode Lordshyppes, pleas it the same to knowe that I receved a pacquet of letters from you by pooste the ij[de] day of this present moneth, and by my letter therein conteigned I perceive that the Kings command and yours is that I should with all convenient deligence not oonly send the Poopes two briefes and there coopies with a pacquete of letters to thabbot of Arbroothe, elect of Dunkell, and with the same I shuld write unto hym shewing howe the Kinggs Grace hath bene soo good Lorde unto hym to opteyn for hym the said Busshopricke of Dunkeld, but also yf I coutte fynde the mean that at the tyme of delyvere of the said brefes to the said elect there might be present a notary whiche wold testifie the same delyveryng and therupon make an instrument in due fourme.

My Lords, because I coutte not be in suretie to haif a Scotts notary redy at the delyver of the said brefes, I sent the said brefes and pacquett with a servant of myn owne, and therupon made letters to the Quene of Scotts and the elect of Dunkeld and send them with the comon notary of the merchies which canne perfitely speke and understande Ffrenche, to thentent he shulde see the delyver of the said brefes (the copies of which lettres I send unto your Lordships, herein closed.)

And as they were riding at Moffett xxxvj miles within Scotland on Weddinsday in the mornyng the iiij[th] daye of this moneth, Sir Alex[r.] Jearden, Knight, toke the said notary and lettres, and because they mentioned of the same brefes whiche my servant had in keping, the same Sir Alex[r.] toke the brefes from my servant, and had the notary and lettres with the brefes and pacquet to the Lord Chamberlain being Wardain, and from hym to the Duke of Albanye in Edinburghe, and there the said notary saw the same brefes and writings in the Dukes haunde. Of whom he desired that aither the said brefes and writings were gevin to hym that he might deliver them according to there superscriptions orels that it wold like hys Lordship to cause them be delivered accordingly for his discharge, seying that he come upon the Poopes message. The said Duke sent the Quene hir letter unopynned and redd the othre lettres to the Counsale openly, and then delivered as well the Poopes brefes as pacquett unto the custodie of maister Gawen Dunbars haunds, beyng clerk of the Conssaill and kepar of the Regestre, to be furthe comyng whenne as they be called for. And as sone as it come to my knowledge that the notary and my servant were arrested I made an other letter to the said Elect reciting the effect of my formour letters, as well sent to the Quene as hym with the Poopes brefes, which letter was delivered to the same Elects hands with all celerite (the coopie of which letter I in likewise send unto your Lordshippes). And anon after the same Duke sent for the Elect and examined hym in the presence of the Counsall, whidder he made laubor to the Poopes Holinesse and the Kinggs Hignes our sovrain Lord for the said Busshoppricke or not, or howe durst he be soo bold as to laubor therefor without licence of the King of Scots, or Governour of Scotland in his nonage, who annswered that he made never laubor therefor, and what laubor as the Quene his sovrain Lady made for his promocion as tutrice and governour to the King hir sonne he knewe not. Whereupon the Duke beyng frett with ire and malice committed hym to warde in the castell of Edinburghe, where as he yit remaynes, and then suffred the said notary and my servant to departe at ther libertes on Thursday last past after they had been kept viij[tn] daies in warde.

My Lordes, seyng the premisses come not to soo good spede as the Kyngs Highness entended they should haif done, there is noo man living more sory for it thenne I am, wherein I did my best deligence for the spede and performance of your commandmentes, as our Lord God knowes. Wherfore I beseche your good Lorshippes to have me excused, for had not bene the sending of the notary, which was taken as a straungier in Scotland, I couthe haife conveyed the writinges to the handes of the said electe without daungier.

For newes, your Lordshippes shall know that I am advertised be myne espies out of Scotland, that the Bisshop of Murraye hath not oonly opteyned the Archbishopricke of Sanctandros, and is come home in Scotland, but also the Duke has commanded hym to warde, to remaigne in the Priory of Pettenwene within eght myle whar he laundyd, and no nerer to come to the courte na counsaile. It is thought that he shalbe kept in strater warde unto the season as he resignes the said Archibusshopricke to the use of a bastard sone of the late King of Scottes, which came home in companye with the said Duke.

The Lord Drommond, captain of the castell of Streveling, was sent for be the Duke to appear afore hym, upon his allegiance, whiche at his commyng was accused for the striking of an harrolde, and also that he with other lordes shuld have bene of counsaile to have made the Kings Grace, our maister, protectour of Scotland, and delyvered the young king to his haundis. And therupon he was committe to warde on Weddinsday last past, and shall abyde assise in Edinburghe upon Monday next comyng.

I assure your Lordshippes that the Quene of Scottes canne gitt noo noble man to be capten of Streveling, ne that will take the charge of keping of the younge King and his broder, for every man refuses her and giffes them to the Duke, which I fere and canne see no remedy, but in conclusion the King and his broder will come and be delivered to the Dukes haundes to their utter destruction by all likelyhoode, and as I am credubly ascertaigned be my secrete espiel.

I trust that at the breking up of ther parliament to gitt knowledge of ther determinaciones, and what ordour shalbe taken emonges them, and therof I shall advertise youe with all spede and diligence.

My Lordes, if suche letters as the Quene of Scottes haif sent with the Poopes legate which hath been in Scotland this yere, passed as well to the Kings Highnes, the French Quene, his and hir sister, as to divers other of you my Lords of the Kings Counsail, to be mean and solicitous to his Highnes for hir help, she is right desirous to haif aunswer again. Albeit whenne she might have holpen herself and husbande with his freyndes, and also meanes founde and devised for the suretie of them and hir childer, she regarded it littell, whiche she nowe sore repentis, making great lamentatioun and weping daily for the same. She is great with childe. It is thought by hir freyndis that thorowe the anguyshe of the premisses she wolbe in great jopardie of hir lyfe, remembering the daungier that her husbande, uncle, and his graundfader standis in at this tyme, as the Holy Trinity knowes, who kepe your good Lordshippes.

At Karlisle, the 14 daye of July,

Yours at commandment,

THOMAS DACRE.

To my Lordis of the Kingis most honourable Counsale.*

The packet of letters addressed by Lord Dacre to Gavin Douglas, intercepted at Moffat and handed over to the Duke of Albany, contained—(1.) A letter from Lord Dacre to the Queen, which as we have seen the Duke had the politeness to send to her unopened. It is interesting, as indicating that the Archbishop of St Andrews having, both by ancient custom, (as stated in the Queen's letter to the Pope before given),† and also by the will of James IV., been made guardian to his family, that was now revoked by the Pope in favour of Gavin Douglas. (2.) A congratulatory letter from Lord Dacre to Douglas. (3.) A very interesting letter from Alexander Trumble or Turn-

* State Papers Scot., Vol. i., No. 13. † Page xv.

bull, factor for Douglas, which details the difficulty he had in getting matters relating to his appointment as Bishop of Dunkeld satisfactorily settled at Rome. The letter intimates that one of these difficulties was the non-payment of "1^{m} ducatis for the composition of the confirmatioun of the Kingis testament." In all likelihood this refers to the will of James IV., which was proved at Rome,* after his death at Flodden; and as Queen Margaret, his widow, was often in great straits for money, it is probable that this fee of 1000 ducats could not be paid at the time it fell due, and it may indeed have been owing to this neglect that no greater attention was given to the Queen's letters in favour of Douglas at the Papal Court. It is well known, besides, that Queen Margaret took all the assets of her husband, James IV., but left his debts unpaid. (4.) A letter from Adam Williamson, the old correspondent of Douglas, congratulating him on his appointment as Bishop, and suggesting that some reward might now be given to himself—such as a prebend's stall in Dunkeld Cathedral—in return for his services. He says very truly, "I spek by tyme, for a dum man gettis seldum land."

The letter from Lord Dacre to the Queen is as follows:—

Lord Dacre to Queen Margaret.

Pleas it your Graice to knowe that the Kingis Highnes my Souerain Lorde your broder is in good health and mery, blessed be our Lord God, who hath, upon your lettres and requestis sent to the Popes Holiness and hym, and for pleassour of you, obteignet the Bysshopriche of Dunkell of his said

* Pinkerton's History, vol. ii. p. 150.

Holiness to Mr Gawen Douglas my Lord your husbandis vncle, as may appere by the Popes breves which I send vnto my said Lord of Dunkell at this tyme, and also a revocacion to the Archebusshop of Saint Andrewes of sich autorities with the legacie of the king, and hath remitt the execucion of the said auctorities and fulfilling of the legacie to my said Lord of Dunkell. Wherefore seyng his Highnes did this at your request, ye can no lesse do than gif unto hym condigne thankis by writing. His Graice regardeth your honour suretie and well, with the King and his broder your sounes his nephieues, above all thingis as ye shall well knowe, whereunto ye maye fathefully trust. And the holy Trinite preserve your Graice. At Kirkoswalde the ijde daye of July.*

Lord Dacre to Gavin Douglas.

My Lord and Cousing: I commend me to you in full hartly maner, ascertanyng you, that this day I receved ane pacquet of lettres from the Kingis Hienes my soucrane Lord by post, wherin amangis vthir there is two brevis with the copie of thame directit be the Popis Holynes, the oone to you and the vther to the Archibischep of Sanct Androis, and also a litell pacquett send to your Lordschip be your factour in the Court of Rome, with a lettir from Maister Adam Williamsoun, whiche I send vnto your Lordschip with my seruand this berar. My Lord, I vnderstand by suche lettres as come to me that the Popis Holynes, at the instant request and gret labour of the Kingis Graice my said souerane Lord maid onto him vpoun the lettres and desyres of the Quenes Graice your soucrane lady his suster, hath elect you Bischeip of Dunkeld.

My said souuerane Lord, for the plessour of the Queene his said suster, and also for the grete wisdome faithfull counsell and stedfastnes that he findeth ye gif, beris, and awe vnto the said Quene, with duetie of all graice to the King

* State Papers Scot., vol. i., No. 13, i.

your maistere and his broder my soucrane Lordis nephieus, hath optenyd the said Bischopryk to you; trasting that your wisdome will induce and counsaile the said Quene and your nephieu hir husband to be sure of the said King and his broder and neuer departe with thame to noone other handis without the hole assent of the Lordis spirituall and temporall seyng what possibilitie they stand in.

My Lord, I vnderstand by the copie of the two breiffis that the effect of the oone sent vnto the Archibischop of Saint Androwes is a speciall reuocation of such auctorite as the Poopes Holynes committed to him, and also of the Kingis legacie, whiche his Hoolines hathe fully remitte to you to be execut and done, which shall sounde and growe to your honor and proffite, and for my said soucrane Lord entendis and is well mynded towardis you, wherefore I hertlie desyre and pray you to deliuer or cause to be deliuerit be ane substanciall persoun afore a notary and recorde the briefe to the said Archibischep, who is fled out of Flaunders and thocht he is kepit secrete in Scotland. Apoun the delivery thereof to mak certificate accordingly.

My Lord, right glad joyous I am of your promocioune and help, as I am bound to be for the great kyndnes and intere favour that hath bene betwixt our antecessours and bloid in tymes passed, which shall never fale on my partie. And of your mynd and recept of these writingis that I maye be certifeid with my said seruand, and thus our Lord God haif you in his keping. At Kirkoswald the ij[de] daye of July.

Your lofyng cosyn,

THOMAS L. DACRE.*

After Lord Dacre heard of the arresting of his servant with the letters he had forwarded, he wrote to Gavin Douglas on the 6th of July from Holm Abbey, as follows:—

* Acta Dom. Concil xxvii., fol 33.

Lord Dacre to Gavin Douglas.

My Lord, I commende me hertely to youe, and witt ye that upon Monday last past I receyved lettres frome the Kinggis Highness my souverain Lord by pooste, emongis whiche there was two breves fro the Popes Holinesse, the one to youe and the oder to the Archebusschop of Sainct Andrewis, and also a pacquet of lettres fro your factor at Rome with the copie of both the said breves, all which writings I sent to youe with my seruant on Twisdaye in the mornyng, with a lettre to youe and one oder to the Quene fro me with the common notarie of the Merchies.

The effect of the one brief sent to the said Archebusshop was, that the Poopes Holines had reuokt all auctorities granted by hym to the said Archebusshop, and also the Kingis legacy, charging hym not to medle nor intromitt with no parte of them. And the effect of your brief is that his Holiness hath admitted and elect youe Busshop of Dunkell, with auctorite to se the Kingis legacy performed. And the nature of my lettre sent to the Quene declared theffecte of the breves, and that she couth no less do then gif thankis by writing to the Kingis Graice my maister, hir broder, for his grete labour made to the Pope at hir desire and requiest. And my lettre to youe send was theffect of the breves, as that ye shuld aithre se or cause the Popes breve be declared to the tharchebusshop of Sainct Andrewis afore a notary and recorde, and vpon the deliuery thereof to certifie me agane by your writing. And because of the faithfull good mynde which ye do bere vnto the young King and his broder your maister, the Quene and hir husband your nephieue, I wrote to youe that seyng your wisdome I trusted you wold neuer gif the Quene and your said nephieu counsale to departe with the King and his broder to noo oder person without the hole assent of all the Lordis spiritual and temporal, but to be sure of them, seyng what possibilitie they stande in. And the premisses is theffect of all the writingis that I sende, saif only of the pacquet which I oppynned not nor sawe.

And as my said seruant and the notary were comyng towardis the Quene and youe on Wednisdaye in the dawyng at Moffett, Sir Alexr. Jardane and Thom Moffett larde of Knok tok them, and there writingis fro them, and had them to the Lord Chamberlane, and fro hym Sir Alexr. toke all the writingis and had them with the notary and my seruant to the Duke. My Lord there is no thing expressed in the lettres but to your honour and promocion, and may well be red and sene when all the Lordis er assembled in the Parliament House togidder, as God knowes, who kepe your Lordship. At thabbey of Holme the vj daye of July.*

The letters of Turnbull and Williamson are as follow :—

A. Turnbull to Gavin Douglas.

Reverendo in Christo Patri, ac Domino, Domino Gavino Dunkeldensi Episcopo, suoque Domino colendissimo.

My Lord, I giueand my seruice to your Lordship in the most humble wise; forsamekle as your Lordship chargit me be your diuers writingis, that in the materis concernyng your Lordship, I suld ask help at my Lord the Bishop of Wlsistir at standis Oratour heir for the King of Ingland, and also to solist his Lordship to labour contrair the promociouns mad in the fauouris of the Bishop of Murray and his legacie, considerand thai ware done and spedd contrare our souerane Lordis priuelage and commoun wele and profit of the realme, I did the samin conform to your Lordships writingis; and as for my said Lord Oratour, I fand his Lordship euir redy in the tyme of neid to do extremlie for your Lordship, and in speciale, anent your Lordships promotioun to Dunkeld: And, howbeit, your Lordship had stark compeditouris and diuers contrare your

* State Papers Scot., vol. i., No. 13, iii.

Lordships said promotioun, and mony effortis and wais maid be small freindis in the hindir hereof: neuirtheles throw the grace of God and our Ladie of Consolatioune, and other gud friendis, and in speciale of my said Lord Oratour, your Lordship was pronuncit Bischop of Dunkeld, *consistorialiter*, on Friday forow Whitsunday, viz. xxv. mensis Maij, *una cum retentione beneficiorum, viz. Prepositure de Edinburgh, et Prebende de Dunbar.* Gif ther was ony brevis of the Papis purchest be my Lord of Murray, direct to the Quenis Grace and your Lordship, declarand the Papis mynd nocht to dispone apone Dunkeld in the fauouris of your Lordship onto the tyme that my said Lord of Murray was in possessioune of Sanctandrois I report me to the samin, the quhilkis or now, I trast your Lordship and the Quenis Grace has ressauit, like as I have writin, diuers tymis to your Lordship, and altherlast, *ex data quinto huius*, and direct the samin to Master Johnne Carre to be seud to your Lordship, with diligens; and with the samin lettres I send to your Lordship the brief *ad portanda arma*, and the copijs of the *Constitutionnis in decima sessione Concilij Lateranensis.* Your bullis of prouisioun of Dunkeld, togidder with the monitour penale *contra Andream Stewart in specie, ac contra omnes alios in genere*, I sall send conforme to your Lordships writing, in all possible haist; had nocht bene I had ane gret impediment in the expedicioun of the said bullis, thai suld haue bene all speid or now, tuiching the quhilk impediment, I wraite to youre Lordship at lenthe *quinto huius.* Dout nocht bot considering as all materis standis, I sall do the best I may; and gif my said Lord the Oratour has done his debt tuiching the inhibitioune and suspensioune of my said Lord of Murrayis falculteis and legacie, your Lordship may consider be the Papis breuis direct to your Lordship, the quhilk breuis I haue sent, and as I traist ye sall ressaue the samin, with your lettres. I wraite to your Lordship to informe the Quenis grace of the thankis done be my said Lord, the Bischop of Wlsistir, and to solist hir Grace to writ to his Lordship, thankand him of his gud deligence, praying his Lordship to perseueir and continew, quhilk has nocht allanerlie desseruit thank, bot bath thank and reward. Item I wraite to youre Lordschip, how that there was ane commissioun made *ex parte Prioris Sancti Andree et aliorum [contra] quos fuit processum ad certas censuras vigore literarum apostolicarum bullis originalibus transumptis minime onestis*, and askit that causs *de nullitate censurarum* to be committit to ane of the cardinals, &c. The said commissioune was proponit be ane Jacobatius, that is Referendir *in vltima signatura Papali*, viz. *quinto huius*. Efter that the Papis Holynes had redd the samin, he deliuerit it to the daitar, onto the tyme that his Holynes war forther mar auisit, and that was mekle be the solicitatioun of the Cardinale Amontane, and has done largelie at all for my Lord of Murray, and yit continewis. I cann nocht say how that commissioune *de nullitate et de retractione promocionis facte in persona Episcopi Morauiensis*, will haue passage. I dred that the Pape will nocht hastelie committ tha materis and caussis, as yit; neuirtheles, ther is diligence done, and sal be done, in the helping of tha materis sa for as be, the cais beand considerit.

I ferlie your Lordship wraite nocht to me to quhilkis jugis your Lordship wald haf had the monitour penale, nor yit *de valore beneficiorum detentorum*. I did the best as I understand, and has committit that monitour penal to my Lord of Cowper and Lindoris, and to the Provost of Abernethy. As for the retentioune of Arbroth, I couth not get *in specie*, becaus it was so recentlie speid *in consistorio*. The help at may be maid in that mater, I sall do my best. Item as tuiching the confirmatioun, and the brieff declaratiouns and absolutiouns respectiue, I haue maid the reformatioun thereof conform to your Lordships last informatioune, bot it will be in gret deficulte and exceddand expenses and we get thame in that forme; I sall spend nothing, nowther in tha materis nor utheris that I ma eschew, bot as or I be frustruate, I will mak honest expenses as efferis. I writ to Jerome Friscobald,* that quhen your Lordschipes bullis of Dunkeld cummis, that he speid the samin to your Lordschip, and that he sal be thankfullie payit of the rest of the bullis and of utheris materis. I will nocht bynd your Lordschip in the bankis *sub penis calumnie apostolice*, and be in danger of thair cursing, so far as I may eschew thairfor. Mak some diligence and finance in the hast your Lordship may, and be reddand him. Your Lordschip can nocht haue ane finale compt quhill that Jerome and I be togidder. I wrote to your Lordschip the bullis ware stoppit for the j^{m} ducatis for the compositioun of the confirmatioun of the Kingis testament. I will nocht consent thairto *aliquo pacto* and I may vtherwayis do. War ane uther man my partie than the Paipe I couth fynd sum remeid. Gif that I may nocht eschew otherwais, or that I haue the bullis taryit, and to haue the Paipe gracious to your Lordschip in other thingis that ar able to occur, I will nocht stand in that mater, for in faithe, I trow verralie had nocht bene the respect of that money, we suld nocht haue gotten our entent in Dunkeld. Thair was so mony impedimentis, and ay the langar able to haue bene the ferrar fra oure purpos. I think it mery as it is.

Item, I haue raisit ane prouisioun apoun the Deanry of Glasgow for Mastir Anthone Ogilby, *certo modo vacantem*, and ane other to Master Johnne Irwyne eftir youre Lordschipis writingis, and I shall send your Lordschip copiis of the samin, with the next cursour.

Item, as for my simplenes, your Lordschip may remember and reward as your Lordschip thinkis tyme and caus. I sal be leile and traist to your Lordschip and your materis sa fer as I haue grace and knawlage. The Italianis has ane proverbe—*fidelis seruus asinus perpetuus*. I waite that I serf

* Several notices of Jerome Frischobald, the banker, and of fees paid to him for Dispensations at Rome, are given in the "Ledger of Andrew Halyburton," 8vo, Edin., 1867.

na Italiane; I traist sickirlie that I serve ane noble, discret, and kind Lord, the quhilk was neuir unkind to naue that deseruit kindnes or reward. Anentis William Douglas dispensatioun writ to me absolut, quhether he is clericus *vel* scolaris. This I have writin of befor diuers tymis at the directioune of your bullis. I sall writ at lenthe in all materis. I gait no writing fra your Lordschip sene the iiii day of Aprile. Pleis your Lordschip to send the tother bill to my Lord of Cowper, and the blissit Trinite conserue your Lordschip eternally. Et sic subscript.

V. R. P. Seruitor ad mandata paratissimus,
A. TRUMBLE.*

Adam Williamson to Gavin Douglas.

To his especiale gude Lorde, Mastir Gavin Douglas, Bischop of Dunkeld, and Abbot of Arbroth.

Humillima recomendatione premissa—My Lord, I mervale that ye neuir wraite to me nor send this lang tyme past; I am redde that ye haue me suspecte, bot, the deid preves the man—*omnis laus virtutis in actione consistit.* Ye ar now Bischop of Dunkeld and that by the noble King of Inglandis writing to the Paipe as apperis, and sum thing by my labour. My Lord, to be schort, send a secret wys man in Ingland and that schortlie, with kynd lettres to the Kingis grace fra the Quene and fra the Erle of Angus and fra you alsa. I ensure you my Lord his Grace will nocht fale the Quene his sistir. Lat hir be radde for na man, his Grace with his wys counsale labouris for the weile of the Quene and of hir childryne, his derest nevois, mair na ye trow. Thocht the Quene haue nocht all thingis that scho desiris at the first, lat hir be content—*quia quod defertur non aufertur.* My Lord, gif the Quene, or my Lord of Angus, or ye think to do anything with the Kingis Grace, cause the Quene to writ kynd lettres to my Lord of York,† for I assur yow he is hir gret frend and may do

* Acta Dom. Concilii, xxvii., fol. 32. † Cardinal Wolsey.

maist with hir broder the King of ony man of lif and merit. He is worthy the autorite that he is in, and that ye wald say and ye knew him alswele as I do. Gif it wald pleis the Quenis Grace to thank him for me, I war mekle bound to hir Graice. He is my singulare gud Lord, I leif heir onlie by him for hir saik. As for the Bischop of Murray his legacy is revokit be the Paipe. He is departit furth of Flandris, and I think that he hydis him in Scotland to mak dissention amang yow. He neuir did gud in Scotland nor neuer sall. My Lord, send a secret wys man in quham ye ma traist, and he sall bring to the Quene and to yow gud tithingis. I besek yow be gud Lord to my sister and to hir husband Ninzeane Inglis. I luk for a Prebend of Dunkeld. I spek by tyme, for a dum man gettis seldum land, and I am youris quhether ye will or nocht. I am affectit to yow abuf ony man in Scotland as God help me, quha preserue yow. At Lundone the xxx day of Junii. Et sic subscript.

tuus ADAM WILLIAMSON. *

The Duke of Albany, being now in possession of evidence that Douglas had obtained the Bishopric of Dunkeld through the influence of Henry with the Pope, deemed this a favourable opportunity of setting aside one who was so nearly related to the Earl of Angus, and so capable of supporting his interest. As stated in Lord Dacre's letter, "being fret with ire and malice," he summoned a meeting of the Lords of Council to be held on 6th July 1515, for the purpose of laying these treasonable papers before them.

Douglas, being aware that his affairs were to be discussed at the meeting, went to see the Regent before it took place. The Secretary of the Council seems to have been present at this interview, and

* Acta Dom. Concilii, xxvii., fol. 32 b.

minuted as follows:—"My Lord Gouernour shew that he was informit be diuers writings from the Court of Rome that the said Postulat was promovit to the Bishopry of Dunkeld be the King of Inglandis writings, and the said promotion solicitat be the Protectour of Ingland, Cardinal de Medicis, and the Orator of Ingland; the quhilk the said Postulat denyit that he knew anything off, and, or he had bene art or part in the said mater he had leuer have bene hangit, and neuer had benefice into the realm."*

Douglas then went to the meeting of the Lords of Council, and was examined in their presence. The following minute was made of the proceedings on this occasion:—

At Edinburgh, the 6th day of June [July] 1515 years, in presence of my Lord Governour, the Lordis of Consale, and the remanent of the Lordis underwritten, that is to say ane noble and honourable man—De Planis, oratour to the maist cristin king of Fraunce; ane maist Reverend, and Reverend faderis in God, James, Archibischop of Glasgw, Chancellar; David, Bishop of Galloway; James, Bischop of Dunblane; Robert, Bishop of Ross; Androw, Bischop of Cathnes; David, Bischop of Ergyle; Johnne, Elect of the Ilis; noble and michty Lordis, Archibald, Erle of Angus; Colyn, Erle of Ergile; Johnne, Erle of Levinax; Hew, Erle of Eglintoun; Cuthbert, Erle of Glencarne; Gilbert, Erle of Cassilis; Venerable faderis in God, James, Postulate of Dunfermling; Patrik, Abbot of Cambuskyneth; Johnne Lord Erskin, Johnne Lord Flemyng, Johnne Lord Hay of Yester, Johnne Lord Drummond, Sir Antone Darsy, Monsr. La Basty, and Baroun of Fareris, Master Gavin Dunbar, Archidene of St Andrews, Clerk of Register, Master James Ogilby, Channoun of

* Ibid. fol 26.

Aberdene, and Master James Wischard, Justice Clerk.—Comperit Master Gavin Douglas, Postulat of Arbroth, and schew how he was ane man of 40 yeris of age or therby, and ane gentilman of gude blude, and has passit his time in Scotland, Ingland, France, and Rome without defamatioun or ony repreif to his honeste, as was knawin to diuers of my Lordis at ware than present for the tyme; howbeit as he was informit, he was delatit to be ane evile man in diuers poyntis, and had committit crymes incontrar the Kingis Majestie and common wele of the realme, the quhilk, he said, God willing, suld nocht be fundin of verite: My said Lord Gouernour herand this narratioun of the said Postulate, answerit first to his rehersis and sayingis that the said Postulate wist weill that my Lord Gouernour held him not sic ane man nor sa mischand for to do agane our Souerane Lord and his realme, and that my Lord Gouernour traistit nocht that ony Scotisman in the realme wald sek help at Inglismen in his doingis, and that he wald be wele content that the said Postulate wald discharge and quyte himself honestly and weile of sic materis; and that the Postulate knew wele when he come to my Lord Gouernour to excuse him, his Lordship said the samin to him, and the Postulat said if his Lordship fand that he askit help at Inglismen in this deid, that is to say in the purchesing of this benefice of Dunkeld or in any vther thingis, he was content that my said Lord suld gar cut off his heid, the quhilk sawis my Lord gart the Postulat confess and rehers agane before the Quene; and my Lord Gouernour said to her Grace before the Lordis of Consale thir wordis, 'Madame, I have gart yow understand this deid quhilk tuichis the King your sonne and my souerane Lord, quhilk is the thing ye suld have maist tendir;' and to thir wordis the Quene ansuerit and confessit it was of verite that the said Lord said to hir sic langage of befor, and said forther to him, My Lord, be ye richt sickir that na person in the warld desiris sa mekle the gude of my barnis as I do, and will nocht sustene na man that wald do aganis thar rycht and privelege of my sonnis croune, bot will help to cause justice be done apoune ony personis that will attempt in the contrar, and prayit his Lordship to do the samin as accordit of his office; and think nocht that euir I was consentand to sic thingis as ar said or siclike, and it will nocht be found that I did onything aganis the privelege of my sonnis croune on my honour, praying your Lordship to give na credence till sic thingis aganis me. And thareto my Lord Gouernour ansuerit, that he was deliuerit to sustene the privilege and rycht of our Souerane Lord to the end of his lyfe at all his power with body and gudis.*

On the 9th of July the meeting again took up the case of Gavin Douglas, when he pleaded that as he was "ane spirituale man," and as he was before a temporal court, he was beyond their jurisdiction. The Lords, however, unanimously overruled this objection. Douglas then produced a letter which had been signed not only by the Queen but by eleven Lords of the Council, preferring him to the Bishopric. The production of this letter caused explanations and protests which are also given in the minute, as follows:—

Anent the actioun proponit be my Lord Gouernour aganis Gawyne, Postulate of Arbroth, that the said Postulate suld purchese the Bischeprick of Dunkeld in the Court of Rome contrare the statutis of the realme, the said Postulate allegit that he is ane spirituale man, and thairfore my Lord Gouernour and Lordis of Consell ar na jugis to him in the said mater: In presens of my Lord Gouernour the Lordis foresaid all in ane voce, be sentence interlocutour decretis and deliueris that nochtwithstanding the said ex-

* Acta Dom. Concilii, xxvii., fol. 26 b.

ceptiouns my Lord Gouernour and Lordis of Consell ar jugis competent to haue the cognitioune of the breking of the Actis of Parliament, and na vtheris.

Copia litere Postulati de Arbroth.

The Qwenis Grace as tutrice testamentar and Gouernour to hir derrest sonne the Kingis Hienes, with the awis of the Lordis vnderwrittin, for diuers and resonable gud causis and consideracionns moving thame gevis and grantis thare full consentis and assentis to ane noble man Master Gawyne Douglas, Postulate of Arbroth, for the gift of the Bischepryk of Dunkeld now vacand be the deces of wmquhile George last Bischep and possessour of the sammyne, quhais saul God pardoune, and preferris him thairto and to be answerit thairof as accordis of the law. Considering he is worthy and abill thairfore baith for his nobilite of blud, vertu, and science, and for the payne and daily labouris he takis and has takin for the weilfare and prosperite of the Kingis persone and liberte of his crowne, and at his power to procure and mak vnite, cherite, and concord amangis the Lordis and Estatis of this realme now standing disiunct and at divisione: And to this effecte our said Souerane Lady and Lordis has writtin in our Souerane Lordis name thare effectuis lettres for the said Maister Gawynes promocioune to the said Bischeprik to the Papis Halynes and his Cardinalis, chargeing be the tenour of this wryte in our saide Souerane Lordis name that na persone nor personis presume or tak apone hand to cum in the contrare hereof in ony wyse, vndir all the hiest payne and charge thai may incur aganis the Kingis Maiestie and his auctorite riall, and als the panis contenit in the Actis of Parliament and priuilege grantit be diuerse Papis to this realme and Kingis of the sammyne quhen ony sic prelacyis and grete beneficis happinis to uaik within the said realme: Certifying thame that cumis in the contrare that the saidis panis sal be execut apoune thame with all rigour without favouris as brekaris of the said priuilege and parttakaris aganis the Kingis Hienes as his conspiratouris and contrare the commoune wele of his realme; and gif neid be that lettres be writtin hereapoune under the signet to mak publicatioune at the Mercat Corcis of Edinburgh, Perth, Dunde, and vther placis neidfull. Subscriuit be our said Souerane Lady and Lordis of Consell in takyn of thare consentis at Perthe the xx day of Januare, the yere of God j^{m} v^{c} and and xiiij yeris. Heir followis the subscriptiounis of the Quenis Grace and Lordis:—Margaret R.; Erle of Angus; Erle of Craufurd; Erle of Eroll; Alex., Erle of Huntlie; C., Erle of Glencarn; Alex., Electus Aberdonen.; Richard, Lord Innerneitht; Jo., Lord Drumond; Willms., Abbas de Cupro; James, Lord Ogilby; Jo. Lo. Hay of Yestir.

Lyoun Kyng of Armis and Master James Urqhart askit instrumentis, as thai allege that thai desyrit him nocht to answere in the said mater bot gif he plesit, hora xi.

Gawyne, Postulate of Arbroth, askit instrumentis that he answerit in the said mater nocht wytht his will, as he allegit, bot because it was decretit that the Lordis foresaide war jugis in the cause.

William, Erle of Erol, askit instrumentis that he put nocht his hand to the lettre purchest be the Postulate of Arbroth for the Bischeprick of Dunkeld for na breking of the Kingis preuilege, bot erar for affirming of his priuilege, and wald nocht consent to nathing at mycht brek his priuilege.

My Lord Glencarne askit instrumentis sielyke.

My Lord Hay of Yestir askit sielyk.

William, Erle of Erole, askit instrumentis that gif he has done onything in tymis bygane, being with the Quenis Graice, that he now reuokit and renuncit the sammyne.

My Lord Drummond askit sielyke.

The Lordis delineris that nochtwithstanding the lettre producit be Gawyne, Postulate of Arbroth subscriuit be the

Quenis Graice and certane Lordis for the promocioune of the Bischepryk of Dunkeld to the said Postulate, that he has brokin and violat the Actis of Parliament maid thairapone, because thai haue fund that it is nocht ane sufficient lettre nor licence to saife him fra the brekyng of the saidis Actis of Parliament for the purchessing of the said Bischeprik of Dunkeld.

The Lordis decretis and deliueris that the Actis of Parliament maid apoune Clerkis purchessing placiis at the Court of Rome without the Kingis licence salbe put to execucioun apoune Master Gawin Douglas, Postulate of Arbroth, in all poyntis efter the forme and tenour of the samin; because he has brokin the said Actis and Statut in the purchessing of the Bischoprik of Dunkeld without the Kingis licence or my Lord Gouernouris of commendacioune or laudacioune to the Papis Halynes for the sammin, as was clerelie vnderstand to the saidis Lordis.*

Douglas, being now found guilty, incurred the punishment of banishment from the kingdom, but it was determined by the Regent and the Chancellor that he should be sent to prison. The Castle of Edinburgh was then selected as the place of his confinement. He was afterwards committed to the custody of John Hepburn (his former rival for the Archbishopric) in the Castle of St Andrews. From thence he was conveyed to the Castle of Dunbar, and again to the Castle of Edinburgh.

The Regent, who seems to have begun his rule in Scotland with great severity, next called Lord Drummond to account for his audacity in striking the Lord Lyon of Scotland when performing the behest of the Council. He found him guilty, and sent him prisoner

* Acta Dom. Concilii, xxvii. foll. 38, 39.

to Blackness Castle, confiscating all his lands and goods.

Such, then, was the unexpected and unfortunate result of the long scheming of Douglas for ecclesiastical preferment.

The Scottish benefices, for which we have seen so much intriguing was practised, were of great value in comparison with the endowments of the present Ecclesiastical Establishment. In 1560, when the value of money was nearly four times higher than at present, the revenues of the Archbishopric of St Andrews amounted annually to £2904, besides 30 chalders of wheat, 41 of bear, 67 of oats, 12 bolls of meal, and 4 of malt. The See of Murray was next in value; after it came Dunkeld, which Douglas in one of his letters before given, describes as "an rycht gud Byschopry of rent." Its annual income amounted in 1560 to £1505, 10s. 4d, besides 4 chalders of wheat,

37 of bear, 64 of meal, and 28 of oats.* It had originally been a monastery of the Culdees, and St Columba was its patron saint. The monastery was greatly enlarged by King David, about the year 1127, who made its head the first bishop. Situated close to the river Tay, the Cathedral, which seems to have been completed soon after the year 1450, with its gray square tower rising up from amidst a mass of trees, must have been an object of great dignity and interest in former times. Even now the ruins of the nave are singularly grand.

One of the predecessors of Douglas was Bishop Sinclair, whose conduct in the war of independence with England procured for him the name of the "warlike Bishop," while Robert the Bruce, sympathising more with his heroic than his ecclesiastical qualities, called him his own Bishop.

Another predecessor of Douglas, Bishop Lauder, by whom the building of the cathedral was completed, made many additions to its furnishings. Canon Myln records that "he procured many priests' vestments of silk, and a deal of silver work, such as six candle-

* The Benedictine Abbey of Aberbrothock to which Douglas was postulated, was in 1560 worth annually £2488, 3s., besides 20 chalders of wheat, 118 of bear, 168 of meal, 27 of oats, and 1 last and 3 barrels of salmon. But from this rental there fell to be deducted allowances to the monks on the establishment, who were paid at Kynloss at the following rate:—" For habit silver, ilk monk haiffand 50 s. be yeir; For thair fische and flesche be yeir, ilk ane haiffand 8d. in the day for thair flesche and 2d in the day for thair fische." They had allowances "for thair fyir, buttir, candill, spice and lentrum meitt. For braid and drink ilk ane of thaim haiffand in the yeir 19 bolls 1 firlot 2 pecs, extending in the haill to 16 chalders 15 bolls 1 firlot."—*Account of Scottish Money, &c., p.* 12, and *Stuart's Records of Kinloss, p.* 159.

sticks, one cup, two phials, three flaggons, a box for the chrism, a cross, in which there was a part of our Lord's cross, a vessel for holding the Eucharist, of considerable weight, and another for the holy water, two instruments for sprinkling the holy water, and two incense censers. There was over against the great altar a painting, representing the twenty-four miracles of St. Colme, and above this two statues of the saint. There were two pillars, on which rested two angels, who held two candlesticks of fifteen branches, according to what is said in the Revelation of St. John. Each of these branches was suspended by a silken rope. He made a pillar for supporting the great wax lights at Easter, with a bishop's chair, and a bench for the choristers." In 1500 Bishop Brown gave various gorgeous dresses, as also a cover for the altar of blue and gold. "He made a pulpit of brass, divided into four divisions, each of which supported the statue of an Evangelist, and when the Gospel was given out, it was in that division which answered to the name of the Evangelist whose Gospel was then read. He made a lesser pulpit, which was supported by the statue of Moses behind, on which there was a candlestick of three branches. He caused the upper parts of the pews to be painted. He renewed the throne of the holy cross, the chancel, the altars of St. Martin and St. Michael. He caused images of the apostles to be made, and portraits of the other saints to be drawn upon the wall all around. As for the kings, noblemen, bishops, and others who had been benefactors to the Church, he caused their figures to be drawn upon the wall behind the altar, that the whole quire might in time of prayers have their eyes upon them. He also beautified all the altars with proper figures, and for the use of each gave proper vestments to the priests. He bought two great bells—the lesser called George, and the greater St. Colme. He procured another, greater, called Maryford, which he left to his successor. A number of the prebendaries contributed vestments, and valuable and weighty silver ornaments. The Prebendary of Finigirth gave two chalices, silver gilt, two silver phials, and a pot adorned with the image of St. Columba, his guardian saint.

The altars in the church were dedicated to, 1. The blessed Virgin, which stood to the right of the principal altar; 2. St. Michael; 3. St. Martin; 4. St. Nicholas; 5. St. Andrew the apostle; 6. the Innocents; 7. All Saints; 8. Stephen the martyr; 9. John the Baptist; 10. St. Catherine; 11. St. John. The 12th is believed to have been the altar of St. Ninians or St. Salvator.*

The Bishops had four mansions or palaces— in Edinburgh, Perth, Cluny, and Dunkeld. The latter stood a little to the south-west of the cathedral. It consisted of several long houses of two stories, thatched after the manner of the times. For greater security to that residence, a castle was erected close to it in 1408. The castle contained "a great hall with vaulted granaries, and a larder"—a precautionary step against any long-continued attack by the Highland clans. Although no vestige of this edifice remains, its site is still called "the Castle Close."

* Myln quoted in Stat. Acc. of Scot., vol. x., p. 972.

In 1508 a wing was built to the palace, and adjoining to it a handsome private chapel. Bishop Brown furnished the palace in 1509, and left the furniture to his successors in office.*

We must now return to the imprisonment of Gavin Douglas, which was deeply felt by his friends, by whom strenuous efforts were made for his release.

The Pope was appealed to, and the following letter of Alexander Turnbull, the agent of Douglas at Rome, addressed to the Earl of Angus, shews the steps which were taken on his behalf:—

Alexander Turnbull to the Earl of Angus.

JHESUS.

My Lord, I commend my seruice oneto your L. in the maist humble wis and emplesit the sammyn to wit, that eftir I gat information at my Lord of Dunkeldin, my maister, was takin and injuriously put in preson, I causit the Papis Halynes to be informit hereapon, and has sped ane breiff of the Papis Halynes direct to the Duk for the delinering and relaxin of hym furth of preson, the copy of the quhilk breff your L. sall resaff; And I purposit incontinent til haf send the said breff hame sa that it mycht haff beyn intimat and present till the Duk, bot efter that thar com heir writing at the Quenis Grace and your L. war remouit of the land, and for certane respectis cummyn in Ingland, I knew nocht to quhat frend I mycht haff send the said breff to that effect at the sammyn mycht haf beyn present till the Duk, and thar is na trast freind now in Brugis that I ma direct my writingis, for Master John Barry the quhilk conwoyit my writingis of befoir has writyn to me and has excusit hym. Thar is laitly past in Ingland a familiar and secretar

* Statistical account of Scotland, x., p. 972.

of the Bisschop of Wlsister * direct be the Papis Halynes wyth the cardinales hat till the Archbisschop of Yorke,† the quhilk was maid Cardinale at the request of the Kingis Grace of Ingland; and your L. mycht fynd the wai for to caus hym to consent to pas in Scotland wyth the Papis brevis, and to present the sammyn to the Duk of Albane for the deliuering of my maister furth of preson, and to haf his ansuer thareapon. I think that war the best wai that we couth fynd, for I dreid that considering as the cais is now, thar is rycht few that will be contentit within our realme to present ony thyng to the Duk til his desplesour ma this way be wroucht. I sal get breuis in diueris formis in the faworis of my Lord, and als sal get speciall command and writing of the Pape till the said secretar to present the said brevis to the Duk; And gif your L. gettis his consent your L. ma solist the Kingis Grace of Ingland to wryt to the Bisschop of Wlsister hereapon, and at the Bisschop ma wryt till his said familiar callit Bonifacius for to accept this mater and tak it one hym for the luff of Almychty God. Remembir apon my L., for war his L. at liberte he wald nocht neglek your L. nor vtheris freindis. I haff sped a breff of the Papis apon the confirmation of the Kingis testament efter my Lordis wryttyng and diuers information send to me thareone, and has send now to the Quenis Grace the copy of the said breff and has writtyn till hir Grace at lentht thareapon, and siclik tuiching vtheris materis. Item, Jerome Friscobald duelland in Brugis causit be his commission Symon de Recasolis and Renald de Recasolis his responsalis in Rome for to ansuer me for the expedition of the bullis of Dunkeldin, and vtheris materis concerning my Lord and freindis. And sen thai bullis war sped, and at thai wnderstand at my Lord was in preson, Jerom has writtin here till his responsalis, and has suspendit that commission, and sa thai will nocht ansure me of a dukat quhill that thai haf vthir command of Jerome; and now is nocht

* Worcester. † Wolsey.

the tym as your L. knawis to want credens considering materis that occurris, for but credens may I do nocht heir for my Lordis and vtheris freindis present, nor yit for myn awin honour; quharfor I beseik your L. to fynde sum way, and caus me to haf credens of part of fynance now in this neid, for Jerome Friscobald has duelland in London a sone callit Leonarde de Friscobald, and Leonarde has Symon and Renald de Recasolis at ansuris til hym here; tharefore your L. ma fynd the wai to caus Leonarde for to wryt to his responsalis for to ansure me of sa mekil fynance as your L. will witschaff, quhill efterwart at we ma fynd sum vthir way; for now passis the Pape furth of Rome to Florens, to Bollone, and to Peis, and we haff mony smal freindis in the court ay waitand thar awantage. For that caus as the Papis Halynes remouis I mon addres me ay to be thar, and that will draw me to the mar large expensis. And wyth the grace of God Almychty I sal do sic diligens efter my power at your L. and vtheris freindis sal be applesit. Baltassar Steward is in the way cumand furth of Scotland here wyth commission and credens fra the Duk til the Papis Halynes contrar my Lord of Dunkeldin as I am informyt; quhen that euer he cummis wyth his credens he will be met. The Papis Halynes and mony vtheris gret men of gud merwalis of the scharp and gret extremite don to my Lord of Dunkeldin and vtheris freindis. The Pape will nocht hastely, as I wnderstand, turne apon my Lord of Dunkeldin, for na information ma be gevin aganis his L., for the Pap has beyn and the Cardinalis sa oft informit of his nobilite, sciens, and vtheris gud nobile properetis, that thai will nocht gif haste credens. And tharfore at your L. be of gud confort and remembir your L. nobill progenitoris, and addres your L. wyth the consal and help of gud freindis to conwict the maleis of your innemys, the quhilk has lawborit and lauboris your L. vtir distruction, the quhilk I traist in God Almychty and your L. gud gouernance sal pas all thare powar. And pleis your L. eftir your L. has considerit this writting to send me ansure thareof; your L. may fynd the way aye quhen any writingis cummys heir to the Bisschop of Wlsistir to caus your writingis send to me to be direct till the Bisschop, for he standis Oratour for the King of Ingland and commonly ilke monetht anis thar cummis writtingis till hym. And as ony thyng occurris, sa at it ples your L. I sall certefy your L. thareof. As the warld standis now, nowthyr ma my Lord wryt to me nor yit I ma get writing conwoit to his L.—God Almychty remeid! This storm is sa wiolent it ma nocht lest. And I get na fynance in hast I mon perfors cum my wa, for I haff lewyt of my credens sen June, and I war rycht way and laichth to depart now quhill my Lord war a free man, and owt of trubill, sa that I mycht vthir wais do. The Bisschop of Wlsistir sped a breiff of the Papis in August direct to the Duk for the deliuering of my Lord, and send the sammyn to the King of Ingland. Gud it war at that breiff war present to the Duk and to haff his ansur, and send the sammyn heir sa that we do heir thareftir. And the glorius Virgyn conserff your L. eternaly. At Rome the ferd dai of Nouember.—Your L. seruitor,

Sr. Alexr. Turnbull.*

The following letter of the Pope to the Duke of Albany is worded in strong language, directly censuring the Duke for the insult he had given to the Holy See by imprisoning Douglas, and awarding pains and penalties to him and all persons aiding openly or secretly in the detention of the Bishop: these penalties to extend to the second generation of their descendants:—

Dilecto filio nobili viro Johanni Duci Albanie Regni Scotie Gubernatori.

Dilecte fili, salutem, etc. Nuper per nos accepto, quod

* *Addressed.*—To my maist speciall Lord my Lord Erle of Angous. MSS. Brit. Mus., Calig. B. v., fol. 97.

nobilitas tua dilectum filium Gawinum electum Dunkeldensem, quem ad supplicationem carissimi in Christo filii nostri Jacobi Scotorum regis illustris ac dilectorum filiorum presidentium Consilii regni Scocie ecclesie Dunkeldensi tunc certo modo pastoris solacio destitute in Episcopum prefeceramus, et pro quo prefatum Jacobum Regem ac te per diuersas nostras in forma breuis literas attencius hortati fueramus vt idem rex assisteret, et tu cum rege et consilio prefatis, eidem Gauino electo in assequenda possessione regiminis et administrationis ipsius ecclesie Dunkeldensis fauorem et auxilium exhiberetis; ac cui antea pro regni Scocie quiete per alias nostras mandaueramus, vt venerabili fratri nostro Andree Archiepiscopo Sanctiandree quem legatum natum dicti regni quoad uiueret cum certis facultatibus creaueramus, nostro nomine inhiberet ne donec aliud sibi mandaremus legatum se nominaret nec sibi concessis vteretur, ad te euocari feceras. Et cum super huiusmodi mandato cuius penitus ignarus erat, eum interrogasses, ipseque Gawinus jurejurando respondisset ipsius mandati sibi per nos facti nullam habuisse nec habere noticiam, sed illius prorsus inscium esse, tu ira accensus, honorisque tui ac proprie salutis immemor, eum temere et iniuriose capiens, demum carceribus mancipari facere seu mandare non formidaueras, in nostrum et apostolice sedis non leuem offensum, atque anime tue detrimentum anathematis, propterea et priuacionis feudorum et inhabilitatis descendentium ad beneficia obtinenda et ecclesiastici interdicti aliasque multiplices penas in constitucione consilii Viennensis contentas, incurrendo: Nos per alias nostras literas eciam in forma breuis nobilitatem tuam in Domino hortandam duximus, vt huiusmodi facinoris atrocitatem celeri remedio corrigere, et opportuna satisfactione emendare studeres, eundemque Gawinum electum quam primum relaxari et ad pristinam libertatem reintegrari procurares. Alioquin expediens nobis ymmo necesse futurum erit pro prefati Gauini electi liberacione et nostri et huiusmodi sancte sedis honoris conseruacione, ad oportuna dicti concilii et aliarum constitucionum apostolicarum prodita a jure remedia contra te, et alios ad detencionem eiusdem auxilium consilium et fauorem, directe uel indirecte, tacite uel expresse prestantes prosilire, eorumque descendentes vsque [ad] secundam generacionem inhabiles, et alios qui cum possent illa negligebant emendare easdemque amplius penas incurrisse declarare et pro talibus nunciari et ab omnibus arcius euitari debere. Nos igitur qui vnicuique in iusticia debitores sumus eidem Gauino electo ne cuius liberacio diucius differatur, de celeris prouisionis remedio succurrere volentes premissa ad memoriam nobilitatis tue de nouo duximus reducenda, eandem nobilitatem tuam quam speciali dilexionis affectu ex visceribus caritatis prosequimur attencius requirentes, quatinus te statim iusticie cui eciam ipse astringeris te exhibeas—etiam ut nos ab huiusmodi cura liberes, prefatum Gawinum electum relaxari et ad prestinam libertatem reintegrari cum effectu facere et emendare nullatenus differas. Alioquin inuiti et contra mentem nostram cogimur pro iusticie debito nedum ad concilii et constitucionum aliaque a iure prodita remedia huiusmodi verumetiam acriores censuras et penas contra te, et quoscunque alios detencioni ipsius Gawini electi auxilium consilium et fauorem directe uel indirecte, tacite vel expresse prestantes, eorumque descendentes usque ad secundam generacionem procedere, et alias in has nostri pastoralis officii partes interponere, prout pro ipsius Gawini electi liberacione et libertatis ecclesiastice et auctoritatis sedis predicti conseruacione conspexerimus expedire. Datum etc.*

In order to trace the steps by which Douglas regained his liberty, and was inducted into office, we must shortly glance at the affairs of Queen Margaret,

* MSS. Brit. Mus. Calig. B. v., fol. 97.

with which it was his fate to be so intimately connected.

The Regent Albany, after his severe punishment of Gavin Douglas and his relative Lord Drummond, kept the Queen also in a kind of captivity in what Douglas from sad experience knew to be, and in a subsequent paper, calls "the wyndy and richt vnplesant Castell and royk of Edinburgh," and deprived her of the custody of her young sons. She at last found this treatment so irksome that she fled to the Border Castle of Blackadder, and afterwards to Harbottle, where she was delivered of her daughter, Lady Margaret Douglas, subsequently the grandmother of King James VI. Soon after this she went to London and was well received at the Court of her brother Henry.

The Regent now became sensible of the imprudence of his conduct towards the sister of the king of England. He sent letters to Margaret, beseeching her to listen to reason, and declaring his aversion to rigorous measures. The Queen replied to his ambassadors that apprehensions for her life had constrained her to quit Scotland, and demanded the tutelage of her sons and the Regency of the kingdom. She related her grievances at the hands of Albany in a long paper which she submitted to his ambassadors, in which the following particulars are very graphically given :—

"And at the comynge of the said Duke into Scotland, he made me fare and pleasante semblance, and afterwards purposed by the advice of his Counseill, to take the King and his broder, my said tender childer from me. And thereupon caused the Lord Dromonde, being Constable of my said Castle of Stirling, whiche had the keping of my said tender childer, to be accused because the said Lorde Dromonde wapped his sleif at an Harrold, and gave hym vpon the breste with his hand, for, because the said Harrold behaved hym otherwise thenne he ought to do, saing that he come in message from the Lordis to my Lady the Kings moder, which was afore the comyng of the said Duke into Scotland.

"And after that also committed the Postulate of Arbroth to warde, because that I wrote a lettre to the Popes Holynes, in commende of the said Postulate to the Bishopricke of Dunkeld, and also, that the Kings Highnes, my derest broder, at my instance wrote anoder lettre to the Popes said Holyness in the favour of the said Postulate, whereupon I come downe to the Holyrodehous to sollicite and labour to the said Duke (sore weeping) for the said Lord Dromonde and Postulate being my counseillouris, but grace got I none, and thenne oder of my counseillouris and seruantis, seing that, withdrew them all from me except my Lord of Anguiss and the Lord Chamberlain.

"And thereupon the said Duke of Albany, by the advice of his counsaill, appointed thre lordis to have the keping of my said childer the King and his broder, as more at large it appereth in a bill of supplication given in to the Kings said Highnes my dereste broder of my matiers aforesaid.

"And for to saye that ever I was aggreable, content, or pleased that the said Duke of Albeny shuld come into Scotland, or that ever he did iustice or meddled with justice, but only vexed and trobled me and my ffreinds it appereth in the said supplicacion whiche I am redy to justifie poincte by ponicte."*

To the Queen's terms the Duke of Albany could not agree, but he offered to set Gavin Douglas at liberty, and to give him a benefice of the value of two or three thousand franks. To this the Queen replied :—

* MSS. Brit. Mus. Calig. B. vi., fol. 117.

"In the furste to lowse Schir Gawen Dowglas, and cause hym be put to libertie, giffand hym ane benefice of ii^{m} or iii^{m} ffrankis.

"I conceyue by the credence of the said Master James that he causes be content for my pleasour to put at large and libertie Mastur Gawen Douglas, and to geve hyme a benefice of ii or iii^{m} ffrankis. I doute not but the Poopes Holynes accepteth and taketh the said Master Gawen for the Bishop of Donkeld, like as his said Holynes signyfyed vnto youe by oon of his breves lately sent and conveyed vnto youe by Carlyll, Harrold de armes. Glad would I be to see the said Bishop at libertie, albeit ye gave vnto hyme noe benefice, but that ye wold suffer hyme to enjoye and occupye his aune promocion; howbeit I doe remyte the reformacion thereof to the Poopes said Holynes, trustinge he will see redress in that behalve as right, and the liberties of Cristis churche dooth require."*

In consequence of these negociations Douglas at last obtained his liberty. His imprisonment had lasted about a year. On the 30th July, 1516, the name of the Elect of Dunkeld appears in the sederunt of the Lords of Council, and again on 15th September.

On the 20th of that month, the Regent, who seems now to have become favourably disposed towards Douglas, wrote the following letter to the Pope on his behalf:—

To Leo X. Sovereign Pontiff.

Most blessed father, we are happy to kiss your feet.

Some time since the church of Dunkeld became vacant by the death of George its late Pastor, who died at home. The President and Chapter, residing at Dunkeld at the time, postulated to the church as their pastor, though as to sacred matters they could not canonically elect, an illus-

* MSS. Brit. Mus. Calig., B. vi., fol. 117.

trious man, Mr Andrew Stewart, by both his parents procreated of royal blood, son of the Earl of Athole, and powerful in those parts.

They committed to his keeping and protection the lands, castles and places belonging to the Bishopric, that by his authority the incursions of the Forest people might be repelled.

But your Holiness, as was reported by the most Reverend Cardinal de Medicis, assumed to the church of Dunkeld Gavin Douglas; who, by the frequent letters of your Clemency to us being at last reconciled to us, is now admitted to the possession of that church.

Lest, however, any tumult or sedition should arise, we have persuaded the other, who under pretence of his being postulated held the forts and castles, to enter into an agreement, which, if confirmed by the authority of your Blessedness, would happily end the whole affair. What we therefore entreat at present is, that all defects of law and deed, and all errors being removed, the contract may be ordered to be observed.

A more full relation will be made by the most Reverend Cardinal of St. Eusebius.

Most Blessed Father, farewell. From Edinburgh, the 28th day of the month of September, in the year of Salvation, 1516.*

All difficulties as to his appointment having passed, Douglas had now to go through the ceremony of consecration as Bishop of Dunkeld.

Alexander Myln, one of the Canons of Dunkeld, and who subsequently was the first President of the Court of Session, wrote the lives of the Bishops of that See. In his book we get some interesting particulars of the proceedings regarding the Bishop's induction into office. Myln states, that James Beaton,

* Trans. from orig. in Epist. Reg. Scot., tom. i., p. 222.

Archbishop of Glasgow, and Chancellor of Scotland, accommodating himself to the new turn of affairs, invited Douglas to Glasgow, where he himself performed the ceremony of consecrating him to the episcopal office; and as he knew that his funds were low from the circumstances in which he had been lately placed, not only paid all the expenses of his consecration, but gave him presents of jewels.*

The narrative of Myln, who was a contemporary, gives but little information as to the consecration of Douglas, a ceremony which forms an interesting episode in the history of the Church in Scotland.

It would appear that about the year 1489, King James IV., either actuated by deep religious feeling, or imitating a similar practice in some of the continental kingdoms, caused himself to be enrolled among the Canons of the cathedral church of St Kentigern at Glasgow. An Act of the Scottish Parliament passed in that year erected Glasgow into an Archbishopric, and a Bull of Pope Innocent VIII. was obtained confirming the same. The Bishops of Dunkeld, Dunblane, Galloway, and Argyll were made suffragans to the new Archbishop, and these sees, with Glasgow itself, were thus withdrawn from the province of St. Andrews.

This measure was strongly opposed by Andrew Forman, Archbishop of St. Andrews; and as the Bull of the Pope was only in favour of the then Bishop of Glasgow (who had died some years before the appointment of Douglas to Dunkeld), there was a difficulty as to whether the consecration of Douglas

* Vitae Episc. Aberd., p. 73.

should take place at Glasgow or St. Andrews. There can be no doubt that Douglas would have much preferred being consecrated by Archbishop Beaton at Glasgow to professing submission at St. Andrews to his old and crafty rival Archbishop Forman.

This prelate, however, was determined to exercise his authority, and treated as a nullity the consecration of Douglas at Glasgow. In a manuscript preserved in the Library of the University of St. Andrews, it is stated that Douglas was duly consecrated in the metropolitan church of St. Andrews by the Archbishop, assisted by John, Bishop of Brechin, and James, Bishop of Dunblane,—"per sacrarum manuum nostrarum impositionem sacrum consecrationis munus impendimus." From the same document it appears that Douglas consented to what was done, for there is added, "quam consecrationem in se humiliter suscipiens eandem ratam et gratam habuit, et presentium tenore habet."

At this time Forman took the opportunity, not only of making Douglas apologise for his long course of opposition to him, but also of exacting from him a promise of obedience for the future. He made Douglas present himself at the Abbey of Dunfermline, and there, on bended knees and with clasped hands, — "genibus flexis, manibus suis junctis et inter manus reuerendissimi Patris sui Metropolitani et Primatis immissis et appositis" —he swore to be submissive to the Archbishop: "Ego Gauinus Episcopus Dunkeldensis ab hac hora et inantea juro quod fidelis et obediens ero tibi Andree Archiepiscopo Sanctiandree, totius regni Scotie

Primati et Legato, meo Metropolitano et Primati, et successoribus tuis canonice intrantibus. Sic me Deus adiuuet, et per hec Sacrosancta Dei Ewangelia."*

Myln gives a graphic account of the circumstances which occurred on Douglas taking possession of his See:—

"After his consecration he first visited St. Andrews, on Michaelmas week, and then the church of Dunkeld. The first night he was very affectionately received by the clergy and laity, who all praised God for so noble, so learned, and so worthy a bishop. He published the bulls at the great altar, gave his blessing, and lodged at the Dean's house, as he had no access to the palace, which, with the steeple, Andrew Stewart's servants held out for him, and they refused to deliver them in their master's name, alleging that they did all by the authority of the Regent. On this account he was forced to have the service of God performed in the Dean's house. To this place he called the Canons, and received their homage, and it was with their whole heart they yielded him homage; on the other hand the Bishop swore to keep all the statutes of the church. After dinner he consulted the gentlemen and clergy who were with him as to what course he ought to follow in that conjuncture. Some advised him to send notice to the Regent, others would have him go in person.

In the midst of these consultations they are informed that Andrew Stewart was in arms, with a design to relieve those who held out the palace. That instant a discharge of cannon shot came from the steeple and palace. Then all the people of rank hurried to the Bishop's defence. These were the worthy Dean, James Lord Ogilvy, David Master of Crawfurd, Colin Campbell of Glenurquhar, Lord Kinfauns, the Prebendary of Alith, and many other church-

* Form. Inst. Eccles. MS., St. Andrews, fol. 53.

men. Notice is sent of these transactions to the Bishop's friends in Angus and elsewhere: upon which the next day there came such crowds from Montrose, from the low parts of Fife, and the country round about, that the town could scarce hold them. But for all their number the Prebendary of Alith had laid up such abundance of every thing, that there was room and provisions for all the men, and also for their horses.

The Bishop elect, not having it in his power to relieve those who held out the palace and steeple, is forced to retire to the woods. Then Bishop Douglas, on his side, summoned them to surrender, under pain of excommunication. For fear of this threat, partly by force, partly by stratagem, the steeple was put into the possession of James Carmichael, of some of the Prebendaries, and of the Bishop's household. This put the people in the palace in great fear: they obtained a truce and a suspension of the excommunication for some hours; but after that time they were still unwilling to surrender; however, by the merits of St. Colme they gave up the palace without bloodshed.

Upon this the Earl and his brother went to court to complain of what had been done; the Bishop went also to defend himself. For some time there were mutual accusations. However, by the wisdom of some of the counsellors they agreed upon these terms: That Andrew Stewart should retain all the Bishop's rents he had levied, and should also have the churches of Alith and Cargill, upon condition of paying some chalders of victual to the Bishop.

From this time the church and the whole province had peace; and though the Bishop was loaded with debts he yet gave himself to good works. His first work was the bridge, one arch of which his predecessor had finished, and his executors drove the piles for other two; Bishop Douglas continued this work. And upon receiving two hundred and forty pounds from Bishop George's executors, the work was brought the length that all travellers on foot had an easy passage. His other good works, spiritual and temporal, I leave to the pens of the higher Canons." *

Being at last in peaceable possession of his See, Douglas engaged with diligence in the discharge of his duty amongst his clergy and people. He also took a prominent part in public affairs, as his name occurs as having been present at several meetings of the Lords of Council. At one of these he was elected, along with the Secretary of the Council, Patrick Panter, to proceed to France and assist the Bishop of Ross, Ambassador there, in renewing the ancient league between the two nations. They departed on the 17th May 1517, and after arranging matters satisfactorily they returned to Scotland about the end of June, as appears by their following letter to Wolsey requesting a safe conduct through England:—

Maist reverend in God, efter dew salutation, We suppois that it is knawin to your Lordschip how be command of oure souerane lord and master the King of Scottis we ar directit nocht anerly for peax and amite betuix the Realmis of France, Ingland, and Scotland, but als for vniversall concorde in the Kirk of God with sufficient auctorite and speciall commande gevin to ws to transport ws quhare it sall be expedient for the premisses; and therapon we in thir partis have spokin with the King of France, and now we vnderstand that the Duc of Albany, Gouernour of Scotland and tutour to oure souerane Lord is discendit in Bertaigne quhais Secretare Gualtere Malynny, as we beleuit, suld have cummyn throw Ingland and brocht to ws ane saufconduct. We herfor thocht necessare to aduertis your Lo. this tyme, to effect that we

* Trans. of Perth Antiquarian Society, I, p. 66.

micht have the said saufconduct according to oure supplicacion for the samyn, quhilk we send to your L. hamely, becaus we knaw weill your L. may greitly further, and is of gude mynde towart peax amangis Cristin princis for rest and vnite of Cristianite, and this we pray your L. at this tyme, as we beleif your L. will for the grete confidens we knaw the said Lord Gouernour has in your L. Maist Reuerend Fader in God, the Haly Gaist haue you in his keping. At Abbayweill the xxvii day of Junii. Be youre gude and laulye frendis, &c.,

Ambassadouris of Scotland.*

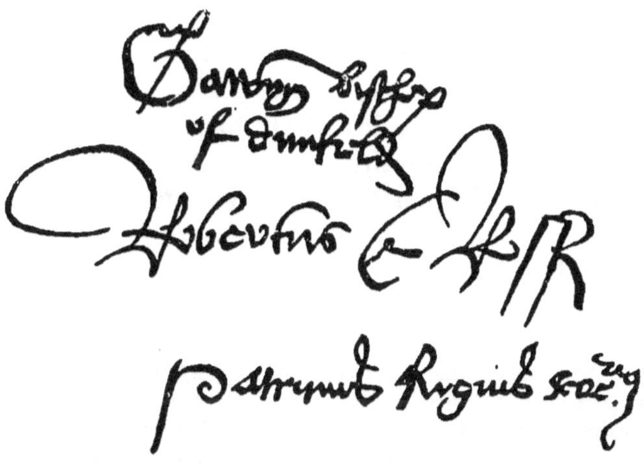

To the maist reuerend in God Archbishop and Cardinale of York, Chancellare of England, Legate of the Lege Apostolique.

The negociations of the Scottish Ambassadors resulted in the memorable treaty of Rouen, by which Scotland and France became mutually bound to aid each other against the power of England.

The Duke of Albany, who had found his regency no easy task, and used to say he wished he had broken

* MSS. Brit. Mus. Calig. B. vi., fol. 174.

all his legs and arms before he had stirred a step towards Scotland, took the opportunity of going to France at this time for the purpose of signing the treaty and visiting his own vast estates in that country.

Before leaving Scotland he delegated his authority to the Archbishops of St Andrews and Glasgow, and to the Earls of Arran, Angus, Argyle and Huntly. The power of Angus now became so great that in 1520 a design was formed by his powerful rival, James Hamilton, Earl of Arran, to seize him, and in all probability afterwards to put him to death. The carrying out of this scheme caused the well-known fight which is recorded in Scottish history under the name of "Clean-the-causeway."

The Earl of Arran and the Hamiltons met in the house of James Beaton, Archbishop of Glasgow, situated at the bottom of Blackfriars' Wynd, to deliberate on the manner of the execution of the plot.*

* The Palace of the Bishops of Dunkeld, and of Gawin Douglas in particular, the friendly opponent of the Archbishop, stood on the opposite side of the same street, immediately to the west of Robertson's Close, and scarcely an hundred yards from Blackfriars Wynd. It appears to have been an extensive mansion, with large gardens attached to it, running back nearly to the Old Town wall. Among the pious and munificent acts recorded by Myln of Bishop Lauder, the preceptor of James II., who was promoted to the See of Dunkeld in 1452, are the purchasing of a mansion in Edinburgh for himself and successors, and the founding of an altarage in St. Giles' Church there to St. Martin. It cannot be doubted that the mansion thus gifted and enlarged was a building well suited by its magnificence for the abode of the successive dignitaries of the Church who were promoted to that exalted station, and that it formed another striking feature in this street of palaces. Its vicinity both to the Archiepiscopal residence and to the Blackfriars' Church—the later scene of rescue of Arch-

The Earl of Angus hearing of their intentions, sent his uncle Gavin Douglas to state that he was willing to retire with his party from the city, if they were permitted to do so in safety. Douglas in the meantime reminded Beaton that it was his business as a churchman to preserve order. The Archbishop purposed, if necessary, to assist the Hamiltons in person, and had put on armour below his ecclesiastical vestments. He made excuses to Douglas, laying the blame of the whole matter on the Earl of Arran, and concluded by saying, "There is no remedy, upon my conscience I cannot help what is about to happen." At the same time he struck his breast with his hand, when the coat of mail was heard to rattle. Douglas perceiving this, said—"How now, my Lord, methinks your conscience clatters."

After leaving the Archbishop, Douglas went back

bishop Beaton by Gawin Douglas—affords a very satisfactory illustration of one of the memorable occurrences during the turbulent minority of James V. This old Episcopal residence has other associations of a very different nature; for we learn from Knox's history that, when he was summoned to appear in the Blackfriars Church on the 15th of May 1556, and his opponents deserted their intended attack through fear, "the said Johne, the same day of the summondis, tawght in Edinburgh in a greattar audience than ever befoir he had done in that toune; The place was the Bischope of Dunkellis, his great loodgeing, whare he continewed in doctrin ten dayis, boyth befoir and after nune." A modern land occupied the site of Bishop Douglas' palace; and the pleasure grounds wherein the poet was wont to stray, and on which we may suppose him to have exercised his refined taste and luxurious fancy in realising such a "gardyne of plesance" as he describes in the opening stanzas of his Palis of Honor, was till recently crowded with mean dwellings of the artisan and labourer, which in their turn have been swept away in an extensive scheme of city improvements.—*Wilson's Memorials of Edinburgh*, p. 339.

to his nephew, and bade him defend himself like a man. "For me," he said, "I will go to my chamber and pray for you."

Sir Patrick Hamilton, a wise and moderate man, brother of the Earl of Arran, now advised his brother to avoid coming to blows, when Sir James Hamilton of Draphane, a natural son of the Earl, upbraided him with cowardice in declining the combat. Sir Patrick then cried out, "Bastard smaik, I shall fight this day where thou darest not be seen:" and followed by the Hamiltons, threw himself sword in hand upon the spearmen of the Earl of Angus. At last the Hamiltons were completely routed, and fled out of the town in great confusion, leaving seventy-two of their number dead on the streets, amongst whom were the Master of Montgomery, and Sir Patrick himself.

Archbishop Beaton, who took part in the fight, and who, Buchanan informs us, flew about as a firebrand of sedition, narrowly escaped. He was taken from behind the high altar in the church of the Black Friars where he had fled for sanctuary, and owed the preservation of his life to Gavin Douglas.

When the Regent Albany left Scotland in 1517, Queen Margaret began to make arrangements for her return thither. After leaving the English Court she proceeded to Berwick, where she met her husband, the Earl of Angus, who had remained in Scotland during her visit to her brother. The Queen had many causes of quarrel with Angus. He had cruelly deserted her when she was on her way to London, and that at the very time when she was laid prostrate by an attack of typhus fever. She now ascertained that during her absence her husband had been guilty of the abduction of Lady Janet Stuart, a daughter of Lord Traquair, whom he was keeping at his Castle of Douglas. She also found that, at the instigation of his uncle, the Earl was drawing her Ettrick Forest rents, had established himself at her house of Newark there, and prevented her from giving her tenants their discharge or receipts. "My Forest of Ettrick," she says, "ought to bring me in 4000 merks yearly, and I shall never get a penny. Much more evil," she continues, "did Angus perpetrate, which she would cause a servant of hers to report to her brother as it was too long to write."*

The Queen now wished to divorce Angus; while at the same time his uncle Gavin came in for a share of her resentment.

In order to be revenged, she used every artifice to bring the Regent Albany back to Scotland, as the only one who was able to punish her husband for his nefarious conduct.

In February 1521, judging from the following letter to Cardinal Wolsey, Douglas seems to have been apprehensive of Albany's return, and of what eventually happened—the loss of his ecclesiastical preferments:—

Gavin Douglas to Cardinal Wolsey.

Maist Reuerend in God, and my gud and maist special Lord, eftir laulie recommendatioun pleis your Lordschipe to wyt that x or xii dais syne their com ane schip furth of

* Strickland's "Queens of Scotland," vol. i., p. 151.

Franche, quhairin come ane Gonsailis, ane seruand of the Dwik of Albaneis, and hes brocht diuers writingis to syndrie of this cuntre assurand thaim that within schortt tyme he salbe within this ralme, quhilk will nother cum for honour nor proffeit to the Kingis Hienes of this realm, for I am assurit he repentis richt sair the last tyme he departit furth of this realm in the fassion as he did. The Castell of Dunbar is bayth with mwnymentis and wyttalis prowidit as evyr wes ony in the yle of Bartane. The said Lord takkis plane part with the freir that seykis pensyoun apon my benefice of Dunkeld, and sais largislie that I sall regret that euir I yeid that gait. In Ingland your Grace and Wisdom ma considder this, and supple oure young King that it cum nocht to syk poynt as men belewis, and evir he cum heir again. And I beseik your Graice that the Kingis Hyenes and your Graice haif me and my afferis recommendit in Royme; and as for vther noweltis thar is nayn bot at all the Lordis in this Realm ar aggreand and at gud poynt, thankat be Almychty God, quha mot haif your Graice eternalye conseruit.

At Edinburgh this penult day of Februar, be your Seruitour, DUNKELD, etc.*

At last, in November 1521, the Duke of Albany returned to Scotland, and was received by the Queen with every appearance of friendship. The Earl of Angus, when he found the Regent was supported with a strong French force, and was well supplied with money and ammunition, fled to the Borders, and took refuge at the Kirk of Steyle,** along with the Lords

* *Addressed.*—To ane mayst reuerend fadir in God, Archibischop of York. *Docqueted.*—Edinr., 28th February, B. of Dunkeld to the Lord Cardinall aduertising a messenger come into Scotland from the D. of Albany, who is soon after expected to be ther.—MSS. Brit. Mus. Cal. B. 1., fol. 77. ** Probably the Church of St. Mary, of Upsetlington, now Ladykirk, Berwickshire.

PGARET

Home and Somerville. From this place Angus sent his uncle Gavin to the Court of Henry for assistance, and at the same time instructed him to report a scandalous intimacy which had sprung up between the Queen and the Regent.*

Douglas accordingly proceeded to London with the following letter from Angus to Wolsey, and a set of instructions to be shown to the King of England. In these instructions it is stated that Angus and his friends had taken an oath "upon the holy Ewangellis," before Douglas and Lord Dacre, that they would never make peace with the Duke of Albany, without the consent of Henry.

The Earl of Angus to Cardinal Wolsey.

My Lord, in my maist humyll maner I recommend my lauchfull seruice to youre Grace, quhom plesit vnderstand I and vtheris has presentlie direct this berar, my derrest uncle, my Lord Bischop of Dunkeld, towart the Kingis Grace youre Soueraine, apoun certane necessare instructiounis the quhilkis I traist salbe acceptable baith vnto his Hienes and youre Grace. Quhairfor, at the vttermaist of my powere, I beseyk youre Grace at my said vncle be thankfullie ressauit and to haue gude and haisty expedition of his materis and directiounis, and at youre Grace plesit schew you his gude Lord and ouris in that behalf, and to geif to him na less credence in euery thyng than to my self presentlie in persoun, for it

* Lord Dacre, writing to Wolsey, says, "There is marvellous great intelligence between Queen Margaret and the Duke of Albany, as well all the day as mich of the night. In manner they care not who knows it. And if I durst say it, for fear of displeasure of my sovereign, they are over tender; whereof, if your Grace examine the Bishop of Dunkeld of his conscience, I trust he will show the truth." The portrait of the Duke of Albany and Queen Margaret here inserted may possibly have been painted about this period.—MSS. Cal. B. vi., 205, dated Dec. 1521.

is na lytill besynes causis him mak sik travale now at sik poynt of necessite, quhen I, and all his frendis in thir partis, mycht sa evill waunt his help and gude counsale. Neuertheles baith we and he, fullie assurit in youre gudenes and hye wisdome, beleving fermlye that his passage towart the Kyngs Hyenes and youre Grace mychtavale gretumly, nocht alanerly to himself and ws, bot alsua to the weilfare of this realme and surtye of the Kingis persoun my Souerane, derest nevo to the Kings Hienes youre maister, has presentlye direct him, fullye instruct in that behalf, vnto his Majesty, as said is. Beseking youre Grace to tak gud hede to the mater, and quhat stede, plesour, or lauchfull seruice I may doo or procure to be done to your plesour in thir partis, I salbe glayd to fulfyll the samyn at the commande of youre Grace, as knawis our Lord God, quha haue youre Grace in his blissit keping eternalye. At the Kyrk of Steyll the xiii day of December, subscriuit with my hand.

Youris, with his lauchfull seruice,

ARCHIBALD, ERL OF ANGUS.

To my Lord Cardinallis Grace of Inglaund.*

Instructions for Bishop Douglas from the Earl of Angus and others. 1521.

Instructions and Commissioun for my Lord of Dunkeld, to be schawin onto the Kyngis Grace of Ingland on the behalf of my Lord of Angus his kyn and freindis, Lord Hwme, Lord Somervel, thar kyn and frendis, for the weil and souerte of thar Souerane Lord; and to apont with his Hienes apon thir articulis efter following, or ony otheris not being heir exprest, as is thocht expedient be the Kingis Grace, his Consale, and avice of the said Bischop for the securite forsaid.

Item, first he sal schaw how the Duke of Albany is cum to Scotland, and throu his pretendit titill to the croune, it is presumyt, he having the keping of the King our Souer-

* MSS. Brit. Mus. Cal., B. vi., fol. 211.

ane your nevo and the reule of his realme and subiectis. gret suspicioun and danger of his person. Quharfor without hasty help and assistance of the Kingis Grace of Ingland, it is thocht til ws that our souerane Lord forsaid standis in gret juperte of his life; the quhilk help and we may haue, we sal de and liff in the querrell for the souerte of our said Soverane, without quhais help it is nocht in our power to perform, and as we may we sall luke to the mater in the meyn tyme.

Item, it is thocht till ws at our said Souerane can nocht be weil and souerlie kepit within his realm, the Duke of Albany beand Gouernour thereof and present in the realme, the said Duk alswa having the Lordis keparis of the Kingis person at his commandment and plesour.

Alsua it is thocht til ws that gif our Souerane suld remane in his awin realme, the Duke being in Scotland and Gouernour tharof, that thir thre Lordis quhilk now hes the name of the keping of the King, and hes nocht in deid, thai or otheris his keparis to be apointit be the parliament of Scotland suld haue the nomination and ponting of al his seruandis about him, sik as cukis and al other men of office, as thai wald ansuer for to God, to thar consciens and to thar Souerane, and nocht the Lordis quhilkis now hes him in keping, ilkane of thame cumand thar four moneth, quhilkis in maner cumis for a schawing or a sycht, seand the said Duke of Albany poyntis all officiaris him self about our said Souerane. And alswa hes keparis of the castell and kepis bath wach and ward abone the King and Lordis keparis of his person. And alsua the Lord kepar for the tyme has na manerof rewle nowther of our Soueranys diet, nor poynting of his seruandis about him, nor abilzement of his person; Quharfor but help and remeid heirof to our apperance, our said Souerane is gane without the mercy of God Almychty.

Item, we think and knawis be experiens that the Quene, be evil and scinistar consale, is mekill inclynyt to the plesour of the Duke in al maner of thingis, and ar neuer syndry bot euery day togidder, owther forrow none or efter; and as it is supposit hes intendit a diuorce betwix the Erle of Angus and the Quene, and quhat consale the said Queyne had gevin hyr be the Bischop of Glasgw, the Abbot of Halyrudehows, and Master John Cantlie, quhom to the said Duke now at his cumyng in Scotland hes gevin to hir thir promotions, the Archbischiprik of Sanctandrois to Glasgw, the Bischoprik of Glasgw to the Abbot of Halyrudehous, and the Abbacy of Kilwynyng to Cantlie and other twa benefices, and als hes had Grissell hys seruand remanand with the Quene thir thre quarteris of this yer for the completing of his purpos; and a gret part of this consale fader frer Henry Chadworth, quhilk the Kyngis Grace of Ingland send to the Quene, knawis in euery behalf.

Item, the said Duk of Albany come at his first hame cummyng to Striueling quhar the Queyn was, and fra thyne to Lithgow bath in cumpany togidder, and syne til Edinburgh, and apon the secund day efter thar cummyng til Edinburgh the said Duk with the Queyn went to the Castell quhar the King was, and thar the capitane deliverit the keys to the Duke, and he deliverit thame to the Quene to dispone at hir plesour, and syne scho gave thame to the Duke agane as hir maist trast for the keping of the Kingis persone.

Item, gif our Souerane can nocht be the consent of the thre estatis of Scotland be transportit furth of his realme, nor yit the Duke of Albany to devoyd the realme, that than thir thre lordis quhilkis suld have the keping of the Kingis Grace, or otheris siclike as sall pless the thre estatis to apoint, to haue the nominatioun and ponting of all officiaris and otheris at ar necessar to be about our said Soueranys person, sik as thai wil ansuer for to God and thar Souerane apon thar allegeance; and at the saidis Lordis being keparis and otheris his officiaris forsaid salbe cleirly relaxit and quytclamyt to haue na melling with the said Duke, onto the tyme our said Souerane be of perfite age as can be thocht. And at the said Duke sal nocht cum be xxx mylis quhar the Kyngis Grace is, nor nane of the Dukis familiars resort in the place quhar he remanys, without quhilk provisioun and help the Kyngis Grace standis in extreme danger of the prosperite of his life.

Item, it is thocht gud by ws, so it stand with the Kyngis plesour and the Consalis, that thar be laubour maid be the Kingis Grace of Ingland onto the Papis Halynes for the securite and sur keping of our Souerane Lordis persoun be his special writingis, to be solistit be his oratouris in the Court of Rome gif it can nocht be done be him self.

Item, the said Erl of Angus, and Lordis Hwme and Somervell, sal weil and trewly tak part in so fer as in thame is for the weil and souerte of the prosper estait of thar Souerane Lord, alsweil be thame self kyn and frendis and parttakkaris, swa that thai may be in souerte of the Kingis Grace that he sal tak na peax nor abstinens of wer with the Duke of Albany without the saidis Lordis bruke thar levingis and all that to thame rychtwisly pertenys in securite, but ony danger of the said Duke, the King thar Souerane beand in sowerte as said is: And for the securite tharof the saidis Lordis ar bodely sworn apon the haly Ewangellis, for thar part, kyn and frendis, befor a reuerend fader, Gawin Bischop of Dunkeld, and Thomas Lord Dacre that thai sal perform, and nocht to trete with the said Duke without the avice of the Kingis Grace of Ingland, bot to remane at the sowerte of thar Souerane Lord swa that the saidis Lordis may be aduertist that his Hienes wil assist to thame, quharof thai ar rycht desyrus to have ansuer in al haste.

Item, gif it sal fortoun, as God forbeid it do, quhilk is to ws mor likly than contrary, that our Souerane be put doun or de, it is than weil knawin that the Duk of Albany wil pretend to the croune. In that cace the saidis Lordis desiris to knaw quhat supple the Kingis Grace wil do thame, and desiring that thar be na peax nor abstinens of weir tane with him without thar securite as said is. And for the mar securite the saidis Lordis hes subscrivit this write with thar handis. At the Kyrk of the Steill, the xiiij day of December, the yer of God j^{m}. v^{c}. and xxi. yeris.

ARCHBALD ERL OF ANGUS.
GEORGE LORD HOM.
JON SOWMERWELL.*

Douglas was at the same time summoned to Rome, as appears from the following letter of Lord Dacre, although the object of his mission is not clear. Sir Henry Ellis thinks that Albany thus arranged matters, probably fearing the talent of Douglas for negociation, and to prevent a long residence on his part as the agent of the Earl of Angus at the English Court;† but from the tenor of the letter of Douglas to Wolsey, dated 1st January 1522, it would appear that he anticipated having to defend himself against certain impeachments.

Lord Thomas Dacre to Cardinal Wolsey.

My Lord, pleas it your Grace, the Busshop of Dunkeld is sommoned to the court of Rome by the meanes of the Duke of Albany, who is right glad thereof, one way seing that his quarrell is so good, and moost speciall that he may lawbor to the Kings Highnes and your Grace to let the Duke of Albany in the acheving of his dampnable mynd and entreprise for the suyrtie of the King his Soueraiu, whiche is in good beleue that with the help of the Kings Highnes and your Grace shall com out of the dangeour of the said Duke and his dampnable purpose, without which it is past remedie, but onelie in the mercie of God. And if it can be thought good for that purpose, that the said Busshop

* MSS. Cott. Calig., B. vi., 223.
† Ellis' Orig. Letters, 3d series, vol. i., p. 286.

remane still and send his proctor to Rome with his answer, with som favorable lettre in his favour fro your Grace to the Kings Oratour at Rome. I trust he wilbe ordred therin aftre your Gracis pleasure, whom it will pleas your Grace to bring to the Kings presence, to the intent that he may shew to his Highnes and your Grace the vehement dangeour that the King his Souerain stands in; and also to declare certain instrucions made by Th'erle of Angus, the Lordes Home and Somervell, on the behalf of them self and other ther kyn, freindes, and partietakers, for the wele and suyrtie of ther Souerain; to the which Articles, standing with the Kings highe pleasure for the partie of the said Lordes, they ar bodely sworn vpon the holy Evangelists to performe the same in the presence of the said Busshop of Dunkeld and me, whom I beseche your Grace may be fauorably herd. I haue graunted to the said Busshop of Dunkeld a saufconduct by the auctoritie of myne office of Wardanre; because the tyme was so shorte, and the dangeour of his message grete, he could not tarie of going and commyng to and fro the Kings Highnes. Howbeit I haue writen to his said Highnes for a saufconduct, which I trust shall mete hym or he com to your presence. And the blessed Trinite preserue your Grace. At the Castell of Norham the xv daye of December.

Yowers wit es serues,

THOMAS L. DACRE.

To my Lord Cardinallis Grace.*

The following letters to Wolsey were written by Douglas while he was engaged in these negociations. The first announces his arrival in England; the second cautions Wolsey against Gaultier Malynne the Duke of Albany's Secretary, who on the part of the Duke requested Wolsey to detain Douglas in

* MSS. Brit. Mus. Cal., B. vi., fol. 215.

London; the third contains the answers of Douglas to the statements of the Duke's Secretary; and the fourth cautions Wolsey against John Duncanson and Evangelista, sent by Albany and the Archbishop of Glasgow to prejudice him against Douglas.

Gavin Douglas to Cardinal Wolsey.

My Lord, in all humble and dew maneyr I recommend my lawfull seruyce onto your Grace, quham plasyt knaw I am cummyn in this realm, send from my lord Erll of Angus, othir Lordis of Scotland and grete personagis to the Kyngis Hyenes apon certan neydfull dyrectiounes, and specially concernyng the weylfar and surte of his derrest nevo the Kyng my Soueran. And gif I, quhilk am onknawyn wyth his Magestye, durst haf presumyt to haf wrytyn onto the samyn, I wald gladly, besekyng your Grace to support me in that behalf, and that it mot plays Yow to shaw me in quhat place and quhat tyme I sall cum to your Grace, and sa furth onto the Kyngis Hyenes, and salbe verre glad to awayt apon your command. And gif it had nocht beyn for this he fest of Crystis natyvyte, and als that I am sumpart accrasyt by the way, I suld haf cummyn strecht to your Grace; besekyng elyke wys the samin to pardon this my hamly wrytyn, and to send ansuer tharof at your plasour. And the blyssyt Lord preserue your Grace in lang and eternall prosperite. At Waltam Cros this Crystynmes evyn. By the hand of your chaplan wyth his lawfull seruyce,

GAWYN, Bischop of Dunkeld, etc.*

Gavin Douglas to Cardinal Wolsey.

Pleiss your Grace, Maister Galteor, Commendator of the Abbay of Glenluse and secretar to the Duke of Albany, callit Gouernor of Scotland, is cum to London, and with him Ross Herald and ane nothir pursauant callit Carrik, quhilk

* State Paper Off. Wolsey's Corresp., iv., 71.

is ane France man borne, and I traist is to pass to France, and with thame thre vthir servandis; quhairfor I beseyk your Grace gif it war your plesour that I mycht haif presense of the Kingis Hienes als sone as thai, and gif I mycht knaw ony of thair directiounis, peraventor I suld informe the Kingis Hienes and your Grace of sik thingis as ye wald think necessair to mak ansuer to thair petitioune; and desiris farthir mot pleis your Grace to remembyr my lytill materis at Rome, and in that behalf to geif credence to this berar my familiar chaiplan and cousing, with quhom youre Grace wald aduerteiss me at youre plesoure quhat ye will comande. And the haly Trinite preserve your Grace eternaly. At London this new yeris evin. Subscriuit with the hand of

Your humble seruytor and
CHAPLAN OF DUNKELD.*

Gavin Douglas to Cardinal Wolsey.

Pleis youre Grace, my chaiplane, quhilk was yisterday at youre presence, schew me that Galtere, this secretar of the Duke of Albanys, has said to youre Grace that I promyst not to cum within this realme, and therfor of his maisteris behalf askit your Grace to withhald me heyre, and lat me pass na farthir. My Lord I beleyf your hye wisdome will not geif credence sa lichtlie aganis me and specialie to the Duke of Albany or ony of his seruandis, quhilkis is capitalle and dedelie inimye to me and all my hous. And thairfor it is na wounder albeyt he say sik thingis for my harme, quhilk divers tymes, and yit daylie baith sayis and dois all that he may or can ymagyn to my distruccioun, and exterminatioun of all my kyn. And as I sall ansuer to God and your Grace, the contrar of it he sayis is playn verite. For baith be mes-

* To the maist reuerand Fader in God and his maist singulare good lorde and maister my Lord Cardinallis grace of York, Legate de Latere and Chancellar of England.—State Papers of Scotland, MSS., vol. I., No. 83.

inger and write I declarit him playnlie I wald pass throcht this realme, and na vther way, and gart schew him quhat day I was appoyntit to entir in the gronde of Ingland, the quhilk I kepit trewlye. And thus youre Grace may consider quhat fauoures he beris to me, or how I suld be intretit gif I war in Scotland vnder his subieccion, or yit gif I pas to France or ony vther part quhair he mon sollist ony thing, quhen he is sa bald within this realme; quhairin I traist he has lytill credence as for to sollist your Grace in my contrar. Albeyt ye haif grantit me the Kingis Hienes saufconduct, the quhilk I traist I haif not forfalt, nor yit your Grace will suffer be brokin. And beside this the mater is petious gif ony kirk man suld be stoppit gangand to Rome for his lauchfull defence, and summond thiddir; and neththeless your Grace knawis full wele I may be lichtlie intretit to remane here, bot na wayis at his commande nor desyre; and full wele wot your hye wisdom quhat is to be done or ansuerit to sik ane petitioun mekle better than I or mony sik can ymagyn. Albeyt gif it mycht stand with your plesour I wald besyk your Grace to ansuer to this Galter, that gif the Duke his maistere wilbe content my action and mater be remittit furth of Rome to your Grace, and before your auditor, quharof I wald be glayd, your Grace suld cause me remane. And ellis quhy or how suld ye hald me fra my lauchfull defence, quhilk is of the law of nature, specialie I havand the Kings saufconduct to pas, as said is. This is my littil avise vnder correctioun of youre Grace, quhom I beseyk to pardon this my sa haymlye wryting. And the haly Trinite haf youre Grace in his blissit and eternall keping. At Lundone this New Yeris day. Subscriuit with the hand of your humble servytor and

CHAPLAN OF DUNKELD.

* To the maist Reverend Fader in God and his maist singular gude Lorde and Maister, my Lord Cardinallis Gracie of York, Legate de Latere and Chancellar of Ingland, &c. MSS. Brit. Mus. Calig., B. vi., fol. 213.

Gavin Douglas to Cardinal Wolsey.

Placyt your Grace, ye had yistyrday syk byssynes that I mycht not schew your Grace quhat I thocht twychyng the cummyng of this Scottis prest Schir John Duncanson, quha yistyrday presentyt wrytyngis to the Kyngs Hyenes and your Grace for an salue conduyt, and is cummyn furth of Scotland wyth gret dylligens apon vij days, and is rycht famylyar wyth the Duk of Albanye and speciall seruand of a lang tyme to the Archbischop of Glasgw; and has brocht wyt hym wrytyngis and dyrectyones fra thaim bayth to be sped in Frans, Flandris, and Rome, as I know by his wordis. Als thar is cummyng wyth hym an Italian callyt Evangilista, the maner of a Lombard in Scotland, to convoy hym at merchandis handis heyr and in Flandris. Gyf your Grace had seyn thar lettre and dyrectyones I trast ye suld knaw mony things tharby; and gif your hye prudens thynkis spedfull at salue conduct be sped her at the instance and subscriptyon of the said Duk, I report me to your gret wysdom; or yit that the said Bischop of Glasgwys materrs and promotion for Sanctandrs suld prosper, consyddyryng he is the mast spyciall man that manteinys and allways hes manteinyt the said Duk. I dreyd alsso this Duncanson is dyrekkyt in my contrary and to do me hurt, and beseks your Grace to provyd the rathar sum remedy tharfor, and gif it mycht stand wyth your plesour that he had na passage for the causys forsaids onto the tyme your Grace knew mare fully his dyrecyones, and gyf your hye prudens plesys so do, I wold nain knew this cam by my desyr, becaus he fenyeis hym famyliar wyth me, quharby perauentur I sall knaw sum pert mayr of his mynd, albeyt I knaw ellis the fynes of the man and nayn mayr dowbyll in our realm. Do as pless your Grace quham God preserue. At Lundon this Epyphanye day wyt the hand of

Your humble Seruytour and

CHAPLAN OF DUNKELD.

To my Lord Cardynalis Grace.*

* Brit. Mus. Cott. Calig., B. vi., fol. 424.

The interference of Douglas in the affairs of Queen Margaret now met with a severe punishment—the loss of his Bishopric and other preferments.

In order to meet the charges which had been brought against her by Angus and his uncle, the Queen sent messengers to Henry, armed with voluminous instructions on her behalf. In these the following statement occurs:—

Item, ye sall geve his Grace to vnderstand of the guid bering that he [the Regent] dois towart me, and how he has put in my handis the disposition of the Bishoprye of Dunkeld now vacand for the delict of hym that had it, and hes geuine me the profittis tharof, and hes gevine to my seruandis ane Abaysy and other benefices for my help and favor, quharfor I pray his Grace richt effectuoslie that he help not the said Dunkeld, considdering the gret evill that he has done to this Realm be his evill counsall, for he has bene the caus of all the dissention and trobill of this Realme, and has maid fals and evill raport of me baitht in Ingland and Scotland, and for that effect the lard of Wedderburn bruder was send to your Grace to that effect; and sen I helpit to get hyme the benefice of Dunkeld I sall help hyme to want the samyn. And considdering the evell that he has done to this realme, and the displessouris he has done to me baitht in word and deid to my vtter dishonour, at his pouer, quhilk he can not deny, I trast that your Grace will not fauor hyme nor mak him na help nor fauor hym, for that salbe your honour and myn; and your guid schawing ye at this tyme guid and kynd brodyr to me, as my trast is ye sall, I salbe your humbill and obeysant sister in all thing, that I ma do your Grace honour and profyt and plesour, and sall gladly take pane apon me to intertene guid peace and concord betwixt your Grace and the King my son your nefue, and othyrwais to haf me excusit with my just querell and defensis to seik remeid odyrwaes and it salbe in your Grace default and not in myn.

MARGARET R.*

In addition to the vexation caused by the loss of his preferments, Douglas had the mortification to find that his mission to secure the support of Henry for the Earl of Angus had entirely failed. He obtained information that Angus, whose castle of Tantallan had been seized by the Regent, had given up his own cause, and was mediating, through the Queen, with Albany for his pardon and his retirement to France. According to Pinkerton he had by this time probably promised to consent to a divorce from the Queen.

In the last letter of Douglas, written at the "Inn of Carlisle," some hostelry of London where he was residing, he betrays great anguish of mind. He complains of the untruth of those that had caused him to labour for the welfare of their young King, and for the security of those who had now brought about their own confusion and perpetual shame. He speaks of himself as weary of life, and promises to God and to Wolsey that he will "never have nor take way with the Duke of Albany, the unworthy Earl of Angus, nor with any other that assists the said Duke, nor will pass into Scotland but at the Cardinal's pleasure, so long as that wicked Duke should be therein, or have rule thereof."

Gavin Douglas to Cardinal Wolsey.

Plesit your Grace, sen I herd the tythingis and wrytingis of yisterday I am and haif bene so dolorus and full of

* MSS. Brit. Mus. Cott. Calig. B. vi. fol. 209.

vehement ennoye that I dar nocht auentor cum in your presence, quhilk causis me thus wryte to your nobill Grace, beseking the samyn of youre grete goodnes to haif compacience of me desolatt and wofull wycht; albeyt I grant I haif deseruyt punycioun, and am vnder the Kingis mercy and youris, not for only falt or demeritt of my avne, but by raisoun of thair ontreuth that causit me labour for the wele of thair Prince, and thair securite, quhilk now has wrocht thair avne confusioun and perpetuall schayme; and has seruit me as your Grace may considdyr, that sollistit the Kingis Hyenes and your Grace to wrytt and doo for thame so oftyn tymes and so largely in diuerss sortis, als wele to thair support and confort, quhairof as now I most nedis vnderly youre mercy. Albeit I dowte not bot your hye prudence consideris profoundly my part thairof, and my hole trew mynde all tyme but ony dissimulance, that in goode fayth am forthir dissauit in this mater then ony vtheris, by raisoun quharof I am so full of sorowe and displesour that I am wery of my avne lyfe; and promittis to God and your noble Grace, as your humle seruand and ane true Christis preist, that I sall neuir have nor tak way with the Duke of Albany, the vnworthy Erl of Anguse, nor na vtheris that assistis to the said Duke, but your express commande and avise; nor neuer sall pass in Scotland but at your plesour, so lang as this wikkyt Duke is thairin or has rewle thairof; and I traist my brother and vther my frendis will vse my counsale. Albeyt yon young wytles fwyll has runnyn apoun his avne myscheyf be continewall persuasioun of wylye subtile men, and for lak of good counsale, schewing to him, I dowte not, mony fenzeit lettres and wounderful terouris; that the Lord Hume and vtheris wald pass in and lefe him allane, and that I wald be takin and haldin heyr, and that Galter the Dukis secretar had appoyntit with the Kingis Hienes for his distructioun, and the Duke to mary the Qwene. I dowte not sik thingis and mekle mayr has bene sayd; and with this the wrytyngis at your Grace causit me send furth of Hamtoun Courte on Sant Thomas daye come not to him quhill the xiiii day of Januar, and so he has remanyt comfortles in the menetyme quhill the tothir subtile folkis had convoyit thair mater. Wald God I had send ane seruand of my avne with tha writingis, or past myself with thame, in caiss I had lyin vii yeris eftir in preson, for I fynd absense ane schrew, and deligence with expeditioun myeht haif done grete goode. Albeyt of verite thair may be none raisionable nor honest excuse that suld causs ony creature brek his lawte or promyt. And I beseyk God that I may see him really punyst for his demerittis and promyssis brokyn mayd to the Kingis Hienes and me his vncle, and sall be glad to sollist the Kingis Hienes and your Grace to this effect at all my powere. Notheless I beseke your Grace to remembre the welefare and securite of the Kingis Grace of Scotland, my souerane lord and maister, and to sollist the Kingis Hyeehnes to that effect, for his Grace has maid no falt but is aluterly innocent. This is and was my principall directioun and causs of my hyddyr cuming, as your Grace full wele vnderstandis, albeit I wald haif procurit as I cowth the weylfayr of my self and frendis besyde, gif thai had not wrocht in the contrar to thair awne distruccioun and myne sa fer as in thame lyis; and gif I durst be so bald as to sollist your Grace and shew quhat wayis war best for the weylfare of the young Kingis Grace my Souerane, I wald be glayd to endeuor myself thairto at the command of your Grace. In caiss now I dar not auentor to propone na sik thingis, by raisoun that I am dissauit be my most tendyr frendis in my fyrst interpryss, incontrar to all goode lyklyhod or naturall equite. Besekking your Grace of your gracious ansuer and quhat ye will command me to doo, and to be my good Lorde, and to lat me knaw gif it be your plesour that I awayt apon your seruice and doo my deuisee as I aucht of dett, and wald be glayd so to doo, for furth of this Realme will I not depart so lang as I may remane thairin with the Kingis plesour and youris, quhat penurite and distress so euir I sustene. And your gracious ansuer herupoun in wourde be message or writing I humly beseyk, or gif it pleis your Grace I cum myself to your nobill presence thairfor; and God Allmychty preserue your Grace eternalye. At the In of Carlyle the last day of Januar. Subscriuit with the hand of

Your humble seruitor and dolorus

CHAPLAN OF DUNKELD, etc.

To my Lord Cardinallis good Grace.*

At this time Douglas drew up the following Memorial for the purpose of being laid before Henry VIII., in which he included every objection he could collect against the Duke of Albany being governor of Scotland. The original document is undoubtedly in his handwriting, and still exists in the Cottonian collection.

Memorial of certain charges concerning the Duke of Albany.

Memorandum—Primus, thare aucht no man to be a Governour of ony realme, or tutor to ane childe within age, les than he mycht be responsable for sik ane charge, and had therwith to mak payment for all sovmes and goodis intromettit and disponit by him. And swith it is, the Duke of Albany has nane heritage of his avne, nothir in Scotland nor in France, quhairby he is, and euir was ane vnsufficient gouernour to the Realme of Scotland and to the Kingis Grace. Besyde this alsua, his fader deyt banneist, forfaltit and rebell to the crovne of Scotland, quhar throcht he is vnhabill to that or ony vther office, heretage, or autorite within the realme of Scotlaund.

Secundlie, he is subdite to the King in France, havand of the said King besyde his wiffis heiritage, (quharthrow he is the Kingis wassell) boith pensioun and officis as one of

* State Papers, Scotland, MSS., vol. i., No. 85.

his capitanis and knichtis of his ordour. Be raison quhairof the realme of Scotland suld nocht only be vnder him as thair gouernour, but also by the samyn raison vnder the Franche king elikewise to quhom he is subiect; and gyf so war that the said king him selfe or ony vtheris wald bynd that induring the tyme of his office he suld no wise mell with him, yit then his naturall fauour vnto his natiue realme and prince, and elikewise the fere and dreyd of his frendis, his goodis and wiffis rentis in tha partis, suld euir inclyne his mynde to the plesour of France, quhairthrow diuers materis wilbe done daylie by him or left vndone that may be preiudicial to Scotland, and na goode apperance to vther realmes besyde.

Thridlie, quhatsumeuer band or promys he now makis salbe allegit for fere and dreyd of the kingis of Inglaund or France, or ellis boith, and therfor sall nocht fayll to brek the said band quhen euir he may se his tym, quhairby maye be no surety to the young king so lang as he is within Scotland. And this is all the moir to be dred that he removis and inputtis at his plesour, all maner officiaris abowte the young Kingis most noble persoun, and has removit his Graice of richt tendir age furth of Striueling Castell quhar he was richt well at eys, to the wyndy and richt vnplesand castell and royk of Edinburgh, and now instantlie removis him agane to Striueling Castell, to the intent that the Castell of Edinburgh quhilk is one of the Kingis cheif strenthis may be in his handis; like as he has thre vtheris the King of Scottis principal strenthis Dunbar, Dunbertane, and Inchgarvy stuft by him with Franchemen, and standing apon the sey at athir cost syde, west sey and est seyis, quhairby Franchemen or ony vtheris quhom he likis may haif fre ische and entre within the Realme of Scotland to quhat novmer he ples, so that therthrow evidentlie nother the Realme nor keparis of the King quhatsumeuer may be in trust suretye quhill this be remedit, and also the saidis castellis ar furneist apoun the Kingis expens richt sumptuouslie, far besyde the old custum by tripill quadrupill moir expens then was wount.

Ferdlie, ony gouernour or tutor aucht to procur the welefare and proffite of the realme and young King that he takis in gouernance and tutele, and suld mak thair caus bettir and no thing wers, quhilk gif he dois and hurtis the realme or cheild, notabyllye by all raisoun and lawis he tynys his office, and aucht to be removit therfra, and so has he done in this sort as eftir followis; quhairfor he is werray suspect and suld alwayis be removit fra ony sik office or autorite, and besyde that, aucht to be compellit to refounde or recompens all the skaythis done by him.

First, not allanerlye spendis and waistis he the Kingis tresour and rentis to his avne vse and at his avne plesour, bot also the furnessing of the castellis foresaid. Neyr thir two yeris by gone he hes furneist certane Franchemen wageouris to the novmer of aucht skoir persounis, gevand euery one of thois, quhilk ar but veray knavis, iiii pundis Scottis in the month of the Kingis cofferis; and De la Bastie, quhom he left vmquhile his deput in his absence, v pundis Scottis euery day, and efter his decess so moche to the Lord Hammyltoun, nothing neding thereof nor no proffite done therwith to the Realme.

Secundlie, he has spendit in his vse the fyfty thousand frankis sent from the France King to the King of Scottis in sobyr recompens of no litill skaith sustenit by the realme of Scotland for the querrell of France; and elikewise diuers vtheris sovmes quhilkis he has ressauit now at his last beyng in France to the support of Scotland, to the valeu as is allegit of twenty or twenty foure thousand Franche crovnis of the son.

Thridlie, the Kingis riche govnys of moist fyne cloith of gold tursit with fynest sabillis he has aualiit, togidder with the hangingis and apparalingis of his chalmeris palit of purpur and weluet crammesyn, and maid clothing therof to sum of his pagis and seruandis, and has conyeit in plakkis the Kingis grete siluer stopis double gilt, that in the hole montis to one richt grete sovme.

Ferdlie, he has sauld and analiit the Kingis thre grete schippis, richt costlie and precious jowellis wourth thre hundreth thousand frankis, and cost I dar say with thair artelyery and ordinance twyis that sovme, besyde vther smalle barkis analiit by him also, and the money tharof spendit by him and to his vse alanerly, and neuir one penny of the samyn returnyt to the Kingis proffit nor the realmes.

Item, diuers landis and heretagis that fallis in the Kingis handis by recognitioun, forfaltour, or vtherwayis, this Duke gevis and sellis sik landis at his plesour quhilk by no wais he may dispone nor analie, nor yit the King himselfe in his les age vnto the tyme he be xxv yeris complete may dispone or analy none sik thingis by the expres lawis of Scotland.

Item, besyde mony vtheris small wardis and mariagis (quhilkis skairsly may be nowmerit), within thir two yheris this Duke of Albany has sauld the wardis landis and mariagis of Drummond, Sanquhare, and Barnbowgall, quhilk war wele wourth fourty thousand pund of Scottis money, and neuir one penny hereof come to the Kingis proffite; togidder now laitlie with the warde and mariage of the airis female of Invervgy bettir than ten thousand pundis Scottis.

Item, besyde all this, he beyng or remanyng in Scotland suld put no goode ordour of justice nor pollecy apperandlie thairin, bot rathare doo thairto distruction dammage and dounputting of all sik as he trustit wald nocht be conform to his mynde, or that wald be contrarious to ocht him plesit doo; albeyt his intent war nevir so wrangwous, as may be well provit apperandlie by the slauchter of the last Chalmerlan, and also by his lettres oft and mony times sent in Scotland to foster discorde and to mak impedimentis to frendschip concorde and vnite, quhilkis scheweth him planely no goode gouernour nor to haif ony zele of goode rule nor welefaire of Scotland, but alanerly to procur his avne avantage. And besyde this also how he sollistis and mantennys the Qwenis Grace to remane from hir husband, aganis the law of God and holy churche, and incontrar hir avne honour and of his bloode, efferis not to be rehersit; and to that effect sollistit certaine Lordis and vtheris his seruandis to geif hir daylie counsale therto, causing thame mene and procure so that the remayning with hir husband was not payit of her dower, and remayning from him makis hir be furneist of the Kingis cofferis with vtheris auantagis besyde, incontrar justice and to the King of Scottis sumptuous cost; in fraude also of the band and contract maid thereupoun betuix boith the kingis and ratifiit euery tyme of trowis, that sche suld be thankfullie payit and content of hir dower.

Item, besyde this also the beneficis and grete prelacciis that wakis it is said that he sellis for grete sovmes of money, quhilk is verray vnlefull, and schewis perfitelie his governament and remanyng in Scotland aluterly in contrar the comon wele tharof, quhilk the moir clerelie may be verifiit by this that the two first yheris he remanyit in Scotland the Realme was neuir in ordour but into trouble and myscheyf, and thre or foure tax or contributioun rasit apoun the pepill by him within the said two yheris; and now elikewise at his last returnyng in Scotland has stent the hole realm to one contributioun and taxt of twenty five thowsand pund Scottis, quhilk manifestlie schewis him no wise necessare but verray improffitable for that realme.

Item, besyde the surfait expensis of the Kingis rentis and casualiteis as is abufe expremit, he has maid one Robert Bertoun, one verre pyrett and sey revare Comptrollar, and ane Maister Johnne Campbell, one bastard bribour quhilk had not vi *d.* wourth of goode of his avne, Thesaurare, the quhilkis as thai allege by thare comptis ar superexpendit so largelie, that the King is in athir of thair dettis ten or twelf thousand pund Scottis; howbeyt God and all the realme of Scotland knawis the Kingis Grace is richt evill furneist in clething and all vther necessaris, on sik one sort (schayme to be rehersit) his Hienes has diuerss tymes within thir two yheris bywent lakkit honest hole hoyssing and dowbillatis, till that his sister the Countes of Mortoun persaving sik disordour, furneist his Grace honorabillie of sik nedful thingis; and also quhen the Qweenis Grace his moder, and sum tyme this ilk Duke of Albany, sent cloith of siluer or gold to mak govnes to his Hienes, his officiaris forsaid wald not furneis lynyng tharto nor pay for the fassoun thereof, and werst of all, allose, it is planely spokin and rehersit the Duke of Ros the Kingis brothir deyt for defalt of sik necessar thingis as belangit to sik one prince, or then was poysonyt.*

Item, all sik thingis beand saddilie rememberyt, sik mysordour and crudelite bypast considerit aucht wele to reduce the cruell exemple of King Rycharde to remembrance; and how a man of sik mynde, and beand suspect be euident tokynnys preceding, havand the hole reule of ony realme, and beand also thairin, may find mony wayis to vsurpe the crovne, and all to layt war to provyde remede tharfor quhen the harme may not be redressit, as God forbyd so suld fall, for als moche as than the said Duke wald or mycht allege and pretend sum coloratt tytill or clame to the crovne, quhare now he has non sik, for in the Kyng of Scottis, God saufe his Grace! restis and regnis the trew ondowtyt bloode of Inglaund Scotlaund and Denmerk.

Item, it is to be rememberit gyf this Duke of Albaneis fader had deit at the faith and pece of his prince, and not rebell nor banneist, yit then he has on live ane eldar brothir, Alexander Stewart Commendatour of Scone and Inchchafferay, within no holy ordouris, but one man habyll to mary, bygottin on the Duke of Albanyis first wife, vmquhile dochter to the Erle of Orknay.

Item, all the statis of Scotland in plane counsale the xxi day of Januar in the yere of God jm vc and xx yheris, by plane act and decrete pronunceit this ilk Duke of Albany to be

* The Duke died at Stirling Castle, in 1515, of some infantile disorder, while his mother was absent in England.

no regent nor gouernor of Scotland les then he returnyt in the realme on the first day of August nixt eftir, quhilk was Lammes day last bypast, and failyeing that he come not in Scotland or then, dischargit him of his office, and thame also of thair athis made to him, and hereupon sent to him thair ambassadour and expres writingis. And so it is that he returnyt not in Scotland quhill the end of Nouember nixt thereftur, and was neuer sens elect nor chosin of new.

By raison quhairof all that he now dois or sall doo in that realme is expres wrong, vsurpit conspirassy and tyranny but ony autorite, like as in maner boith his doyngis and wourdis to the ilk Scottis ambassadour proportis, saying prowdly quhen he herd of this act and the forsaid writingis, 'quhat ar thai in Scotland that dar be so bald for to degraid me of ocht, albeyt I remanyt furth of Scotland this xxvii yheris, so hardy that ony tharin presvme or attempt sik thing, I knawe thame all well eneuch.'

Item, it is nowise to be foryett how the Archibishop of Glasgow now beyng Chancellar of Scotland intendis and procuris by all maner wayis how his brothir dochter childerin, the Erle of Arans sons, may attayn to the crovne of Scotland, like as by his wourdis quhen he baptist the first childe may be wele coniectoure, quhare he said thus "Quho wayt then I may leyf till I see and put the crovne on this childis hede." By raison quhairof, he beyng of sik mynde is aluterlye suspicious and our dangerous a persoun to bere ony autorite in Scotland, nor to mell with the Kingis maist noble persoun by himself or ony him pertenys.

Item, finalie it is to be reducit to remembrans how in the [tyme] of Alexander the thrid King of Scottis, in his youth the King of Ingeland Henry the Thrid then beyng his fader of law and not so tendir of bloode as his vncle, come in propir persoun to Werk Castell apon Twede, as the Scottis cornikle rehersis, and thare maid to be removit from the Kingis counsale all sik suspect officiaris as was not profitable, and made vtheris to be chosen in thar stedis or placis.

Item, abufe all this is to be considerit that the Kingis Hienes, movit of verre raisoun, naturall equite and piete, suld and may also by all lawis procure and defend the welefare and surety of his deirest nevo the yong Kyng of Scottis and his realme, without ony mandatt or vther commissioun had or axit therto, but onlye by raisoun that his Grace is one coniunct persoun and so tendir of bloode to the said young King, and thus persute may be maid or deducit befor the Popis Holynes, and he to interpone his decrett and autorite therto; or than by quhatsumeuir vther lefull fassoun or waye the Kingis maieste thinkis most expedient. But all wayis the caussis abufe expremyit bene none evill ground, but verre lefull and just fundament for the samyn, and ar dowtles of verity euery wourd.*

Whilst Douglas was in the midst of these negociations, the death of Andrew Forman, Archbishop of St Andrews, and Abbot of Dunfermline, took place.

The eager expectant of these benefices was the Chancellor, James Beaton, Archbishop of Glasgow, who dreaded the rivalry of the Bishop of Dunkeld. He therefore exerted his utmost endeavours to accomplish his ruin. Unfortunately for Douglas at this time, war was declared by the English against the Scots, the latter joining with France in an alliance against the Emperor Charles V. and Henry VIII. Douglas was therefore now resident in an enemy's country, which was represented to his disadvantage at home.

Beaton accordingly got the following proclamation drawn up in the name of the young king, James V., with the advice of the Lords of Council and the three Estates of Parliament.

* Brit. Mus. Calig., B. iii., fol. 309.

Proclamation of James V. against Gawin Douglas, Bishop of Dunkeld.

We, James by the grace of God, King of Scots, to all and several our lieges who shall see this letter, give our testimony and solemn assurance: Know that by the Lords of our Council and three estates of the kingdom, before and in presence of our dearest cousin our tutor and governor John, the noble Duke of Albany, &c., it is decreed and promulgated, as follows: At Edinburgh on the 21st day of February, in the year of our Lord 1521, in presence of the illustrious prince, John Duke of Albany, royal tutor and governor, the Lords of the royal Council and the three Estates of the kingdom have resolved, decreed and ordained, Forasmuch as Gavin Douglas, Bishop of Dunkeld, not only without the permission and leave of our sovereign Lord the King, his Tutor and Regent of the kingdom, and three Estates of parliament, but even in direct opposition to the orders of the said Regent, has entered England with the intention of residing there, with treasonable intents against this kingdom, as from unequivocal indications may be conjectured, having joined the English, the enemies of this kingdom even after the declaration of war. By this conduct, according to the statutes of parliament, he has incurred the crime of high treason; and that no indulgence may be shewn to rebels plotting rebellion so audaciously, in pursuance of the decree of the foresaid Lords, our royal letters have been despatched to the Vicar-General of St Andrews, the judge ordinary having jurisdiction over the foresaid Bishop of Dunkeld, the said metropolitan see being vacant, that the Dean and Canons of the Church of Dunkeld, and all others having interest, under pain of ecclesiastical censure shall make up an inventory of the revenues of the foresaid Church, and shall shew and exhibit the names of those in possession of such revenues and emoluments, and none of the Canons nor the Dean aforesaid shall intromit therewith unless by special order and authority of the foresaid Vicar-General; nor shall any one else intromit therewith unless he shall find sufficient caution for the safe keeping of the revenues: lest he that aims at the subversion of the whole kingdom should derive from the patrimony of Christ means for the prosecution of his crimes: Provided always, however, that divine worship in the church of Dunkeld shall not on that account be the less attended to. And lest the man, persevering in a malevolent intention, should from time to time devise new plots, as in past times he added fuel to the flames of civil discord, and now has voluntarily withdrawn from the kingdom, nor shews any disposition to return to reason, in terms of the said act, and proclamation following thereon, all and several the lieges of the kingdom of whatever condition, degree, ecclesiastical or secular rank are prohibited under the penalty of high treason from assisting or supporting him by money, or from holding communication with him by letters or messengers. And since no man should have greater influence with our most holy Lord the Pope and his most holy College of Cardinals than our King and his illustrious Tutor, and the devout loyalty of the whole kingdom to his Holiness, it has been decreed by the advice of the said three estates to send letters to our most holy Lord the Pope, lest he should appoint and institute the foresaid Gavin, thus conspiring against the state, to the Archbishopric of St Andrews and the monastery of Dunfermling, or either of them, in violation of the privileges formerly conceded to this kingdom by the supreme Pontiffs. And lest such letters should be said to have emanated from any private influence, the petition of three estates of the kingdom concerning the premises are to be herewith sent, and at the same time the present proclamation under the testimony of the great seal of our sovereign Lord the King. This proclamation issued by authority of the said estates, in the presence of our said Cousin and Tutor, we James, by the grace of God King of Scots, with consent and authority of our said Tutor, approve ratify and confirm. Given under the testimony of our great seal.*

. A letter was also written by Beaton to Christian II., King of Denmark, in which he besought that monarch to command his ministers at Rome to dissuade the new Pope, Adrian VI., from nominating Gavin Douglas for the Archbishopric.†

That Douglas had some hopes of this preferment appears from the following extract of a letter of Lord Dacre to Cardinal Wolsey, dated the 14th of March 1522: "Please it your Grace I aduertised you of two schyppes of warre of the Duke of Albanyes which was redie to depart; which the xi[th] day of this month went furth, a bark and v marchantis shippes with them that lay within the kee at Leith. In which shippes of war th'erle of Angus and his brodre is gone towardis Ffraunce. The Lord Flemyng and Thomas Hay the Kingis Secretary in ther company. Beseching your Grace to be good and gracius to the Bishopp of Dunkell, in whom I verely trust is nothing but troughe, and that it wald pleas your Grace to write in his fauor to the Popis Holines for the Archbisshopricke of Saint Androwes, seing that it is bruted in Scotland, that he is postulate therof, and, if it could be purposed, it shuld mak mervellous grete brek in Scotland, for he which has the gift of the Duke is the man that rewles him moost of any living."‡

* Trans. from orig. in Epist. Reg. Scot. i., p. 328. It is satisfactory to find that the Scottish Parliament, in February 1524, about eighteen months after Douglas's death, passed an Act to the effect that the charge above made against him for treasonably passing into England was "in all the punctis therein contenit vane, vntrew, and had na veritie." Scots Acts, ii., p. 290.

† Ibid., tom. i., p. 333. ‡ State Papers Scot., vol. i., No. 87.

Whilst Douglas resided in London, he enjoyed the friendship of Polydore Vergil, the historian of England, who was the friend of Wolsey, and was on terms of familiarity with the persons most eminent for rank and learning at the Court of Henry. Vergil in his history of England alludes to Douglas as follows:—

"Of late one Gawine Dowglas, Bishop of Dunchell, a Scottishe man, a manne as well noble in ligniage as vertewe, when he understoode that I was purposed to write this historie, hee camme to commune with mee; in forthe with, we fell into friendshippe, and after he vehementlie requiered mee, that in relation of the Scottishe affaires, I showlde in no wise follow the president of an historie of a certaine contriman of his,* promisinge within few dayse to sende mee of those matters not to be contemned, which in deade hee perfourmed. . . . . But I did not longe enjoy the fruicion of this mie frind, for in the year of our Lord MDXXII., he died of the plague in London."†

The sad event which deprived Vergil of his friend, and Scotland of one of her ablest men, took place in September 1522, in the house of his old friend Thomas, Lord Dacre, in St Clement's parish, near London. At the time of his death he was in the forty-eighth year of his age. His will is dated the 10th, and probate was granted on the 19th of September.

Agreeably to his own injunctions, Bishop Douglas was buried in the Hospital Church of the Savoy, on the

* The "History of Scotland," by John Major or Mair.

† Vergil's Eng. Hist. (Camden Society), i., p. 105.

left side of Thomas Halsey, Bishop of Leighlin, who died about the same time, and the following inscription was placed on their tomb :—

"Hic jacet Thomas Halsey Leglinensis Episcopus, in basilica Sancti Petri Romae Nationis Anglicorum penitenciarius, summae probitatis vir, qui hoc solum post se reliquit, vixit dum vixit bene. Cui laevus conditur Gavanus Dowglas, natione Scotus, Dunkeldensis Praesul, patria sui exul, Anno Christi 1522." *

Holinshed † states that Douglas enjoyed "an honest pension to live on" from Henry VIII. but this may be doubted, as there is no allusion to it, nor to any arrears accruing from it, in the general inventory of his means and effects. On the contrary, the Bishop seems to have been reduced to straits, as in his will there is mention made of some of his silver plate being pledged to various persons.

The will of Bishop Douglas, which is preserved in the charter-chest of the ancient family of Lindsay of Dowhill, is very interesting, as being almost the oldest document of the kind respecting a Scottish person of note, and it is fuller and more precise than many subsequent ones. It is as follows :—

* Here lieth Thomas Halsey, Bishop of Leighlin, Penitentiary of the English nation in the Church of St Peter's at Rome, a man of great probity, who left only this character behind him—he lived, while he lived, well. On his left is buried Gavin Douglas, a native of Scotland, Bishop of Dunkeld, an exile from his country. In the year of Christ 1522.

Owing to a fire which happened in the Savoy Chapel in 1864, the brass tablet which marked the spot of the interment of the two bishops was removed from its place. The tablet is still preserved, and a cut from a rubbing from it is here inserted.

† Chronicles, vol. iii., p. 676.

Hic iacet Thomas · Halsey Leghlinen epūs · in basilica
scti petri Rome nationis Anglicor penitēciari' summe
probitatis vir q' hoc solū post se reliquit vixit dum vixit
bene · cū laevus conditur Gawan' Dolbglas natione
Scotus Dunkelley presul patria sua exul: A° · xpi · 1522

Will of Gavin Douglas, Bishop of Dunkeld, 1522.

INVENTARIUM omnium bonorum quondam Reverendi in Christo patris, et domini, Gawini, miseratione divina, Episcopi Dounkeldensis, factum apud hospitium domini Dacris in partibus Anglie, in parochia Sancti Clementis prope Landonium, decimo die mensis Septembris, anno Domini millesimo quingentesimo vicesimo secundo, coram his testibus, Henrico Grahame, Johanne Baxtar, domino Jacobo Hendersoune, Capellano, et Magistro Davide Douglas, Presbitero, ac notario publico. IN PRIMIS, res et bona in palatio Dunkeldensi, magister Robertus Grahame, Canonicus ejusdem, habet sub inventario manu publicorum notariorum signato. Item, bona in Clony, Silvester Rettray in Gudy habet inventarium eorundem manu magistri Alexandri Douglas Canonici Dunkeldensis conscriptum. Item, bona in Crawmond, Archibaldus Douglas, germanus noster, habet in custodia. Item, bona in hospitio Ville Sancti Johannis, dominus Thomas Paule Capellanus habet sub inventario. Item, bona in hospitio Edinburgi, dominus Johannes Geddes, Capellanus, habet in custodia.

Item, fatetur se habere *in bonis*, viz., in integris procurationibus sue Diocesis Dunkeldensis, Anni Domini millesimi quingentesimi vicesimi primi, nonaginta quatuor libras monete Scotie, salvo justo calculo. Et de quotis testamentorum ejusdem anni, extendentibus per bonam estimationem ad summam centum librarum, salvo justo calculo ut prefertur. Item, fatetur se habere de firmis terrarum suarum termini Penthecostes ultimi elapsi, extendentibus in pecunia ad ducentas quinquaginta libras, in manibus Magistrorum Georgei Hepburne, Decani Dounkeldensis, et Roberti Grahame canonici ejusdem, quos constituimus nostros vicarios generales, factores, et procuratores ad lites, causas, et negotia nos tangentia, et concernentia. Item, fatetur se habere de decimis garbalibus Ecclesiarum parochialium de Littill Dounkeldensi, et Capeth, extendentibus ad decem et novem celdras victualium farine et ordei, viz. de croppa anni instantis, viz. anni etc. quingentesimi vicesimi secundi, et de eisdem Ecclesiis viginti octo celdrarum avenarum pro pabulis equorum, pretium bolle farine pretium bolle ordei ac pretium bolle avenarum, Summa Item, fatetur se habere in decimis garbalibus Ecclesie parochialis de Cargill ejusdem croppe, extendentibus ad triginta duas celdras farine, et ordei, pretium bolle farine pretium bolle ordei Summa Item, in decimis garbalibus Ecclesie de Ouchtergavyn, extendentibus ad decem celdras, et octo bollas farine et ordei, pretium bolle farine pretium bolle ordei Summa Item, in decimis garbalibus Ecclesie de Tibbermure viginti octo celdras farine, et ordei, pretium bolle farine pretium bolle ordei Summa Item, in decimis garbalibus Ecclesie de Forgundyny, extendentibus ad triginta celdras farine, et ordei, pretium bolle farine, pretium bolle ordei Summa Salva tamen semper estimatione equitantium decimas garbales predictarum Ecclesiarum. Item, fatetur decimas garbales Ecclesie de Alithe concessas et allocatas nobili et potenti domino de Glammys, pro solutione dotis. Item, in manibus Archibaldi Douglas germani nostri, pro assedatione garbalium Ecclesiarum Parochialium de Abirlady, et Abercorne, de croppa anni instantis, extendentium ad summam tringintarum quinquaginta duarum marcarum monete Scotie predicte, ut patet in dicta assedatione. Item, fatetur se habere in manibus Hugonis Douglas burgensis de Edinburghe, pro assedatione decimarum garbalium Ecclesie de Crawmond ejusdem anni, extendentium ad summam ducentarum quadraginta marcarum monete predicte. Item, fatetur se habere in manibus Davidis Berclay de Cullerny, pro assedatione decimarum Ecclesie Parochialis de Strathmiglo, extendentium ad summam ducentarum quadraginta marcarum. Item, fatetur sibi deberi pro decimis garbalibus Ecclesiarum de Boncle, et Prestoune, per intromissores earundem, summam octoginta marcarum. Item, fatetur se habere in vestibus corporeis in partibus Anglie, unam togam le tany satyn cum le soumyeis. Item, unum par le chimeris,* de nigro le satyn. Aliud par le chimeris de panno laneo violeti coloris, cum capucco † utrique pari convenienti, pretium xl s. monete sterlingorum. Item, unam togam luteam cum strictis manicis furritam, cum le blakliuyen, pretium v. merkis; Aliam togam de tanny grauss,‡ cum parte interiori de chalmelett. Item, unam cinctam togam de le satyn, pretium. . . . Et alteram togam de panno laneo nigro, pretium. . . . Item, duo collobia curta, sive clamides vulgariter le chimeris, unam de black satyn, et aliam de chalmelet, pretium xxvi s. viii d. Item, unam togam laneam in Scotia violeti coloris furritam, cum le soumyeis. Item, unum capuceum de satyn rubei coloris ex parte exteriori, et nigri coloris ex parte interiori. Item, aliud capuceum de le bleue welvott, et aliud de nigro welvott. Item, octodecim rochetas.§ pretium ciii libras, duo paria galgarum,|| tres camisias,¶ duo birreta.** Item, fatetur se habere unam pelvim†† argenteam, cum lavacro,‡‡ ponderis iii li. iii unciarum, summa viii librarum; unum ciphum §§ argenteum cum coopertorio, ponderis ii li. xiiii unciarum, summa v li. viii s. xi d.; unam cratheram argenteam cum coopertorio, ponderis xi unciarum, summa xxxiii s. x d. Item. vii coclearia |||| argentea, ponderis viii unciarum, i quarterii, summa xxiii s. Item, quinque annulos aureos, cum gemmis, ponderis duarum unciarum, summa iiii librarum. Item, unam calicem ¶¶ argenteam, cum patera, ponderis xi unciarum, summa xl s. Item, duos urceolos *** argenteos, ponderis trium unciarum, summa x s. Item, unam pelvim argenteam, impignoratam venerabili viro Willielmo Holgill, Preceptori Hospitalis Sancti Johannis de Savoye predicte, pro Summa

* A vestment without sleeves. † A mantle with a hood.
‡ Thick silk, (Fr. gros.) § Surplices. || Breeches.
¶ Albs, or garments of white linen. ** Caps.
†† A baptismal vessel. ‡‡ A hand basin. §§ A goblet.
|||| Spoons. ¶¶ A chalice. *** Cruets.

quinquaginta duorum nobilium, continentem pondus octo librarum. Item, fatetur se habere duos ciphos argenteos, cum crathera, et coopertorio,* impignoratos Johanni Johnesoune civi Londonii, pro viginti nobilibus aureis, pondus cuiuslibet ciphi xxiii unciarum, et pondus crathere cum coopertorio. . . . . †

Item, fatetur se habere in pecunia monitata, duodecim scuta gallicana aurea, de pondere lii s. Item, fatetur se habere duos mulos, unum masculum, et aliam femellam, et duos equos, unum, viz. pili albi, et aliam pili bruneti.

SUMMA OMNIUM BONORUM.

DEBITA QUE SIBI DEBENTUR.

In primis, Anthonius Duninaldis mercator, Londinii commorans, tenetur sibi astrictus in summam undecim librarum sterlingorum, de resta majoris summe pro excambio facto ex oppido de Deip ad Civitatem Londoniensem, ut patet ex tenore obligationis dicti Anthonii. Item, quoad reliqua debita que in partibus Scotie sibi debentur, refert se compotis sui Camerarii, et granatariorum suorum.

Debita que aliis debentur.

In primis, sponse quondam Roberti Richardsone, burgensis de Edinburghe, ducentas marcas, et ultra, ad bonum computum. Item, Johanni Ermar, burgensi de Perth, et uxori Willielmi Bell, penes eorum debita, refert se suo priori testamento ante suum recessum, necnon camerario suo Dounkeldensi, et Domino Thome Paule granatario suo apud Perth, quoad solutionem eorundem, et defalcationibus, et acquitantiis eorundem desuper receptis. Item, penes debita Magistri Edwardi Cunynghame, et quantum ad solutionem eorundem, refert se Domino Johanni Geddes presbytero, et acquittantiis dicti Magistri Edward desuper exhibitis. Item, fatetur se debere Magistro Matheo Geddes, pro

* A cup with a lid.

† Something here is wanting to complete the sentence.

pecunia mutuata, viginti quinque marcas monete Scotie. Item, diversis civibus Londonensibus, pro suis cotidianis sumptibus in esculentis, et poculentis, ut patet in libris dictarum, extendentibus ad xli noble, xvii grotis, iii d., summa xiii li. xvii s. viii d. Item, Richardo Wilkensoune hospiti suo, decem le nobillis, quatuordecim grossos, summa li s. Item, pro custodia equorum domui et familie sue, ad gramina, viii s. Item, pro liberatione et redemptione Margarete Crichtone de le Comptoure, tempore egritudinis eundem tunc custodientis, summa viginti trium solidorum, pro cujus solutione prestitit fidei-jussores. Item, Domino Dacris, decem libras. Item, scissoribus pro galigis, et factura vestimentorum, xiii s. iiii d. Item, lotrici vestimentorum Domini, v s. iiii d. Item, Domino Thome Paule granatario de Perth, summa septem librarum, quinque solidorum, x d. deliberata Georgeo Geddes Senescallo, pro necessariis Domini misse Dunkeldensi.

SUMMA DEBITORUM.

SUMMA OMNIUM BONORUM DEBITIS ABSTRACTIS.

CUM nichil sit certius morte, nec incertius hora mortis, hinc est quod Ego Gawinus, indignus Episcopus Dunkeldensis, eger corpore, sanus tamen mente, condo Testamentum meum in hunc modum: *In primis*, do et lego animam meam Deo omnipotenti, beatissimeque Marie, et Sancto Columbe patrono meo, totique celesti contubernio, corpusque meum sepeliendum in choro Ecclesie Hospitalis Sancti Johannis baptiste de Savoie, prope London. Item, do et lego prefato Hospitali unum par le chimeris de nigro le satyn, cum capucco eiusdem. Item, do et lego Ecclesie parochiali Sancti Clementis pro jure funerali, meam togam de le tany satyn furitam cum le soumyeis. Item, do et lego sacerdotibus in die sepulture mee indigenitalibus, et pro cereis et reliquis necessariis ad nostras exequias spectantibus, summam trium librarum xiii s. iiii d. Item, do et lego Magistro Matheo Geldas Capellano nostro, togam laneam violeti coloris in Scotia furritam, cum le soumyeis. Item, Magistro David Douglas Capellano, togam meam de le tany grauss, cum le chalmelett ex parte interiori. Item, Margarete Douglas consanguinee nostre, cum Petro Carmychell avunculo nostro, tricentas marcas. Item, Christiane Douglas consanguinee nostre apud Elchok, ducentas marcas. Item, Henrico Grahame consanguineo nostro centum marcas. Item, Johanni Baxtar centum marcas, si bona adhuc extendunt ultra solutionem debitorum, sin autem quadraginta libras secundum modificationem Executorum. Item, Georgio Geddes familiari nostro, quadraginta marcas. Item, Hugoni Johnesoune familiari nostro, quadraginta marcas. Item, Magistro David Douglas, decem libras. Item, domino Jacobo Hendersone, decem marcas. Johanni Buyde, alias Delamott, decem marcas. Item, Johanni M'Cuddy coquo, quadraginta solidos. Item, do et lego mulos et equos meos antedictos meis servitoribus non habentibus equos, equaliter inter ipsos distribuendos. Residuum omnium bonorum meorum do et lego in dispositione Executorum meorum, viz. Archibaldi Douglas germani nostri, et Magistri Roberti Grahame Canonici Dunkeldensis, quos, ut memini, constitui meos Executores in priore meo testamento, veluti pro presenti constituo, quibus addo et constituo Georgeum Douglas consanguineum meum, et magistrum Matheum Geddis, Vicarium de Tibbirmure coexecutores. Insuper constituo venerabilem et egregium virum dominum Willelmum Halgill, preceptorem dicti Hospitalis de Savoie, superiorem et moderatorem bonorum meorum antedictorum in partibus Anglie existentium, ut ipsi disponant hujusmodi bona pro salute anime mee, prout respondere voluerint coram summo Judice, in districto examine. Nolo insuper in aliquo derogare priori meo Inventario vigore constitutionis presentis Testamenti, et executorum in eodem, sed volo quod utrumque sortiatur effectum pro mea ultima voluntate perimplenda.

pro Registratione, viii s. iii d. ob.

PROBATUM fuit presens Testamentum coram nobis Johanne Alen, juris utriusque doctore, canonico ecclesie Cathedralis Lincolniensis, Reverendissimi in Christo Patris, et domini, domini Thome miseratione divina, titulo sancte Cecilie, sacrosancte Romane ecclesie Presbiteri Cardinalis, Eboracensis Archiepiscopi, Anglie primatis, magnique Cancellarii ejusdem, ac Sedis Apostolice nati, atque etiam de latere inibi Legati, Commissario Generali, sufficienter et legitime in hac parte deputato, xix die Mensis Septembris, Anno Domini millesimo, quingentesimo xxii°., et per nos approbatum, insinuatum, legitimeque pronunciatum pro valore ejusdem; Commissaque fuit administratio omnium et singulorum bonorum, et debitorum testatoris suprascripti defuncti, Magistro Matheo Geddes, uni executorum in hujusmodi testamento nominato, de bene et fideli administrando eadem, et de perimplendo predictum testamentum, necnon de vero et pleno computo, calculo, sive ratiocinio, nobis aut alii judici, vel judicibus in ea parte competentibus, cum ad hoc debite requisitus fuerit, reddendo, in forma juris jurato, salvo jure cuiuscunque. Datum Londonii, sub sigillo prefati Reverendissimi Patris, quo in hac parte utimur, die et anno predictis.

Hume of Godscroft affirms that Douglas had a natural daughter married to Sempill of Fulwood,* and in the will of the Bishop there is mentioned one *consanguineus* and certain *consanguineae* of the name of Douglas, besides his brother, Archibald Douglas. It is not improbable that some of these may have been his own offspring, as such terms have occasionally signification similar to "nepotism." According to the sentiments of the age, transgressions of this kind were treated with indulgence, whether among the clergy or laity. Patrick Hepburn, Bishop of Moray,

* Hist. of House of Doug., p. 220.

had two sons legitimised in one day, and five daughters in another.

Among the estimates of the character of Bishop Gavin Douglas, to be found in the writings of authors of note, perhaps the most interesting is that given by John Lesley, Bishop of Ross, the Scottish historian, who flourished not many years after Gavin's death, and who thus expresses himself concerning him:— "If he had not mixed himself up with the national tumults, he would have been truly worthy of being consecrated in the writings and memory of all, on account of his fragrant wit and singular erudition."

On the whole, it will be admitted that the opinion formed by Lesley is a just estimate of the character of Gavin Douglas; and though his varied accomplishments must be acknowledged by all, we cannot agree with the indiscriminate panegyrics which have been paid to his memory by later biographers.

In 1513, when Douglas completed his translation of Virgil, he bade adieu to his poetical studies—

> "And will direct my labours euermoir
> Vnto the common welth and Goddis gloir."

He accordingly appears on subsequent occasions rather as a statesman than as a poet, and in that capacity his conduct was not free from blame. It will always be a subject of the greatest regret that a man of his genius and learning should have forsaken his tranquil literary labours, and wasted his abilities on intrigues, some for his own aggrandisement, and others occasioned by the selfish policy of his nephew, the Earl of Angus, which rendered him, in the latter part of his life, the victim of persecution and calamity.

Of Bishop Douglas no portrait is known to exist. In H. M. Record Office there is preserved a detached seal of a circular form, with a full length figure of a bishop within a Gothic niche. In base, a shield quarterly, first Angus, second Abernethy, third Brechin, fourth Stuart of Bonkil; on an escutcheon surtout, Douglas. Round the seal is the following inscription—

S. ROTVNDV GAWINI EPISCOPI DOVNKELD.

ACCOUNT OF THE WRITINGS OF BISHOP GAVIN DOUGLAS.

THE extant literary works of Bishop Gavin Douglas are not commensurate with his acknowledged ability and learning. His contemporaries represent him as having been eminently skilled in divinity and in the canon law. His translation of Virgil attests his accurate knowledge of Latin; while the request of Lord Sinclair, that he would also translate Homer, shows that he was considered as well acquainted with Greek. His poetry exhibits an exuberant imagination; and it has been well observed that, in this particular, his faults are those of superabundance, rather than deficiency. With qualifications of such a high order, it might reasonably have been expected that, had political matters not intervened, he would have enriched our literature to a greater extent.

In his youth, Douglas selected Ovid as his favourite author; and, as before stated, his first literary labour was a translation of the "De Remedio Amoris" of that poet; but of this work no trace can now be discovered. It has been supposed that he found the exercise of translating this book desirable to cure him of a youthful attachment, which, by the rules of the Popish Church, he could not continue consistently with his intention of entering into holy orders.

In 1501, when he was in his twenty-seventh year, Douglas finished the 'Palice of Honour,' the longest of his original compositions. It may be described as an allegorical poem, displaying great power of invention, and a ready command of striking imagery. Its outline is as follows :—

In a morning in May, the poet, rising early, enters a delightful garden, where fragrance was exhaled from the flowers, and where the melody of birds gave additional charm to the scene.

"In broider'd beds unnumber'd flowers were seen.
Of Nature's couch the living tapestry ;
And, hid within their leafy curtains green,
The little birds pour'd forth such harmony
As filled my very heart with joy and glee;
A flood of music followed, wave on wave,
Which Echo answered from her airy cave ;
And sprinkled o'er the laurels blooming near,
The silver dew-drops shone, like diamonds bright and clear.

Whilst in this paradise my senses fed,
And filled my heart with every rich delight,
Up from the sea Eöus raised his head—
I mean the horse to whose ætherial might
Is given to draw the golden chariot bright
Of Titan, which by night looks dark and dead,
But changeth in the morn to ruby red ;
Whilst birds, and fields, and flowers, on holm and hight.
New life assume in glittering vests bedight.

* Bishop Sage's Life, p. 14.

The daisy sweet, the marigold and rose.
That all the night their silken buds did close.
Lest icy rimes their tender twigs should sear,
Expanded fragrant: and, as Titan rose,
Each ancient tree his greeny glories shows,
Emerging joyous from the darkness drear:
All living things the kindly warmth did cheer:
The idle grasshoppers both chirpt and play'd,
The sweet laborious bees melodious music made.

Delightful was the season, May's first hour,
The glorious sun uprising in his power,
Bathed with a kindly heat all growing things:
Nor boisterous Eolus, with blast and shower,
Nor Saturn, with his aspect sad and sour,
Dar'd in that place unfurl his icy wings;
But sweet Favonius thither fragrance brings,
And little streams, half-hid in moss, do run,
Making a pleasant chime, and glancing in the sun." *

A sudden light now gleams from the skies, and the poet falls into a swoon in which he has a remarkable vision. He finds himself transported into a desert, through which rushed a hideous flood. In this doleful region, he begins to complain of the cruelty of Fortune, when the goddess Minerva appears, attended by many fair ladies and gallant men. After the cavalcade passes, the poet sees two caitiffs approach, who prove to be the arch-traitors Achitophel and Sinon. The latter informs the poet, that the party are passing through this wilderness on their way to the Palace of Honour. He inquires how such

* This and several other passages are from a modernized version of the original given by P. Fraser Tytler, Esq., in his *Lives of Scott. Worthies*, vol. iii p. 154, which are, in illustrative contrast to the original, not without interest.

wretches are associated with so polished a court, when Achitophel answers that they were there as hail and thunder often occur in the lovely month of May. After describing the death of Actæon, which the poet witnesses, he descries Diana, mounted on an elephant, approaching, attended by a train of chaste and true virgins, 'flouris of feminitie.' They pass by the poet, who remarks that the number of Diana's followers is somewhat scanty. He now finds the desert become still more loathsome to him, when at length he observes a shining light in the northern sky, and hears distant music. At last, he sees the court of Venus approach, with the goddess seated on a gorgeous car. He then describes in eloquent terms her matchless beauty.*

Venus is attended by her son Cupid, and by Mars, mounted upon a barded courser 'stout and bald.'

"The mighty Mars a barded courser bore,
Grim was his look, his body large and square,
His sinewy neck in breadth a span or more,
Round which did shortly curl his crisp brown hair;
His limbs well-knit, and of proportion fair
Were clothed in panoply of radiant steel.
On Venus still he gaz'd with amorous air,
And she her knight him call'd in woe or weal,
Whilst o'er his noble form her love-lit glances steal."†

A train of lovers, happy and unhappy, follow the amorous queen, and the poet, ruminating on their

* Miss Strickland is of opinion that the poet is here describing the charms of Margaret Tudor, the young Queen of James IV., afterwards married to his nephew. *Queens of Scot.*, i. 103.

† Tytler's Scot. Worthies, vol. iii., p. 158.

fortunes, recites a ballad on the inconstancy of love. Venus, hearing these unwelcome sentiments, bites her lip; and her party, finding the poet in his retreat, bring him before their queen. A court is constituted, and a clerk called Varius arraigns the poet for studiously endeavouring to defame Venus and her followers. He objects to the competence of the court, as ladies are not usually invested with judicial functions; and what is very amusing, the author here pleads in jest what he did seriously enough in earnest fifteen years afterwards, that he was 'ane spiritual man,' and that he ought to be remitted to his judge ordinary.*

Venus, much irritated, finds him guilty, and he is greatly alarmed at the punishment which is to be awarded to him. He expects either death, or a transformation into the form of some wild animal.

At this juncture, the court of the Muses comes on the scene, attended by all the famous poets both ancient and modern. Venus then relates to Calliope the case of the poet. At the suggestion of Calliope, it is agreed to pardon him, on condition that he shall write a short ballad of a more cheerful nature than the one which procured his arrest. This he does extempore in a strain, which is so far satisfactory, that he is at once set free. He thanks Calliope for her mediation, who, taking a fancy for him, puts him under the charge of a sweet nymph, and, in the company of the Muses, he sets out on a voyage round the world. They at length reach the

* See *ante*, p. lxii.

Castalian font, where he finds such a crowd pressing to drink that he could not taste a drop.

"Beside that fount, with clearest crystal blest,
Alighted down the Muses bright of hue,
Themselves to solace and their steeds to rest;
And all their followers on the instant drew
To taste the stream, which sparkling leapt to view.
Thro' freshest meads with laurel canopied.
Then trembling to the well renowned I flew,
But the rude crowd all passage there defied,
Nor might I snatch a drop of that celestial tide.

Our horses pastured in a pleasant field,
Verdant and rich, beneath a mountain green,
Where, from the mid-day heat a shade to yield,
Some ancient cedars wove a leafy screen;
On the smooth turf unnumbered flowers were seen
Weaving a carpet 'neath umbrageous trees;
And o'er their channels, pav'd with jewels sheen,
The waters gliding did the senses please,
Mingling their quiet tunes with hum of honied bees.

On many an instrument of breath or string
These gentle ladies play'd or playing sung;
Some sat beneath the trees in lovely ring,
Some solitary stray'd the flowers among;
Ev'n the rude elements in silence hung.
And wooed their music with intense delight;
Whilst from their charms such dazzling rays were flung,
As utterly amaz'd all mortal sight,
And might have thaw'd the heart of sternest anchorite.

Far doth it pass all powers of living speech
To tell the joy that from these sights I took;
And if so high the wondrous theme doth reach,
How should my vein the great endeavour brook!
We may not soar so high, my little book.

But pass we on:—Upon the field I spied,
Woven of silk, with golden post and hook,
A goodly tent unfold its wings of pride,
To whose delightsome porch me drew my lovely guide."*

A fine pavilion is here pitched, where Ovid, Virgil, and other poets recount the deeds of ancient heroes. The Muses then resume their travels, until they reach a charming valley.

At last, the rock is seen which is the end of their journey. It is of slippery marble, with only one passage to the summit. The nymph and the poet commence the ascent, but on nearing the top, they find a deep abyss full of brimstone, in which many wretched creatures lay dead, and others were sweltering in the flames. The nymph informs him that these are people who, pretending to pursue the path of honour, but really following pleasure, fell into this sorrowful lake. The nymph now seizes the poet by the hair, and carries him to the top of the rock, in the same way that Habakkuk was conveyed to Babylon. From this eminence he sees the misery of the world, and a goodly vessel wrecked on a sandbank, with many of the crew perishing in the waves. His guide informs him that this ship is called 'The Carwell (or ship) of the State of Grace,' and gives him an outline of the Christian faith. One of the peculiarities of the poem is the unnatural blending of Christian subjects with the heathen mythology, and it is somewhat incongruous to find a nymph of Calliope's train expounding the scheme of redemption.†

* Scott. Worthies, vol. iii., p. 160.

† In his Virgil, Book IV. c. 6, he describes the priestesses of Bacchus as nuns.—Vol. ii. p. 193.

On turning in another direction, he sees the Palace of Honour,—a place of such transcendant beauty as to defy description. In a garden, he sees Venus seated on a throne, covered with precious gems, and a mirror placed before her, surrounded by three golden trees. In this mirror might be viewed the deeds of every one, and all the events of sacred and profane history. Some of these are enumerated, and the poet then passes to the description of games, hunting, hawking, etc., and the necromancy of Roger Bacon, and other famous magicians. Venus observes him while looking into the mirror, and recognises him as once having been her prisoner. She now asks how he likes this place, and then reminds him of his promise to write some poetry to free himself when he was in danger. She gives him a book to put in rhyme, by which, doubtless, the poet meant Virgil. This he accepts, and engages to obey her commands.

The struggles of many questionable characters to intrude into the Palace are next described; such as Sinon, Achitophel, Jugurtha, and Tryphon. Catiline, whom he sees trying to get in at a window, is driven back by a blow bestowed on him by Cicero with a heavy book.

Looking in at a small orifice, the poet discovers a hall in the palace of more magnificence than anything to be found on earth, which he thus describes:—

"In high relief of rich and massive gold,
The borders round the doors and windows shone;
Each tower and turret, beauteous to behold,
Of polished ivory form'd: ne was there one
That did not show inlaid its walls upon

Bright shapes of birds, 'midst sweet enamell'd flowers,
And curious knots, carved in the snow-white bone,
With matchless cunning by the artist's powers.—
So perfect and so pure were Honour's lordly bowers.

But pass we on—the nymph and I did wend
Straight to the hall, and climb'd a radiant stair,
Form'd all of topaz clear from end to end.
The gate was shut, but through a lattice there
Of beryl, gazing, a transcendant glare
Broke dazzlingly on mine astonished sight.—
A room I saw—but oh, what tongue shall dare
To paint that chamber, so surpassing bright!
Sure never such a view was given to mortal wight.

From every part combined, roof, wall, and floor,
A flood of light most gloriously was cast:
And as the stream upon mine eyes gan pour,
Blinded I stood awhile: that sight surpast
Aught that in Eastern story read thou hast
Of richest palace, or of gorgeous stall:
On diamond pillars, tall as any mast,
Clustering, and bound with ropes of rubies all,
The sapphire arches leant of that celestial hall.

The very benches, forms, and footstools mean,
Were shap'd of smaragdine and precious stone,
And on the carpet brilliant groups were seen
Of heroes old, whose steely corslets shone
Embost with jewels;—near them, on a throne
Sat Honour, mighty prince, with look severe,
And deep-set awful eye, whose glance alone
So full of might and glorious did appear,
That all my senses reel'd, and down I dropt with fear.

Within her snowy arms that Lady sweet
Me caught, and swiftly to the portal hied;

For wing'd with love and pity were her feet,
And soft she bore me to inhale the tide
Of the fresh air. She deem'd I would have died,
So sudden and so deadly pale I grew;
But fondly each reviving art she tried,
And bath'd my brow with Heliconian dew,
Till, faint and slow, mine eyes unclos'd to meet her view."*

The nymph explains to the poet the meaning of Honour as understood in this its headquarters, and apostrophizes virtue in two eloquent stanzas. After describing some of the historic characters who were seen in the palace, the nymph now proposes to take the poet into the garden, which was surrounded by a moat, having as the only means of entrance a plank laid across. The nymph passes over this primitive bridge in safety, but the poet, when he attempts to follow, falls into the water, which causes him to awake from his dream. After musing on the glorious palace and all its beauties, the author concludes by writing a ballad in praise of honour. A poetical address to King James IV. completes the work.

Douglas is supposed by Bishop Sage to have taken the plan of his Palace of Honour from the Picture of Cebes, but the resemblance is comparatively slight. There is equally little connection between his poem and the 'Sejour d'Honneur' of Octavien de St. Gelais, unless it be in their respective titles. Dr. Irving remarks that "the successive appearance of the different courts described in the Palace of Honour may possibly remind some readers of the Triumphs of

* Scott. Worthies, vol. iii., p. 167.

Petrarch, in which various shadowy trains succeed each other in a somewhat similar manner."* It may, however, with more probability be surmised, that Douglas had before him Chaucer's "Temple of Fame," when he drew the outline of his Palace of Honour. Chaucer's allegory takes the form of a dream, in which the poet finds himself in the Temple of Venus, whence he is carried, not by a nymph, but by an eagle, to a magnificent palace built upon a mountain of ice, and supported by rows of pillars, on which are inscribed the names of the most illustrious poets. Many of the names given by Chaucer are to be found in Douglas; yet, on the whole, the arrangement and versification of the two poems are so unlike, that to Douglas must be accorded the praise of having conceived and successfully completed an original design.

It has been supposed that Bunyan may have borrowed the idea of his Pilgrim's Progress from that of the Palace of Honour. In his famous allegory, the Christian hero, like the poet in that of Douglas, is conducted by supernatural beings through a great variety of strange scenes. In both the journey ends at a place of celestial glory, while there is a *limbo* or abyss by the wayside, a little before the ultimate object is reached. There is, however, a marked contrast between the poet, joining the gorgeous, though incongruous, cavalcade trooping to the Palace of Honour, and Christian wending his way through Despair and the Valley of the Shadow of Death to the Shining City.†

* Hist. of Scot. Poetry, p. 277.

† Essay on Scot. Poetry, by Prof. Nichol, p. xxvi.

The next poem of Douglas is his allegory of the progress of human life, to which the title of "King Hart" has been given. This poem was first printed by Pinkerton from the manuscripts of Sir Richard Maitland, preserved in the Pepysian Library, in Magdalen College, Cambridge. In 1784 Pinkerton went to Cambridge, and transcribed the MS., a great part of which he published in 1786, under the title of "Ancient Scotish Poems, from the MS. Collections of Sir Richard Maitland of Lethington, Knight."*

In this collection King Hart forms the first poem. Pinkerton's edition of it, however, contains important errors, some of which are due to the obscurity of the MS., and some to misreadings of the editor himself.

These difficulties led Pinkerton to suppose that it was written by Douglas before his Palace of Honour. Dr. Irving, in his History of Scotish Poetry, considers that, as the versification is superior to the Palace of Honour, and as the author does not enumerate it among his early works, it was written by Douglas after his translation of Virgil was completed. Douglas, however, in concluding his version of Virgil, takes a farewell of poetical composition ; and we may therefore assume, if we are to attach importance to this declaration, that King Hart was written between 1501, when the Palace of Honour was finished, and 1512, when the translation of Virgil was begun.

King Hart (or the heart of man) is represented as a mystical king in all the bloom of youth, and sur-

* 2 vols. 8vo.

rounded by attendants, who are personifications of the propensities of early manhood. The king, although a feudal monarch, is still far from enjoying freedom, as these "ythand servitouris," or busy attendants, govern him without any hope of his getting quit of them. He has also five servants, who are the five senses, appointed to guard him from his enemies. Notwithstanding all the care which is taken of the king, he is sometimes betrayed. Honour, coming to his gate, is denied admittance by the attendants, as the king was feasting; but by means of some contrivance, Honour gains access, and climbs up to the great tower, stating that his presence would add to the embellishments of the castle.

The palace of Dame Pleasance is next described. This Queen, with a legion of fair attendants, passes by the castle of King Hart, whose sentries are alarmed at the number in her train, and report what they saw to the king. Youthhead and Fresh Delight, two of the king's attendants, volunteer to ascertain of whom this party may consist. They set out, but are so surprised with what they encounter that they are easily made prisoners.

"Youthheid forth far'd—he rode on Innocence,
A milk-white steed that ambled as the wind:
Whilst Fresh Delight bestrode Benevolence,
A palfrey fair, that would not bide behind:
The glorious beams had almost made them blind,
That forth from Beauty burst beneath the cloud
With which the goddess had herself enshrined,
Sitting, like Eastern queen, in her pavilion proud.

But these young wights, abased at the sight,
Full soon were staid in their courageous mood;
Instant within them died all power and might,
And gazing, rooted to the earth they stood;
At which Fair Calling, seeing them subdued,
Seized on their slackened rein with rosy hands:
Then to her castle swift away she yude,*
And fastened soon the twain in Venus' silken bands."†

The king sends out new messengers, who are also captured. At last, becoming enraged, he arrays his host for battle with Dame Pleasance and her army. In the contest the king's party are defeated, and King Hart himself being injured by an arrow, is handed over to Dame Beauty to have his wound dressed, but the more she tries to cure it the worse it becomes. Many of the king's subjects are taken prisoners and confined in dungeons. King Hart is also imprisoned in a grated chamber, near the donjon, where he listens to the mirth that proceeds from the halls of the Queen. By means of Dame Pity, who at this juncture treacherously deserts Dame Pleasance, King Hart and his retainers are set free, and now take possession of the palace, making Dame Pleasance herself a prisoner. The Queen, after an interview with King Hart, finds that he is deeply smitten with her charms, and the first canto ends with their espousals and marriage feast.

The second canto begins with a striking description of Age, in the form of an "auld gude man," coming to the castle and seeking admittance. When the news of his arrival is carried to the king by Wantonness, the

* Went. † Scott. Worthies, p. 146.

king is grieved, but is still more so when he finds that Youthhead, Disport, and Fresh Delight desert him. Conscience then arrives, and breaks in without question or resistance. Sadness also intrudes, and whispers something in the king's ear. Dame Pleasance now loses all patience, and, whilst her royal husband is asleep, collects her train and deserts him. Wisdom and Reason now counsel the king to return to his own castle, where he finds but little comfort. Languor welcomes him at the gate. Strength creeps out at a postern; and, as he departs, Decrepitude, with a hideous host, is seen coming over the moor. They carry the castle by storm, and mortally wound the king, who prepares for death, and makes his last will and testament. To Queen Pleasance he bequeathes his palfrey Unsteadfastness; to Gluttony his "meikle wamb" and diseased liver; to Rere-Supper (or a second supper) he leaves his worn-out stomach; to Chastity his conscience, to be scoured from the rust which had long clogged it; to Freedom his threadbare coat; to Foolhardness his broken brow; and to Dame Danger a spear which had lost the head.

Like the Palace of Honour, King Hart is a work which in its execution is quite original. In it, however, may be traced some ideas which show that Douglas was familiar with Piers the Plowman, the famous poem of John Langland, written more than a century before. In *Passus* ix. of that poem, Lady Anima is enclosed in a castle, with Do-well, Do-bet, and Do-best as her keepers. Inwit or Conscience is the seneschal of the castle, whose sons, corresponding to the five senses of Douglas, are appointed to guard Lady Anima.—

Work-well and Go-well, See-well, Say-well, and Hear-well. The castle is afterwards explained as Caro, or the body; Lady Anima as Life, and dwelling in the heart of man. Various other allegorical characters, similar to those mentioned in King Hart, are to be found in the twenty divisions of Langland's long poem.

Of the poem called *Conscience*, which, in the present volume, follows King Hart, there is little to be said. The original is also preserved in the Maitland Manuscript, and is written on folios 192 and 193. It is an invective against the growing desire of churchmen for wealth. As occasionally Douglas has shown in his ideas similarity to those in the poem of Piers Plowman, it seems not improbable that he may have been familiar with the account given in that poem (B. xx. 519), of an angel proclaiming woe to the Church, on its receiving Constantine's gift of "lordeshipe and rentes."

This poem was probably the means of another piece of the same kind being written, which is still extant, the author of which is however unknown. It is as follows:—

ON CONSCIENCE.*

Quhen doctouris preichit to win the joy eternall,
  Vnto the hevin eftir our Lordis assense,
Thay causit justice, but bud or favour carnall,
  Thay causit be pvnist fleschly vyle offense,
  Gaif benyfice to Clerkis of Conscience;

* Bannatyne MS., fol. 89 *b*, and Ramsay's Evergreen, i. 159.

And sa the Feind had sic invy thairon,
Gart scraip away of Conscience the Con,
And sa behind wes levit bot Science.

Than wer all Clerkis for Sciens promovit,
And thay that wald to study maist apply:
Bot yit the Feind at Sciens was commovit,
Gart scraip away of Sciens the Sci;
And sa levit Ens be his fals slie invy,
Quhilk suld be for gold or geir exponit,
Quhairby benefice ar now of dayis disponit,
But Sciens or Consciens for to sell and by.

O soveraine Lord! and most excellant King,
Gar put the Con and Sci agane till Ens,
And rewll thy realm with justice in thy ring;
Gife benefice to Clerkis of Consciens,
Of wisdom and honour to stand at thy defens;
Se in thy court that Consciens ay be clene,
For corruptioun befoir thy dayis hes bene
Aganis justice, with vthir grit offens.

The most remarkable of the works of Bishop Douglas is unquestionably his *Translation of the Æneid of Virgil*, which he began in 1512, and finished according to his own statement

'Apon the fest of Marie Magdalene,'

the 22d of July 1513, so that it was a task of only eighteen months, during two of which he was unable from business to proceed with his labours.

It was at the request of his cousin Henry, Lord

Sinclair, that Douglas undertook this work. At the end of the translation there is a poetical address to his Lordship, in which he is represented as a liberal and learned patron of literature and science. When we consider the state of learning when Douglas wrote, and the shortness of the time which he took to finish this translation, it must be admitted that the effort was a great one, and the work is one of which Scotland may always be proud.

That Douglas should have selected Virgil as his favourite author is not surprising, as that poet was the most popular of all the classical writers. The works of Virgil passed through ninety editions before the year 1500, and in the time of Douglas they were the delight of young and old. The characteristic of the Æneid is a sustained loftiness – a great subject adequately conceived by a great mind, and unfolded in language of the utmost elegance. The translation of Douglas, on the other hand, is written more in a homely and familiar style, and has that diffuseness which is characteristic of all the early poets of our country. Its author had it in view to make his favourite classic easily understood by his countrymen; and in this way he has loaded his translation with expletives, sometimes far beyond what are necessary. In one or two instances, he has modernized the ideas of Virgil. For example, he describes the Sibyl as a nun, and makes her admonish Æneas to count his beads. To suit the exigencies of his verse besides, he has in many places altered proper names in such a way as to render them hardly recognisable.

Although Douglas has discharged his duty as a translator with great fidelity, he has not escaped censure. The learned Francis Junius, author of the 'Glossarium Gothicum' and other works, in a letter to Sir W. Dugdale,* remarks: "In my perusing of this Prelate his book (to say so much by the way), I stumbled on manie passages wherein this wittie Gawin doth grossly mistake Virgil, and is much led out of the way by the infection of a monkish ignorance then prevailing in church and commonwealth." Dr. Irving remarks on this criticism very truly that, in the passages which depart most widely from the original, Douglas has not been misled by his ignorance of the language, but by his adherence to the diffuseness prevalent in his own time. The learned Ruddiman also states that, from careful observation of his skill in explaining many words throughout his whole translation, he shows "how great a master he has been of the Latin tongue."

The charge brought against Douglas by Junius is not deserved, for in only one or two instances can he really be blamed for positive mistranslations, and these are not such as seriously to detract from the merits of his work.† Junius certainly appears to have studied Douglas' Translation very carefully, and left in MS. a glossary of its obsolete words which still exists among his books bequeathed to

* Life of Sir W. Dugdale, by W. Hamper, p. 383.

† One of these mistranslations may be noticed at p. 22 of vol. iii., where the word "viscum," in Æn. vi. l. 205, is rendered as "gum or glew," in place of "the mistletoe," which Virgil there refers to.

the Bodleian Library. It was consulted by Ruddiman, who informs us that in it "many of the hardest words are wholly omitted: he has mistaken the meaning of others, and very rarely gives the original of any." *

While to Douglas belongs the honour of being the author of the first metrical translation of a Classical writer in Britain, he was soon followed by others, in emulation of his success. One of these was the Earl of Surrey, the great improver of the English language after Chaucer, and the earliest writer of English blank verse. The Earl translated the second and fourth Books of Virgil, and this work seems to have been suggested by the prior version of Douglas, as he frequently copies it. This is particularly observable in the second Book, where many lines are adopted with hardly any alteration. The following passage in Douglas may be compared with the corresponding passage in Surrey, and is only one out of many which are given by Dr. Nott as establishing the fact of the Earl's indebtedness to his Scottish predecessor.†

DOUGLAS.

The Greikis chiftanes, irkit of the weir,
By past or than sa mony langsum yeir,
And oft rebutit by fataile destany,
Ane huige hors, like ane greit hill, in hy
Craftelie thai wrocht in wirschip of Pallas.

SURREY.

The Greeks' chieftans all irked with the war
Wherein they wasted had so many years,

* Preface to Douglas' Virgil, p. 3.
† Works of Earl of Surrey, by Dr. Nott, Vol. i., p. 227.

And oft repulsed by fatal destiny,
A huge horse made, high raised like a hill
By the divine science of Minerva.

Besides many passages shewing considerable descriptive power, there may be instanced, as specimens of the felicity of Douglas in his version of Virgil, those detailing the destruction of the Palace of Priam and the death of that king in the second Book; the complaint of Queen Dido, and the account of her death in the fourth Book; the spirited account of the funeral games in the fifth Book; and the passage in the sixth Book where Æneas and the Sibyl arrive in the Elysian fields.

For a specimen of diffuseness, the following translation of the line Æn. v. 429 may be taken:—

"Immiscentque manus manibus, pugnamque lacessunt."

Now, hand to hand, the dintis lichtis with a swak;
Now bendis he wp his burdoun with a mynt,
On syde he bradis for till eschew the dint;
He etlis yondir his avantage to tak,
He metis him thar, and charris him with a chak;
He watis to spy, and smytis in all his mycht,
The todir keppis hym on his burdoun wycht;
Thai foyne at vthir, and eggis to bargane.*

In concluding his translation, Douglas intimates his belief in the perpetuity of his fame, and takes farewell of his poetical studies:—

Thus vp my pen and instrumentis full yoyr
On Virgillis post I fix for evirmore,
Nevir, from thens, syk materis to discryve;
My muse sal now be cleyn contemplatyve.†

* Works, ii., p. 249. † Vol. iv. p. 223.

The following lines by Sir Walter Scott, may fitly close this short notice of Douglas' best known work :—

> "A bishop by the altar stood,
> A noble lord of Douglas blood,
> With mitre sheen and rocquet white;
> Yet show'd his meek and thoughtful eye
> But little pride of prelacy;
> More pleased that, in a barbarous age,
> He gave rude Scotland Virgil's page,
> Than that beneath his rule he held
> The bishopric of fair Dunkeld."*

In the Prologues to the thirteen Books of which Douglas' translation of Virgil consists, we find descriptive passages equal, if not superior, to any which exist in the whole range of Scottish poetry. The dreary picture of winter in the seventh Prologue, the glowing description of May in the twelfth, and the beauties of an evening in June in the thirteenth, have justly attracted much attention, and show that their author was a man of accurate observation and original thought. His other prologues display a great knowledge of human nature, and contain pointed observations on the manners and pursuits of mankind.

The *First* Prologue narrates the story of his undertaking the translating of Virgil. He extols the merits of that Poet, and laments his own unworthiness to follow so distinguished a guide. He attacks the celebrated William Caxton for publishing a translation of a French book purporting to be a translation of Virgil. This work, by Guillaume de Roy, was

* Marmion, Canto vi., 11.

simply a kind of romance made out of the Æneid, with some trifling additions, the whole forming but a small volume. Douglas gives a full account of the deficiencies of the author, viz :—the omission of the greater part of the first three Books, with the total want of the fifth ; his statement that the storm in Book I. was sent forth by Æolus and Neptune, whereas Neptune saved Æneas from the storm ; his perversion of the story of Dido ; his rejection of the descent of Æneas to the shades as fabulous ; his confusion of the Tiber with the Tover ; and his substitution of Crispina for Deiphobe as the name of the Sibyl ; summing up the whole by the assurance that this book is no more like Virgil than Satan resembled St. Augustine :

"Nor na mar like than the devill and Sanct Austyne."

Douglas then enlarges on the difficulty he experienced in his own translation from the imperfections of the Scottish language, and the Prologue is concluded by his asking a charitable criticism from his readers.

The *Second* Prologue is a short address to Melpomene moralizing on the destruction of Troy.

The *Third* Prologue is descriptive of the contents of the third Book of Virgil, and invokes the assistance of the Virgin for its completion.

The *Fourth* Prologue contains thirty-five stanzas. It is directed against the danger of unbridled love. Of this he quotes many instances from the Scriptures and the Classics, and especially refers to the unfortunate Dido, the account of whose fate is described in the following Book of Virgil.

The *Fifth* Prologue, being introductory to the games

described in the fifth Book of Virgil, exemplifies the amusements that are suited to the tastes of different classes of men.

The *Sixth* Prologue is adapted to the subject treated in the corresponding Book of the Æneid, which is the account of the visit of Æneas to Hades. The poem begins by an apostrophe to Pluto, "Patron of the deip Acheron." The author then cautions his readers not to treat the subject of this book lightly, but to read it more than twice. He gives a comparison of the Christian and Pagan religions, and an account of the belief in Purgatory, the origin of which has been attributed to Virgil. He avows his strong belief in Christianity, and his detestation of "fals goddis." As for Pluto, he "sall hym hunt of sty."

The *Seventh* Prologue is a description of winter, and is one of the most picturesque of his poetical pieces. He describes the country as melancholy and dreary; the trees destitute of foliage; rivers in heavy flood, and the little rills, so sweet and quiet in summer, turned into torrents tearing down their banks. The earth is now barren, hard, and unlovely, and the decay of nature begins to remind man of "wintry age and all subduing death."

The following passage, from a version by Fawkes, gives a modern aspect to a favourable specimen of the beauties in the original:

"Now reign'd the power of keen congealing frost,
When all the beauty of the year is lost;
The brumal season, bitter, cold, and pale,
When short dull days and sounding storms prevail.
The wild north wind, tremendous from afar,

O'erwhelm'd imperial Neptune in his car,
Their scatter'd honours from the forests tore,
And dash'd the mad waves headlong on the shore.
Fierce, foaming rivers, swell'd with torrents brown,
Hurl'd all their banks precipitately down;
Loud roar'd the thunder of the raging floods,
Loud as gaunt lions bellowing shake the woods.
Th' unwieldy monsters which the deeps contain,
Sought safety at the bottom of the main.
Strife-stirring Mars, regressive in his sphere,
Sustain'd the cold dominions of the year;
And black Orion dimm'd the face of day,
Leading the luckless mariner astray.
Saturn, whose boding aspect, chill and wan,
Frowns in dread vengeance on the race of man,
Denouncing dearth, and desolating pest,
Held high his course progressive in the east;
And blooming Hebe, Juno's daughter gay,
Was ravish'd of her beautiful array.
Incessant rains had drench'd the floated ground,
And clouds o'ercast the firmament around:
White shone the hills involv'd in silver snow,
But brown and barren were the vales below:
On firm foundations of eternal stone
High rugged rocks in frosty splendor shone;
The hoary fields no vivid verdure wore,
Frost warpt the world, and beauty was no more.
Wide-wasting winds that chill'd the dreary day,
And seemed to threaten nature with decay,
Reminded man, at every baleful breath,
Of wintry age, and all-subduing death." *

While such is the state of matters out of doors, the Poet hurries to warm himself at the fire; its cheerful

* Original Poems and Translations, p. 269.

blaze lights up his chamber, and casting his eyes around, he sees his Virgil lying on a desk, still far from completion. He then resolves to make up the delay, and resumes his work of translation—

"Quhen frostis days our fret bayth fyrth and fauld."

The *Eighth* Prologue is one of the most remarkable of his productions, from the excess of alliteration which he employs, and the antiquated words with which it is filled. It is thus one of the most difficult of his poems to understand fully, or to read pleasantly.* In it the author takes a cynical view of the world, and complains bitterly of the wrong-doing which is everywhere rampant. He describes himself falling asleep, and, in a dream, hearing a melancholy looking sage moralizing on the wickedness of the age. The Poet informs the sage that, while all mankind have their aims and foibles, his ambition is to see his task of translation finished. The sage hereupon gives him a roll in which many hidden mysteries are unfolded, but the Poet tells him plainly that he cannot understand them. The apparition then takes the Poet to a field where they find a hidden treasure. While beginning to pick up the hoard his vision ceased, and all the wealth disappeared so completely that—

"I fand not in all that field, in faith, a be bike."

When he could make nothing of the treasure, he turned to translating the eighth Book of Virgil.

* In the copy of the Edition of Douglas' Virgil, published in 1710, which belonged to the celebrated Horne Tooke, now in possession of the Editor, so many words are marked as unintelligible that he apparently had made but little of this Prologue, and he has written on the margin—"Alliteration with a witness! in this Prologue."

The *Ninth* Prologue, after praising virtue and honesty, shews that heroic verse is the poetry most suited to exalted subjects, and the language to be employed should be grave and sententious. The Poet illustrates this by the belongings of Knights and Nobles "of estait." He pays a well-merited complaint to the sustained elevation of Virgil's "wark emperiall," and entreats his readers' pardon if his translation has not done justice to the original.

The *Tenth* Prologue is a religious poem in thirty-four stanzas. In it are shown the perfections of the Deity, in language of considerable elegance. The author then enunciates the mystery of the Trinity, and concludes by stating his firm belief in the Christian religion, and that he himself will

> "Woirship nother idoll, stok, nor elf,"

although he is constrained to describe scenes of this kind in Virgil.

The *Eleventh* Prologue, of twenty-four stanzas, treats first of knightly chivalry, which should be founded on right and justice; not seeking occasions of contention, but, at the same time, possessing fortitude and courage. Spiritual chivalry is then described, which, it is enjoined, should not be a merely passive state, but christian knights ought to persevere in good works to the end of their days, and should strive to reach the land of promise

> "Hecht till Abraham and his seyd."

The *Twelfth* Prologue—

> "Where splendid Douglas paints the blooming May,"

is certainly the finest effort of his muse, and his description of country life and scenes, here given, is not surpassed by any other Scottish Poet. Its first editor, in 1553, characterises it as "ane singular lernit Proloug," and from that time to the present it has met with the highest encomiums. In 1752, an elegant English version was published by Francis Fawkes,* and in the same year one was printed in the Scots Magazine by Jerome Stone, Schoolmaster of Dunkeld.† We quote once more a passage from the version of Fawkes, as a specimen of the beauties in the original :—

"All gentle hearts confess the quickening spring,
For May invigorates every living thing.
Hark! how the merry minstrels of the grove
Devote the day to melody and love;
The ouzle shrill, that haunts the thorny dale,
The mellow thrush, the love-lorn nightingale,
Their little breasts with emulation swell,
And sweetly strive in singing to excell.
In the thick forest feeds the cooing dove;
The starling whistles various notes of love;
The sparrow chirps, the clefted walls among:
To the sweet wildness of the linnet's song,
To the harsh cuckoo, and the twittering quail
Resounds the wood, the river, and the vale;
And tender twigs, all trembling on the trees,
Dance to the murmuring music of the bees.
Upspring the airy larks, shrill-voiced and loud,
And breathe their matins from a morning cloud,

* A description of May. From Gawin Douglas, Bishop of Dunkeld. By Francis Fawkes, A.M. It is also to be found in his Original Poems and translations, 1761, p. 225.

† Scots Magazine, 1755, p. 294.

To greet glad Nature, and the God of day,
And flowery Venus, blooming queen of May;
The songs of praise their tuneful breasts employ,
Charm every ear, and wrap the soul in joy.
Thus sung the sweet musicians on the spray:
  Welcome, thou Lord of light, and lamp of day:
Welcome to tender herbs, and myrtle bowers,
Welcome to plants, and odour-breathing flowers:
Welcome to every root upon the plain,
Welcome to gardens, and the golden grain;
Welcome to birds that build upon the breere,
Welcome, great Lord and Ruler of the year;
Welcome, thou source of universal good,
Of buds to boughs, and beauty to the wood;
Welcome, bright Phœbus, whose prolific power
In every meadow spreads out every flower;
Where-e'er thy beams in mild effulgence play,
Kind Nature smiles, and all the world is gay."

The *Thirteenth* Prologue is descriptive of summer and the "joyous moneth tyme of June." The poet, in a calm evening, enters a garden, and seats himself under a green laurel. Whilst engaged in studying the stars he falls asleep, when an aged man appears to him, crowned with bay leaves—

. . . "that was als stern of speche
As he had been ane medysyner or lech."

He informs the Poet that he is Maphaeus Vegius, and requests him to translate his supplement to Virgil. The Poet then represents that, as he had finished Virgil, he thought he had given sufficient time to unprofitable studies, and reminds Maphaeus of St. Jerome, who was—

"Dung and beft intill hys sleip
For he to gentilis bukis gaif sik keip."

Maphaeus then informs him that he cannot be excused; that he must translate his book, or he would suffer for it. With his club Maphaeus then

"Twenty rowtis upon my rigging laid."

after which the Poet promises obedience. He then awakes from his dream, and states his anxiety to fulfil the promise made in his sleep to Maphaeus.

Besides his poetical works, Bishop Douglas is said to have written others on historical subjects, to which the title of "Aureæ Narrationes" was given, but they are not known to exist. Bishop Sage was of opinion that these "Narrations" were referred to by Douglas himself in an address to Lord Sinclair, concluding his Virgil:

"I have alsso a schort comment compild
To expon strange historeis and termes wild." *

The comment thus referred to, however, consists merely of explanations of words and passages in Virgil, which Douglas had begun but did not finish. These were written by him on the margin of the Cambridge Manuscript, and extend no further than to the end of the first Book of the Æneid. They are printed at the conclusion of vol. ii. of this edition of his works.

The historical views of Douglas may be in part gleaned from the following notes which he furnished to the writer of English history, Polydore Vergil.

Vergil was a native of Urbino in Italy, and in 1501 was appointed collector of the tribute known as Peter-

* Vol. iv. p. 228.

Pence, payable in England to the Pope. He was afterwards nominated to the Archdeaconry of Wells. In 1509 he was so anxious to obtain information about Scottish history, that he wrote directly to King James IV., stating that he knew no trustworthy work on the subject, and desiring to be furnished with an authentic list of the Kings of Scotland, that he might put them in their proper order in his history.*

As already related, Vergil was on terms of familiarity with the persons most eminent for rank and learning at the Court of Henry VIII.; and when Douglas was living as an exile in England in 1522, Vergil made his acquaintance. In the previous year the History of Scotland was published by John Major; and as that author in his work treats the well-known story of Gathelus and Scota as a fable, Douglas agreed to furnish Vergil with some notes relative to the subject, which were duly inserted by Vergil in his History of England, which appeared in 1534, and was dedicated to King Henry VIII. The notes of Douglas introduced by Vergil were to the following effect :—

"Gathelus, the sonne of Neolus, king of the Atheniens, flienge from the harde servage of his father, departed into Ægipte to aid Pharao against the Æthiopians, unto whome Moses was sente from Godde, with the which benefit the Ægiptian kinge beinge stirred, gave his daughter named Scota in marriage to Gathelus, whoe forthewith serchinge new dwellinge places arrived in Spaine, and inhabited that coste which after him was called Portugallia, as who woulde saye the porte of Gathelus, terminge his subjects Scotts, according to the name of the noble woman his wife, Scota.

* Epist. Reg. Scot. i. p. 139.

Thus havinge issew and propagation of discent, three hundred yeare after, the Scotts beinge brought into Irelond bie their kinge Simon Brechus, weare the beginning of a newe kingdom, and finallie, before the comminge of Christe, camme into Albion. It followed consequentlie that the Pictes not long after camme allso owte of Scithia in to Albion, and that these two externe nations had issewe of stemme and encrease of kingdom in that coste of the Ilond which is now called Scotlonde, from which time they allways mantayned warrs with the Brittons, with the Romains, and Julius Cæsar especiallie, the Scottes remayninge still inviolate, as not disturbed from their degree. Finallie this was therein written, that owlie theire Kinge Rewtheres having evel succes at home in his troubles with the Brittons, didde once avoyded his contrie and fledde into Irelonde; and that within a while, after haveinge encreased his power with Irisshe menne, retowrned to his former possessions; and that in this beehalfe Beda was nott of sufficient perseveraunce, which calleth this retorne the firste comminge of the Scottes in to Albion. All this was donne beefore the comminge of Our Savior.

As soon as I hadde redde these thinges, accordinge to the olde proverbe, I seemed to see the beare bringe foorthe her younglinges. Afterwarde, when for recreation wee mette together, as wee weare accustomed, this Gawine demaunded mie opinion. I aunswered, that as towchinge there originall I wowlde not greatlie contende, seing that for the moste parte all contries weare woonte to drawe the principles of there pedegree ether from the Goddes or from heroicall nobles, to the ende that they which afterwarde beinge not easie of beeleefe minded to skanne and derive theim, when they showlde hardlie find enie thinge of more certeintee, they showld rather bee constreyned to beeleve it firmelie then enie farder to labour vainelie. But to bee shorte, this in noe wise kanne agree that the Scottes and Pictes, two mightie people, showlde soe longe reigne in the llond, showlde performe so manie battailes, showlde so often foyle the Britons and Romains, moleste them, and vanquisshe them, and yet noe antique or grave writer once make rehersall of theim; especiallie seeing that Cæsar, Tacitus, Ptolome, and Plinie (levinge to reherse the others) doe eche wheare in there histories make mention of the people named Trinobantes, Cenigmani, Segontiaci, Ancalites, Bibroci, Brigantes, Silures, Iceni, Ordolucæ, Vicomagi, Elgouæ, with the other contries of Brittaine; but of the Scottes and Pictes not a woorde, bie cause as yeat they weare not in this region, which forsothe is to bee thoughte the verie cause whie late writers have soe slacklie used the memoriall of theim. Wherefore I towlde him, even as frindlie as trewlie, that as concerninge the Scottes and Pictes beefore there comminge into Brittaine (which Bedas in his time hadd well assigned), it showlde not bee lawful for me to intermeddell, bie reason of the prescrit which is incident to an historien, which is that hee showld nether abhorre the discooveringe of falsehoode, nether in anie case alowe the underminiuge of veritee, nether to gyve suspition of favor nor yeat of envy.

This Gawine, noe doubte a sincere manne, didd the lesse dissent from this sentence, in that it plainelie appeared to him that reason and trewthe herin well agreaed, so easlie is trewthe allwaise discolowred from feyned phansies." *

Although Douglas did not agree with the historical views of Major, that author in 1516 dedicated to him and Robert Cockburn, Bishop of Ross, his Commentary on the Fourth Book of Sentences of Peter Lombard. Prefixed to his previous work on the First and Second Books of the same Commen-

* P. Vergil's English History (Camden Soc.), vol. i. p. 106.

taries,* Major inserts a dialogue of which the title is as follows:—"Dialogus de materia theologo tractanda. Dialogus inter duos famatos viros M. Gauuinium Douglaseium virum non minus eruditum quam nobilem, Ecclesiæ Beati Ægidii Edinburgensis Præfectum, et Magistrum Dav. Cranstonum in Sacra Theosophia Baccalaureum, optimé meritum." "This dialogue," says the Rev. Mr. Lorimer, "is very curious, and throws some valuable light upon the theological spirit of Gavin Douglas, who appears from it to have been no admirer of the scholastic method of theologizing. He is introduced as saying that he could not see what advantage theology could derive from so many frivolous positions and subtleties, which could give no entrance into the science, but only mystified and darkened it. He quotes Æneas Sylvius, who had been bold enough to say that the works of Aristotle would perish some day by the hand of all-destroying time; and he thinks that his friend Major would be better employed in preaching than writing commentaries on the Sentences. He complains of the multitude of such books. Many were beginning to speak against that whole manner of treating the topics of theology. It was absurd to have more regard to the authority of Aristotle on

* Paris 1509, fol. That there was an official connection between Major and Douglas appears from the following extract from the Register of the Scottish Privy Seal (iv. fol. 41):—"Presentacio directa Episcopo Candide Case et Capelle Regie pro collacione habenda Magistro Johanni Maro in theologia doctore super Thesaurario dicte Capelle Regie nunc vacante per decessum quondam Domini Johannis Craufurd, ad presentacionem Regis spectante, etc. Apud Edr. vltimo Decembris, anno vc ixo, et regni Regis xxijo. Gratis Magistro Gawino Dowglace."

such subjects than to the doctors of the Church; he therefore wished much that Major would abandon such studies, and return to his native country, to cultivate the vineyard of the Lord, and by preaching to scatter far and wide that evangelical seed from which the souls of the faithful would reap the best fruits." *

According to Dempster,† Douglas also wrote some dramatic poems founded on incidents in sacred history, which he designates, "Comoediæ aliquot sacræ," but these are not known to exist.‡

One of the peculiarities of the works of Bishop Douglas, is their philological value. So far back as the year 1638, Lisle, the Anglo-Saxon scholar, states, in the preface to his "Ancient Monuments of the Saxon tongue," that he improved more in the knowledge of Saxon by the perusal of G. Douglas' Virgil than by that of all the old English he could find, poetry, or prose, because it was nearer the Saxon and further from the Norman.§ In 1710, Ruddiman published

* Precursors of Knox, p. 220. † Hist. Eccl. Gent. Scot. p. 221.

‡ The Rev. Mr. Scott, one of the biographers of Douglas, was of opinion that to him might be attributed the authorship of "The Flowers of the Forest," one of the finest of the Scottish songs, as it describes the disasters of the Scots at the battle of Flodden, in which Douglas lost several of his relations. It is however admitted, that although the tune and two detached verses are ancient, the rest was composed by Miss Jane Elliot, a lady belonging to the county of Roxburgh.

§ "At length," he says, "I lighted on Virgil, Scotished by the Reuerend Gawin Dowglas, Bishop of Dunkell, and vncle to the Earle of Angus; the best translation of that Poet that euer I read. And though I found that dialect more hard than any of the former (as neerer the Saxon, because farther from the Norman), yet with helpe of the Latine, I made shift to vnderstand it, and read the his glossary of the words in the same work, which was an era in Scottish philology, and was the foundation of the elaborate Dictionary of the Scottish Language, afterwards published by the Rev. Dr. Jamieson.

The origin of the literary language of Scotland has long been a subject of interesting inquiry among Scottish philologers, and various theories have been promulgated as to its independent origin, which are now no longer tenable. It is unnecessary to enter into these on the present occasion, but it may be remarked that there is every reason to believe that the broad Saxon dialect, derived from the Teutonic invaders of Britain, was at one time general from London to the Forth, and northwards on the Eastern coast as far as Aberdeen.

The venerable father of English typography, William Caxton, writing at London in 1496, tells us in the preface to his "Buke of Eneydos," so much maligned by Douglas, that, to make himself intelligible to "comyn people," he had to "vse old and homely terms," and to provide himself with a stock of these he took up a book written in "olde Englysshe," when he found that "certynlye it was more lyke to Dutsche than Englishe." This statement of Caxton is interesting as showing the change that had, ere his time,

booke more than once from the beginning to the end. Wherby I must confesse I got more knowledge of that I sought, than by any of the other. For as at the Saxon inuasion, many of the Britans, so at the Norman many of the Saxons fled into Scotland, preseruing in that Realme unconquered, as the line Royall, so also the language, better than the Inhabitants here, vnder conquerors law and custome, were able."—*Preface*, p. 16.

come over the language in the South of England, owing to Anglo-Norman and other influences. In the ancient Kingdom of Northumbria, which stretched from the Humber to the Firth of Forth, the language remained more pure, and resisted that propensity to change which more or less affects all living languages. It was in the dialect common to this extensive district that nearly all the English metrical romances of mediæval times are written, and with it the language of the earlier Scottish Poets, Barbour and Wynton, is almost identical. "Did we not know the age of G. Douglas," says Sir Walter Scott, "we should certainly esteem his language older than that of Chaucer, when in fact it is nearly two centuries later." "This observation," remarks George Chalmers, "is equally true of Dunbar and Lindsay, and this fact is amply sufficient to preclude a late theory that the Scottish poets took the lead in improvement, leaving Gower, Chaucer, and Lydgate far behind." *

In his account of the dialect of the southern counties of Scotland (p. 51), Mr J. A. H. Murray observes, "after the final establishment of Scotland as a distinct nationality, and much more after the decline and extinction of the 'langage of the Northin lede' in England, the written language of Scotland became more and more conformed to that type of the northern speech which was spoken on the shores of the Forth, in Edinburgh, Linlithgow, Stirling, Dunfermline, and St Andrews, the centre of political and ecclesiastical government and of the education as well as the commerce of the kingdom; and, as a conse-

* Int. to Works of Sir D. Lyndsay, vol. i., p. 146.

quence, it came more and more to assume characteristics of its own, distinct from the old northern tongue which had been common to southern Scotland and northern England."

Douglas was the first native writer who applied the name of "Scottis" to the language he employed, and he informs us that he had to the best of his ability "written in the langage of Scottis nation;" but, while he used the broad and widely-spread dialect common at an early period to the north of England and southern Scotland, his works present certain peculiarities, which may be easily explained. In his preface to Virgil, he complains of the rude simplicity of the language of his country, which he found unsuited for the work of translation. He accordingly, in his version of Virgil, does not scruple to Scotticise a Latin word, while in his earlier poems, the use of words derived from this language is easily observable; a fault that tends to give an air of affectation to writings where they are freely introduced. Words such as *amene*, *condict*, *degest*, *defundand*, *depured*, *facund*, *venust*, and many others of the same kind, never obtained currency, and cannot be said to have enriched the language. Besides, the familiarity of Douglas with French has led him to introduce many expressions from that language, as a cursory glance at the glossary of the present edition will sufficiently prove. Words such as *abilyement*, *arrace*, *balein*, *barbare*, *cahute*, *dedeinyie*, *gloir*, *mobilis*, *orloge*, *poun*, *scripture* (a writing case, *éscriptoire*), *velis* (calves), *bew schirris* (fair sirs), are a few out of many which are freely employed by Douglas in his works. His admiration for Chaucer, whom he sometimes closely imitates, appears to have induced Douglas to adopt some of the grammatical forms used by that poet, which are unusual with Scottish authors; and the Rev. Mr. Skeat observes, that the poetry of Douglas is not to be regarded as pure Scottish, but as Scottish much affected by Anglicisms. This is the more surprising, as Douglas in his first prologue professes to be "kepand na Sodroun bot oure awin langage;" and Mr. J. A. H. Murray remarks, that "not only does he use the y-prefix to the past participle (which the Northern dialect had dropped before the 12th century) in y-beried, y-clepit, y-conquest, y-fetterit, y-forgit, y-lowpit, y-markit, y-sowpit, y-womplit, y-wymplit, y-drad, y-plet, y-bound, y-boundin, y-brokin, y-graven, y-slain; but he has even the *peculiarly* Southern forms which retain the prefix and drop the terminations—y-baik, y-be, y-bore, y-clois, y-draw, y-schroude, y-set—for the Northern bak-en, be-en, bor-en, clos-it, draw-en, schroud-it, sett-en or sutt-en. Some of these forms were indeed more "Sodroun" than the literary English of his own day; but all are Chaucerian, and show how deeply Douglas had drunk of him who was, more even than Virgil—

In that art of eloquence the flude."*

In concluding this short notice of the works of Bishop Gavin Douglas, the following tribute to his literary merits, by Sir David Lindsay of the Mount, may not unaptly be added as showing the respect in which he was held by his contemporaries:—

* P. 47.

Allace! for aue, quhilk lamp was in this land,
Of eloquence the flowand balmy strand,
And in our Inglis rhetoric the rose;
As of rubies the Charbuncle bin chose!
And, as Phebus dois Cynthia presell,
Sa Gawin Douglas Bischop of Dunkell,
Had, quhen he was into this land on live,
Abufe vulgar Poeitis prerogative,
Baith in practick and speculatioun.
I say na mair, gude reidaris may discriue,
His wourthy warkis in nomber ma than fiue,
And specialy the trew translatioun
Of Virgill, quhilk bin consolatioun
To cunning men, to knaw his greit ingyne,
Als weill in natural science as diuyne."*

* Complaynt of the Papingo, ll. 22-36. Here Lyndsay describes the writings of Douglas as being in "*our Inglis.*"

NOTICES OF THE MANUSCRIPTS AND PRINTED EDITIONS OF THE WORKS OF GAVIN DOUGLAS.

Of the *Palice of Honour*, the earliest of the works of Douglas, no manuscript is known to exist. The first edition was printed in London, by William Copland. It appeared without a date, and bears the following title:—

The | Palis of | Honoure, compyled by | Gawyne dowglas Bys- | shope of Dunkyll.

¶ Imprinted at London in | flet stret, at the sygne of | the Rose garland by | wyllyam | Copland.

❡ God saue Quene Marye.

From the circumstance that this edition is of the same size, and has the same ornamentation on the title page as the edition of Douglas' Virgil, which this printer published in 1553, we may conclude that both issued from the press about the same time; and copies of the two are sometimes bound in one volume.

It is not paged, but consists of 39 folios. On folio 3, there is a spirited cut of the Royal Arms of

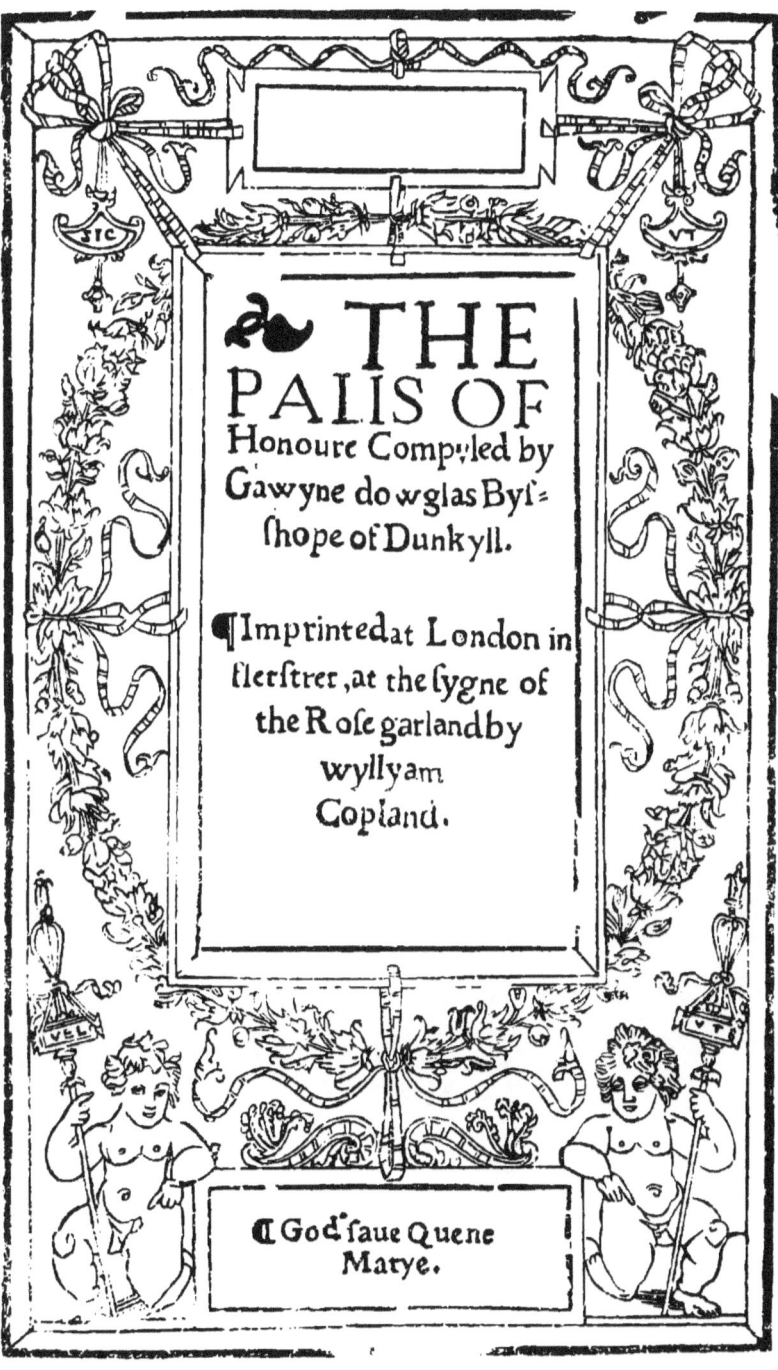

THE PALIS OF Honoure Compyled by Gawyne dowglas Byſ=ſhope of Dunkyll.

¶ Imprinted at London in fleetſtret, at the ſygne of the Rose garland by wyllyam Copland.

¶ God ſaue Quene Marye.

Scotland, which is given in facsimile at p. 6 of this volume. On the margins are a number of explanatory side notes, which are wanting in the Edinburgh edition, but are supplied in the present reprint.

A list of the variations of this edition from the Edinburgh edition of 1579, was given in the reprint of the same edition, published by the Bannatyne Club in 1827; and will be found in the notes to the present volume. This London edition is very rare, and a copy at the Roxburghe sale brought the sum of twenty guineas.

The Edinburgh Edition of 1579, has the following title:—

¶ Heir beginnis | ane treatise callit the Palice | of Honovr compylit | be M. Gawine Dowglas | Bischop of | Dunkeld.

Imprentit at Edin- | burgh be Iohne Ros | for Henrie Charteris. Anno 1579.

Cvm privilegio regali.

In the address to "the Reidar" prefixed to this edition, it is stated that it is more correct than the one printed in London, and also than "the copyis set furth of auld amangis ourselfis," of which latter all have now disappeared. Curiously enough, Mr. Laing recovered a few leaves of one of these editions, which he supposes to have been printed in Edinburgh, by Thomas Davidson, about or before the year 1540. These fragments, however, present no variations of interest.

The Edinburgh Edition is of greater rarity, as not

more than two or three copies are known to exist, one of which is preserved in the Library of the University of Edinburgh, and another in that of the Faculty of Advocates. The copy in the University was presented to his *alma mater*, by William Drummond of Hawthornden in 1626. At the end there is a woodcut, a copy of which is given at page 82 of this volume.

A reprint of this Edition, with the Prologues to Virgil, formed the second volume of a series of the works of the Scottish Poets, published in Perth, by R. Morrison & Son, in 1787. This edition is understood to have been edited by the Rev. James Scott, one of the ministers of Perth, who prefixed a life of the author, and some illustrative notes.

A more correct reprint of the Edinburgh Edition was published by John Pinkerton in 1792. It appeared in the first volume of his "Scotish Poems reprinted from scarce editions." Pinkerton gives a few variations of the text from the London edition. These he puts at the foot of each page. To each of the Divisions of the Poem he prefixes an "Argument," or short synopsis of its contents in an imitation of the old Scottish language. These will be found in the notes to the present volume. From their being apparently in old Scottish, they have misled Lowndes and other bibliographers, who represent them as one of the peculiarities of the Edinburgh edition of 1579.

A facsimile reprint was made of the Edinburgh edition, for the Bannatyne Club, in 1827. It was presented to the Club by Mr. John G. Kinnear. Prefixed to this beautiful volume, as above stated,

Frontispiece

in Fragment of an unknown Edition of
"The Palice of Honour."
Supposed to have been printed at Edinburgh
circa 1540.

ay the grace
ings end.

eambyl. And novv nixt efter
the Palyce of HONOVR
n.&c.

Tailpiece

at end of the Prologue of " The Palice of Honou
in same Fragment.

is a list of the variations of the Edinburgh from the London edition of 1553.

The Poem of *King Hart,* and the verses on *Conscience,* exist in the folio Maitland Manuscript, preserved in the Pepysian Library in Magdalen College, Cambridge.

This MS., and another in quarto, were long preserved by the family of the Scottish Poet, Sir Richard Maitland, and in these venerable volumes not only Maitland's Poems were engrossed, but several by Dunbar, and his contemporaries. It was supposed by Pinkerton that Sir Richard's great-grandson, the Duke of Lauderdale, had presented these MSS. to Samuel Pepys, Secretary of the Admiralty in the time of Charles II., who bequeathed his library, in 1703, to Magdalen College, Cambridge. The Lauderdale MSS. were, however, sold by auction at London in 1692, and the catalogue of them, reprinted by Mr Laing in vol. ii. of the Bannatyne Miscellany, proves that they had been purchased by Pepys at that time.

The folio MS. seems from various dates between 1555 and 1585, to have been about thirty-three years in formation, and to have been written by various persons. It is much stained by sea water, and some leaves are injured at the lower corners. Most of the leaves were inlaid in the time of Pepys himself, by which means, various side-notes have been cut away, amongst these the notes to King Hart, with three exceptions.

Pinkerton, in 1786, included "King Hart" in his

"Ancient Scotish Poems, never before in print: But now published from the MS. collections of Sir Richard Maitland, of Lethington, Knight, Lord Privy Seal of Scotland,"* but he has in several instances misread the manuscript. He has however supplied several of its defects with considerable ingenuity. In the MS. these poems occur without any titles, nor has "King Hart" (which begins on fol. 226), any division into Cantos. This division was made by Pinkerton, who, in addition, prefixed to each Canto an "Argument," or synopsis of its contents, in imitation of the old Scottish language. These will be found in the notes to the present volume. As in the case of "The Palice of Honour," they have proved somewhat misleading. Mr. P. F. Tytler, in his account of the poem, describes Pinkerton's "Arguments," as "Douglas' nervous and condensed description of his own poem."†

The verses on *Conscience* are written on folios 192-193 of this MS.

MSS. OF VIRGIL'S ÆNEID.

Of the *Translation of the Æneid of Virgil*, several excellent copies exist in Manuscript. Those at present best known, are as follow:—

I. *The Cambridge MS.*, preserved in the Library of Trinity College, Cambridge, (Gale's MSS. O 3. 12).

This MS. is a small folio, written about the year 1525. It is in the original binding, and has the name, "John Danyelston, Rector of Dysart," written on the title.

* 2 vols. sm. 8vo, Lond. 1786.

† Lives of Scottish Worthies, vol. iii. p. 142.

The first buke

[illegible]

The batalis and the man I will discrive
Fra Troys boundis first that fugitive
By fate to Ital come and coist Lavyne
Our land and sey cachit with mekil pyne
By fors of goddis abuf fra euery steid
Of cruell Juno throu auld remembrit feid
Gret payn in batail sufferit he alsso
Or he his goddis brocht in Latio
And belt the cite fra quham of nobill fame
The latyne pepill takyn hes thar name
And eik the faderis princis of Alba
Cam, and the wallaris of gret Rome alsua.
O thou my muse declar the caus quhy
Quhat maieste offendit schaw quhairby
Or yit quharfor of goddis the drery quene
Sa feil dangeris sik travell maid sustene
A worthy man fulfillit of pyete
Is thar sik greif in hevynly myndis on hie
Thar was ane antyant cite hecht Cartage
Quham ... of Tyre held in heritage
Cummyn to Itale standand far on plane
The mouth of lang Tibir our forgane
Myghty of mobillis full of studyis seyr

Musa in Greik signifeis an inventioun ... [illegible]

Quhat is Latium or Latio ... [illegible]

Its heading is as follows :—

"Heyr begynnys | the wark of Virgyll Prynce of Latyn Poetis | in his twelf bukis of Eneados | compilit and translatit furth of Latyn | in our Scottis Langage | by ane richt nobill and wirschipfull Clerk | Master Gawyn Dowglas | Provest of Sanct Gylys Kyrk in Edinburgh | and Person of Lyntoun in Louthiane | quhilk eftyr was Bischop of Dunkeld."

The Colophon of the MS. at page 905, is as follows :—

"Heir endis the thretteyn and final Buke
of Eneados, whilk is the first correck
coppy nixt efter the Translatioun
wryttin be Master Matho Geddes
Scribe or Writar to the
Translatar."

Master Matho Geddes was the Bishop's Chaplain. and one of his executors, to whom the administration of his affairs was granted at London in 1522. This MS. had apparently been carefully made, and seems to have been in the hands of Douglas himself as it has several marginal glosses or notes in the Bishop's handwriting. They are printed at the end of vol. ii. This MS. was printed by George Dundas, Esq., Advocate, afterwards Lord Manor, to be presented to the Bannatyne Club in 1839.

II. The MS. known as *The Elphynstoun MS.*, from which the present Edition has been printed, is preserved in the Library of the University of Edinburgh.

It is a folio volume, consisting of 377 folios, written in a neat, legible hand, and in orthography it is equal, if not superior to the Cambridge MS. That it is an early MS. is shown by the circumstance that at the bottom of the first page, the name, "W. Hay, 1527," occurs. There are bound along with it, in the same volume, several poems by Sir D. Lyndsay, transcribed in 1566.

It has the following inscription on a blank leaf:—"This buik partenis to David Andersone, burges of Abirdene, be gift of Mr. Wm. Hay, Person of Turreff, 1563." The volume was presented to the Library in 1692, as appears from the following note:—"Liber Bibliothecæ Edinburgenæ ex dono generosi Juvenis Joannis Aikman, filii Magistri Gulielmi [Aikman] a Cairnie, causarum patroni, D. Gavini Douglasii, Castri Caledonii Episcopi, versio Scotica Aeneadum Virgilii, anno 1513 facta, unaque Dauidis Lindesii Equitis Aurati opuscula quaedam compacta." The MS. has no title or heading at the beginning, nor a colophon at the end. The name of the transcriber, "M. Joannes Elphynstoun," occurs on the last page.

Elphinstoun seems to have found his task of transcription somewhat irksome. At the end of the 13th Book (p. 728), after writing, *Explicit Liber decimus tertius Eneados*, he adds, *Quod Bocardo et Baroco*,—the names of the most difficult forms in Logic. Sir W. Hamilton remarks of Bocardo, "that so intricate was this mood considered, that it was looked upon as a trap, into which, if you once got, it was no easy task to find an exit. During the middle ages it was the name given in Oxford to the Academic jail or *carcer*—which still remains as a relic of the ancient logical glory of that venerable seminary." (*Lectures, vol. iii.*, *p.* 443). On the last leaf (p. 736), Elphinstoun thus concludes: *Opere finito, sit laus et gloria Christo,* followed by his initials and signature.

III. The MS. known as *The Ruthven MS.*, preserved in the Library of the University of Edinburgh.

It is a folio volume, of 600 pages, neatly and distinctly written, and may have been executed between 1530 and 1540. At the top of the blank leaf fronting the title, is the signature of "W. Dns. Ruthven," who was afterwards raised to the peerage as Earl of Gowrie, but was beheaded 3d May 1584.

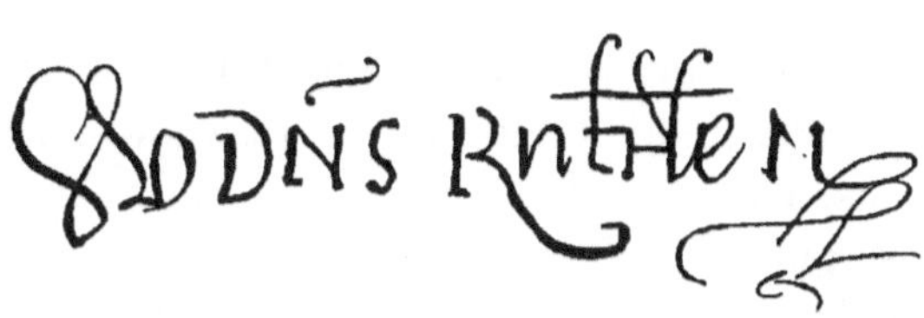

This MS., from the following inscription, was added to the Library in the name of the graduates of 1643. "Ego donatus sum Academiæ Edinburgenæ a Magisterio candidatis, A.D. 1643."

It commences as follows :—

"Here begynnys the Buke of Vergile | Contenand in the self xiii. Bukis translatit | out of Latyne be ane reuerend | Fader in God, Gawane Douglas, Bischop | vmquhile of Dunkeld."

It ends with the lines beginning "*Off Mantua*," etc., as given at the last page of the text of vol. iv. This MS. was used by Ruddiman for the edition of 1710, who states in the Preface that "there are few of our amendments which are not owing to, or at least confirmed by an old and excellent MS. belonging to the Library of the College of Edinburgh, and on this occasion we acknowledge our obligations and return our most hearty thanks to that learned Society, and their Honourable Patrons the Lord Provost and other Magistrates of the City, who were pleased most courteously to allow us the use of that valuable MS. so long as it could be favourable to our design."

IV. *The Lambeth MS.*, preserved in Library of the Archbishop of Canterbury at Lambeth Palace. It is in excellent preservation, and is somewhat more modern than the preceding, having the date of transcription 1545-6. It commences as follows :—

"Heir begynnys the proloug of Virgile, Prince of Latin poetry, in his tuelf buks of Eneados compilit and translatit furth of Latin in our Scottis language, by ane right nobill and worshipful Clerk, Maister Gawyn Douglass, Provost of Sanct Gyles Kirk in Edinburgh, and persoun of Lyntoun in Lauthian, quhilk eftir was Byshop of Dunkeld, written Anno 1545. 2º Februarii."

On the last page the Colophon is as follows :

"Heir endis the Buk of Virgill writtin be the hand of Johanne Mudy, with Maister Thomas Bellenden, of Auchinoull, Justice-clerk, and endit the 2° Februarij, anno m v^{c} xlv."

It bears the signature of "Edmund Ashefeyld," as its possessor in 1596. The scribe seems to have begun to copy the "Comment," or the side-notes of the Cambridge MS., as the first two of them occur in their proper places on the margin. In vol. ii. of this Edition, lines 13 to 16 of p. 47 occur in this MS. as a side-note, in place of being put in the text, as they are found in the Elphinstoun MS.

V. *The Bath MS.* is preserved in the library of the Marquis of Bath, at Longleate, Wilts. Its colophon, as follows, has the date 1547 :—

"Heir endis the buke of Virgil, Prince of Latin Poetis, in his tuelf Bukis of Eneados translatit furth of Latyne in our Scottish language be ane rycht nobil and worshipful clerk, Master Gawane Dowglas, Provest of Sanct Gelis Kirk in Edinburgh, and Person of Lynton in Louthian, quhilk eftir was Bischop of Dunkeld ; and als endis the xiii Buke translatit as said is, with the Prolougis therof, written be me, Henry Aytoun, Notare publick, and endit the twenty-twa day of Nouember, the ȝeir of God mv^{c} fourty-sevin ȝeiris."

This MS. seems to have been partially collated with the first printed edition of 1553 by Urry, the editor of Chaucer, for the edition by Ruddiman, which appeared in 1710.

PRINTED EDITIONS.

The first Edition of the Translation of Virgil was published in London in 1553. It bears the following title :—

"The | xiii Bukes of Eneados of | the famose Poete Virgill, | Translatet out of Latyne | Verses into Scottish Me- | tir, bi the Reuerend Fa- | ther in God, May- | ster Gawin Douglas | Bishop of Dunkel and | vnkil to the Erle | of Angus. Euery | buke hauing hys | perticular | Prologe.

¶ Imprinted at Londō 1553."

This edition, in 4to, is printed in black letter, and contains 381 folios. It is remarkable for the inaccuracy of its text. There is no mention of the printer's name, nor of the source from which it is taken, but it was from the press of William Copland.

Having been printed thirty-three years after the death of the author, it varies much from the manuscript copies which exist. There are no means of knowing for certain who edited the book, but it is probable that it was Copland himself who performed this duty. William Copland, the younger brother probably of Robert Copland, was one of the original members of the Stationers' Company of London, and published various books of a religious character, along with poems and romances. The first issue from his press, in 1548, was a work by Henry Forth, on the Lord's Supper ; his next publication, the same year, was a translation from Zwinglius, entitled,—"A detection of the blasphemies and errours of them that say they offer vp the bodye of Christ in their Masse."

The anti-Roman Catholic feeling shewn by the publication of these works is also exhibited in the edition of Virgil. In the Prologues, wherever Douglas alludes to the Virgin Mary, to Purgatory, and to some Roman Catholic ceremonies, the passages are either completely altered, or entirely omitted. The two following examples, which occur in the first Prologue, may be given :—

DOUGLAS.

Throw praier of thi Moder, quene of blis.

ED. 1553.

Throu Christ thy sone bring us to hewynly blys.

DOUGLAS.

In Christ is all my traist and hewynnis Quene.
Thou Virgyne modir and madyne be my muse.

ED. 1553.

In Christ I trest, borne of the virgine quene.
Thou saluiour of mankind be mye muse.

The other instances will be found in the Notes to Vols. ii., iii., and iv. of this edition.

As shewing still further the liberties taken by Copland, he, from motives of delicacy, omits the account of the adventure of Dido and Æneas in the fourth book of Virgil,—a passage extending to no less than 66 lines. At the end of the sixth book there is a note inserted by Copland, descriptive of the general characteristics of the preceding books of the Æneid, and of the virtues of Æneas, as he is subsequently depicted. The note, which is printed on a separate leaf, seems to have been afterwards cancelled, as it is frequently found wanting in the copies extant of this early edition. The poetical address to Lord Sinclair, at the end of the work, is also wanting in the B. L. edition. A series of quaint side-notes have been supplied by Copland, which are given in the present text.

In 1710, the well-known folio edition, by Thomas Ruddiman, of the translation of the Æneid appeared. It bears the following title :—

"Virgil's Æneis, translated into Scottish verse by the famous Gawin Douglas, Bishop of Dunkeld. A new edition. Wherein the many errors of the former are corrected, and the defects supplied from an excellent manuscript. To which is added a large glossary, explaining the difficult words, which may serve for a dictionary to the old Scottish language. And to the whole is prefixed an exact account of the Author's Life and Writings, from the best histories and records. Edinburgh : Printed by Mr Andrew Symson and Mr Robert Freebairn, and sold at their shops. MDCCX." Folio.

Some interesting particulars may be gleaned of the history of this edition in Chalmers' Life of Ruddiman, in addition to what is to be found in the work itself. Chalmers informs us that "about the time of the Union Robert Freebairn, the Edinburgh bookseller, undertook to publish an edition of Gavin Douglas' Virgil, which eventually appeared in 1710. The publisher found several learned men, whom, as they were proud to lend their aid, he is studious to thank for their various contributions. He acknowledges obligations to Dr Wm. Nicolson, Bishop of Carlisle, to Sir Robert Sibbald, Dr Pitcairne, Dr Drummond, and Mr John Urry, of Christ Church, Oxford. The elaborate life of our great poet, which is prefixed to the work, was contributed by Bishop John Sage, who probably desired the concealment of his authorship, and who died in the subsequent year. The publisher, however, thought himself obliged by gratitude to acknowledge how much indebted he had been to the care of the judicious Thomas Ruddiman, who, in his opinion, "deserved all respect and encouragement from the patrons of virtue and letters." The fact is that Freebairn owed more to Ruddiman than he mentions. It was Ruddiman who superintended the work, corrected the press; who wrote "The large Glossary, explaining the difficult words, and serving for a dictionary to the old Scottish language."

"In his pocket-book, Ruddiman charged Freebairn for correcting G. D. [Gavin Douglas' Virgil], writing the Glossary, &c., a hundred pounds Scots, of which he acknowledged to have received forty-eight pounds. By this document is the authorship ascertained, and by this evidence it is proved that Ruddiman was allowed £8, 6s. 8d. sterling, for performing one of the most elaborate works in our language."*

Ruddiman, who was about thirty-four years of age, seems to have entered upon the work with great ardour, and to have brought together a great amount of philological knowledge, bearing upon the elucidation of the old Scottish language. But, notwith-

* Chalmers' Life of Ruddiman, pp. 44, 45.

standing all his care, the edition contains many errors and misprints. These were owing to his use of the black letter edition of 1553, in printing the text, and he informs us that he had proceeded to page 45 before he was aware that there existed any MS. of Douglas' Virgil in Scotland. As before observed, he thanks the University authorities for the use of one of the MSS. contained in the Library: this was "the Ruthven MS.;" but he does not seem to have been aware of the existence of the other and older MS. which that Library contains, and which has been used in preparing the present edition. On the whole, the edition of Ruddiman was a great work for the period at which it appeared, and it is still commended by authors who have occasion to consult it.

"The Æneid of Virgil, translated into Scottish verse. By Gawin Douglas, Bishop of Dunkeld. Printed at Edinburgh, 1839," 2 vols., 4to.

This sumptuous edition was presented to the members of the Bannatyne Club, as a joint contribution, by Andrew Rutherfurd, Esq., advocate, afterwards Lord Rutherfurd, and George Dundas, Esq., advocate, afterwards Lord Manor. These volumes contain only the text of Douglas' Translation of the Æneid, and the Cambridge MS. was taken as the basis of the work. Mr Dundas, the editor, intended in a third volume to have given a new and more elaborate Glossary than that of Ruddiman; this intention, however, was not carried out, and the work remains as an excellent text, but without introduction or notes of any kind.

¶ Heir beginnis
ane Treatise callit the PALICE
of HONOVR, Compylit
be M. GAWINE
DOWGLAS
Bischop of
Dunkeld.

I  R

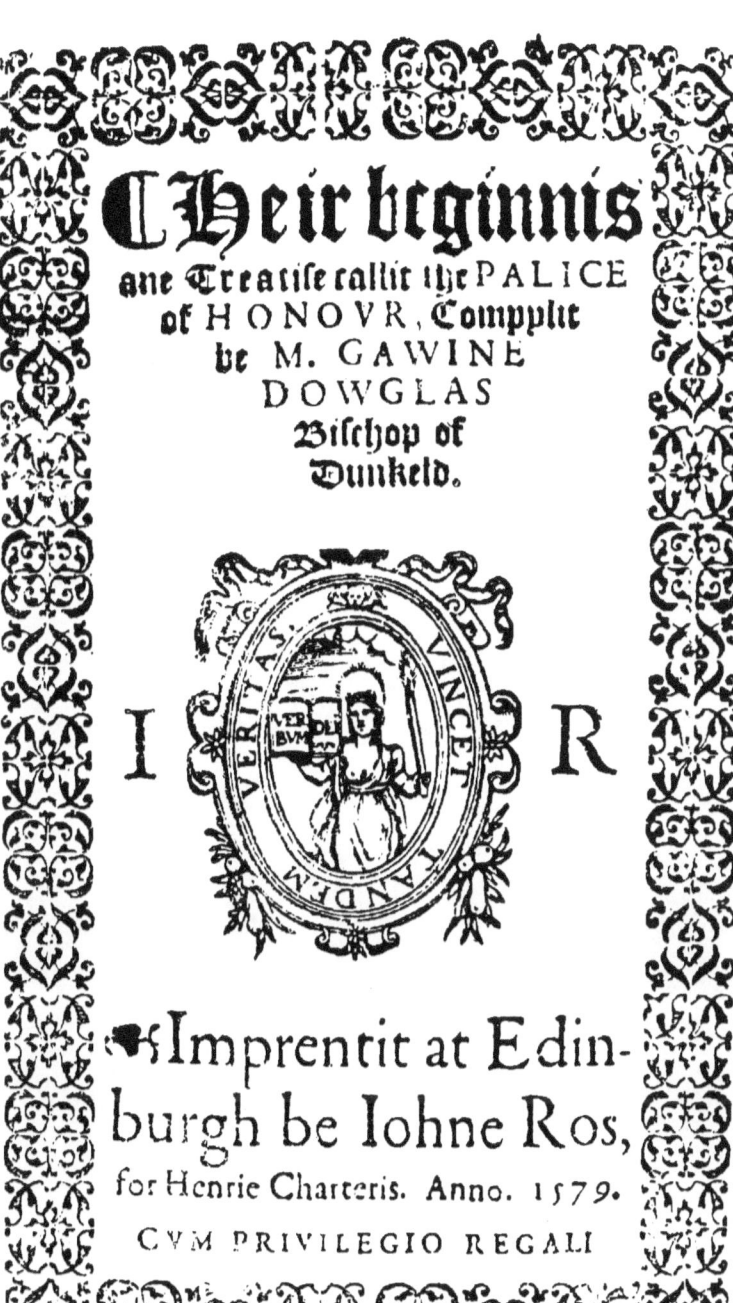

¶ Imprentit at Edin-
burgh be Iohne Ros,
for Henrie Charteris. Anno. 1579.
CVM PRIVILEGIO REGALI

THE

PALICE OF HONOUR.

TO THE REIDAR.

QVHEN we had sene and considderit the diuers Impressiones befoir Imprentit of this Notabill werk to haue bene altogidder faultie and corrupt: not onlie that quhilk hes bene Imprentit at London, bot also the Copyis set furth of auld amangis our selfis: We haue thocht gude to tak sum panes and trawellis to haue the samin mair commodiously and correctly set furth: to the Intent, that the beneuolent Reidar may haue the mair delyte and plesure in reiding, and the mair frute in perusing, this plesand and delectabill werk.

THE PROLOGVE.

WHEN paill Aurora with face lamentabill
Her russat mantill borderit all with sabill,
Lappit about the heuinly circumstance,
The tender bed and arres honorabill
Of Flora, quene till floures amiabill,
In May I rais to do my obseruance,
And enterit in a gardyne of plesance,
With sol depaint as paradice amiabill,
And blisfull bewis with blomed varyance.

Sa craftely dame Flora had ouirfret
Hir heuinly bed, powderit with mony a set
Of ruby, topas, perle, and emerant,
With balmy dew bathit and kyndlie wet;
Quhill vapours hote, richt fresche, and weill ybet,
Dulce of odour, of fleuour maist fragrant,
The siluer droppis on daseis distillant,
Quhilk verdour branches ouir the alars ȝet,
With smoky sence the mystis reflectant.

The fragrant flouris blomand in thair seis,
Ouirspred the leuis of natures tapestreis;

Abone the quhilk with heuinly harmoneis
The birdis sat on twystis and on greis,
Melodiously makand thair kyndlie gleis,
Quhais schill noitis fordinned all the skyis,
Of repercust air the echo cryis
Amang the branches of the blomed treis,
And on the laurers siluer droppis lyis.

Quhill that I rowmed in that paradice,
Replenischit, and full of all delice,
Out of the sey Eous alift his heid,
I mene the hors quhilk drawis at deuice
The assiltrie and goldin chair of price
Of Tytan, quhilk at morrow semis reid;
The new collour that all the nicht lay deid
Is restorit, baith foullis, flouris, and rice
Recomfort was, throw Phebus gudlyheid.

The dasy and the maryguld vnlappit,
Quhilks all the nicht lay with their leuis happit,
Thame to reserue fra rewmes pungitiue;
The vmbrate treis that Tytan about wappit
War portrait, and on the eirth yschappit
Be goldin bemis viuificatiue,
Quhais amene heit is maist restoratiue;
The greshoppers amangis the vergers gnappit,
And beis wrocht materiall for thair hyue.

Richt hailsome was the sessoun of the ȝeir,
Phebus furth ȝet depured bemis cleir,
Maist nutritiue till all thingis vegetant.

God Eolus of wind list nocht appeir,
Nor auld Saturne with his mortall speir
And bad aspect contrair till euerie plant.
Neptunus nold within that palice haut.
The beriall stremis rynning men micht heir,
By bonkis grene with glancis variant.

For till behald that heuinly place compleit,
The purgit air with new engendrit heit,
The sol enbroude with colour, vre, and stone,
The tender grene, the balmy droppis sweit,
Sa reioycit and comfort was my spreit,
I not was it a vision or fantone ;
Amyd the buskis rowming myne alone,
Within that garth of all plesance repleit,
A voice I hard preclair as Phebus schone ;

Singand, O May thow mirrour of soles,
Maternall moneth, lady and maistres
Till euerie thing adoun respirature,
Thyne heuinlie work and worthie craftines
The small herbis constranis till incres.
O verray ground till working of nature,
Quhais hie curage and assucurit cure
Causis the eirth his frutes till expres,
Diffundant grace on euerie creature.

Thy godly lore, cunning incomparabill,
Dantis the sauage beistis maist vnstabill,
And expellis all that nature infestis ;
The knoppit syonis with leuis aggreabill,

For till reuert and burgione ar maid abill;
Thy mirth refreschis byrdis in thair nestis,
Quhilks the to prise and nature neuer restis,
Confessand ȝow maist potent and louabill
Amang the brownis of the oliue twystis.

In the is rute and augment of curage,
In the enforces Martis vassalage,
In the is amorous lufe and harmonie,
With incrementis fresche in lustie age.
Quha that constranit ar in luifis rage,
Addressand thame with obseruance airlie,
Weill auchtis the till gloir and magnifie.
And with that word I raisit my visage
Soir affrayit, half in ane frenesie.

O Nature Quene, and O ȝe lustie May,
(Quod I) tho, how lang sall I thus foruay
Quhilk ȝow and Venus in this garth deseruis?
Recounsell me out of this greit affray,
That I may sing ȝow laudis day be day,
ȝe that all mundane creatures preseruis
Comfort ȝour man that in this fanton steruis,
With spreit arraisit and euerie wit away,
Quaiking for feir, baith pulsis, vane, and neruis.

My fatall weird, my febill wit I wary,
My desie heid quhome laik of brane gart vary,
And not sustene so amiabill a soun,
With ery courage, febill strenthis sary,
Bownand me hame and list na langer tary;

Out of the air come ane impressioun,
Throw quhais licht in extasie or swoun,
Amyd the virgultis all in till a fary,
As feminine so feblit fell I down.

And with that gleme sa desyit was my micht,
Quhill thair remanit nouther voice nor sicht,
Breith, motion, nor heiring naturall ;
Saw neuer man so faynt a leuand wicht,
And na ferly, for ouir excelland licht
Corruptis the wit, and garris the blude áwaill
Vntill the hart, that it na danger aill.
Quhen it is smorit, memberis wirkis not richt,
The dreidfull terrour swa did me assail.

ȝit at the last, I not how lang a space,
A lytle heit appeirit in my face,
Whilk had tofoir bene paill and voyde of blude,
Tho in my sweuen I met a ferly cace ;
I thocht me set within a desert place,
Amyd a forest by a hyddeous flude
With grysly fische, and schortly till conclude,
I sall discryue (as God will giue me grace)
Myne visioun in rurall termis rude.

FINIS PROLOGI.

DIEU ET
MON
DROIT

THE PALICE OF HONOVR,

COMPYLIT BE

M. GAWINE DOWGLAS,

BISCHOP OF DUNKELD.

THE FIRST PART.

THOW barrant wit ouirset with fantasyis,
Schaw now the craft that in thy memor lyis,
Schaw now thy schame, schaw now thy badnystie,
Schaw thy endite reprufe of rethoryis,
Schaw now thy beggit termis mair than thryis,
Schaw now thy rymis, and thine harlotrie,
Schaw now thy dull exhaust inanitie,
Schaw furth thy cure and write thir frenesyis
Quhilks of thy sempill cunning nakit the.

My rauist spreit in that desert terribill,
Approchit neir that vglie flude horribill,
Like till Cochyte the riuer infernall,
With vile water quhilk maid a hiddious trubil,
Rinnand ouirheid, blude reid, and impossibill

That it had been a riuer naturall;
With brayis bair, raif rochis like to fall,
Quhairon na gers nor herbis wer visibill,
Bot swappis brint with blastis boriall.

This laithlie flude rumland as thonder routit,
In quhome the fisch ȝelland as eluis schoutit,
Thair ȝelpis wilde my heiring all fordeifit,
Thay grym monstures my spreits abhorrit and doutit.
Not throw the soyl bot muskane treis sproutit,
Combust, barrant, vnblomit and vnleifit,
Auld rottin runtis quhairin na sap was leifit,
Moch, all waist, widderit with granis moutit,
A ganand den, quhair murtherars men reifit.

Quhairfoir my seluin was richt sair agast,
This wildernes abhominabill and waist,
(In quhome nathing was nature comfortand)
Was dark as rock, the quhilk the sey vpcast.
The quhissilling wind blew mony bitter blast,
Runtis rattillit and vneith micht I stand.
Out throw the wod I crap on fute and hand,
The riuer stank, the treis clatterit fast.
The soyl was nocht bot marres, slike, and sand.

And not but caus my spreitis wer abaisit,
All solitair in that desert arraisit,
Allace, I said, is nane vther remeid,

A discription of the inconstance of fortune

Cruell fortoun quhy hes thow me betraisit?
Quhy hes thow thus my fatall end compassit?
Allace, allace, sall I thus sone be deid

In this desert, and wait nane vther reid,
Bot be deuoirit with sum beist rauenous.
I weip, I waill, I plene, I cry, I pleid,
Inconstant warld and quheill contrarious.

Thy transitorie plesance quhat auaillis?
Now thair, now heir, now hie and now deuaillis,
Now to, now fra, now law, now magnifyis,
Now hait, now cauld, now lauchis, now beuaillis,
Now seik, now haill, now werie, now not aillis,
Now gude, now euill, now weitis, and now dryis,
Now thow promittis, and richt now thow denyis,
Now wo, now weill, now firme, now friuolous,
Now gam, now gram, now lowis, now defyis,
Inconstant warld and quheill contrarious.

Ha, quha suld haue affyance in thy blis?
Ha, quha suld haue firme esperance in this
Quhilk is allace sa freuch and variant?
Certes nane; sum hes no wicht? surelie ȝis.
Than has my self bene gyltie? ȝe, I wis.
Thairfoir allace sall danger thus me dant?
Quhidder is become sa sone this duillie hant?
And ver translait in winter furious?
Thus I beuaill my faitis repugnant,
Inconstant warld and quheill contrarious.

Bydand the deid thus in my extasie,
Ane dyn I hard approching fast me by,
Quhilk mouit fra the plague Septentrionall,
As heird of beistis stamping with loud cry,

But than, God wait, how affrayit was I!
Traistand to be stranglit with bestiall.
Amid a stock richt priuelie I stall,
Quhair luikand out anone I did espy
Ane lustie rout of beistis rationall.

The Quen of Sapyence wyth hyr court.

Of ladyis fair and gudlie men arrayit
In constant weid, that weill my spreitis payit,
With degest mind, quharin all wit aboundit.
Full soberlie thair haiknayis thay assayit
Efter the faitis auld, and not forwayit.
Thair hie prudence schew furth and naithing roundit
With gude effeir quhairat the wod resoundit.
In steidfast ordour, to vesie vnaffrayit
Thay ryding furth with stabilnes ygroundit.

Amiddis quhome borne in ane goldin chair,
Ouirfret with perle and stanis maist preclair,
That drawin was by haiknayis all milk quhite,
Was set a Quene, as lyllie sweit of swair,
In purpour rob hemmit with gold ilk gair,
Quhilk gemmit claspis closit all perfite.
A diademe maist plesandlie polite
Set on the tressis of her giltin hair,
And in hir hand a scepter of delite.

Sine nixt hir raid in granit violate
Twelf damisellis, ilk ane in thair estait,
Quhilks semit of her counsell maist secre,
And nixt thame was a lustie rout, God wait.
Lords, ladyis, and mony fair prelait,

Baith borne of hie estait and law degre,
Furth with thair Quene, thay all by passit me
Ane esie pais, thay ryding furth the gait,
And I abaid alone within the tre.

And as the rout was passit one and one,
And I remanand in the tre alone,
Out throw the wod come rydand catiues twane,
Ane on ane asse, a widdie about his mone,
The vther raid ane hiddeous hors vpone,
I passit furth and fast at thame did frane,
Quhat men thay wer? Thay answerit me agane,
Our namis bene Achitophel and Sinone,
That by our subtell menis, feill hes slane.

Craftye Synone and false Architefel.

Wait ȝe (quod I) quhat signifeis ȝone rout?
Synon said ȝee: and gaue ane hiddeous schout
We wretchis bene abiect thair fra I wis.
Ȝone is the Quene of Sapience but dout,
Lady Minerue, and ȝone twelf hir about
Ar the prudent Sibillais full of blis,
Cassandra eik Delbora and Circes,
The fatall sisters twynand our weirdis out,
Judith, Jael, and mony a Prophetis.

Quhilks groundit ar in firme intelligence,
And thair is als into ȝone court gone hence
Clerkis diuine, with problewmis curius.
As Salomon the well of sapience,
And Aristotell fulfillit of prudence,
Salust, Senek, and Titus Liuius,

Wyse and lerned men.

Pithagoras, Porphyre, Permenydus,
Melysses with his sawis but defence,
Sidrach, Secundus, and Solenyus.

Ptholomeus, Ipocras, Socrates,
Empedocles, Neptenabus, Hermes,
Galien, Auerroes, and Plato,
Enoch, Lameth, Job and Diogenes,
The eloquent and prudent Vlisses,
Wise Josephus, and facund Cicero,
Melchisedech with vther mony mo.
Thair veyage lyis throw out this wildernes,
To the Palice of Honour all thay go.

Is situat from hence liggis ten hunder,
Our horsis oft, or we be thair, will founder.
Adew, we may na langer heir remane.
Or that ȝe pas, (quod I) tell me this wonder,
How that ȝe wretchit catiues thus at vnder
Ar sociat with this court souerane?
Achitophell maid this answer agane,
Knawis thow not? Haill, eirdquaik, and thunder
Ar oft in May with mony schour of rane.

Architetel confessis hys awne craftenes, deceyt, and abused wit.

Richt sa we bene into this companie
Our wit aboundit and vsit was lewdlie,
My wisdome ay fulfillit my desire,
As thou may in the Bybill weill espy:
How Davids prayer put my counsell by,
I gart his sone aganis him conspire,
The quhilk was slane, quhairfoir vp be the swire

Myself I hangit, frustrat sa foulelie.
This Synon was a Greik that raisit fire.

First into Troy, as Virgill dois report,
Sa tratourlike maid him be draw ouirthort
Quhill in he brocht the hors with men of armis, Sinons craftines.
Quhairthrow the toun destroyit was at schort.
(Quod I) Is this ȝour destanie and sort?
Cursit be he that sorrowis for ȝour harmis,
For ȝe haue bene schrewis baith, be Goddis armis,
ȝe will obtene na entres at ȝone port,
But gif it be throw sorcerie or charmis.

Ingres to haue (quod thay) we not presume,
It sufficis vs to se the Palice blume,
And stand on rowme, quhair better folk bene charrit,
For to remane, adew, we haue na tume,
This ilk way cummis the courtis, be our dume,
Of Diane and Venus, that feill hes marrit.
With that they raid away as thay war skarrit;
And I agane maist like ane elriche grume
Crap in the muskane aikin stok misharrit.

Thus wretchitlie I maid my residence,
Imagining feill syse for sum defence
In contrair sauage beistis maist cruell,
For na remeid bot deid be violence
Sum time asswagis febill indigence,
Thus in à part I recomfort mysell,
Bot that sa litle was I dar not tell,
The stichling of a mouse out of presence
Had bene to me mair vgsum than the hell. Feare.

Ȝit glaid I was that I with them had spokin,
Had not bene that, certes my hart had brokin
For megirnes and pusillamitie.
Remanand thus within the tre all lokkin,
Desirand fast sum signes or sum tokin
Of Lady Venus, or hir companie;
Ane hart transformit ran fast by the tree
With houndis rent, on quhom Diane was wrokin,
Thairby I vnderstude that scho was nie.

Thay had befoir declairit hir cumming
Mair perfitelie, forthy I knew the signe
Was Acteon, quhilk Diane nakit waitit
Bathing in a well, and eik hir madynnis ȝing.
The Goddes was commouit at this thing,
And him in forme hes of ane hart translatit.
I saw (allace) his houndis at him slatit;
Backwert he blent to give them knawledgeing,
Thay raif thair lord, misknew him at them batit.

Sine ladyis come with lustie giltin tressis,
In habit wilde maist like till fostaressis.
Amiddis quhome heich on ane eliphant,
In signe that scho in chaistitie incressis,
Raid Diane, that ladyis hartis dressis
Till be stabill, and na way inconstant,
God wait that nane of thame is variant,
All chaist and trew virginitie professis
I note, bot few I saw with Diane hant.

Intill that court I saw anone present
Jephteis douchter a lustie lady gent,

Offerit to God in her virginitie.
Polixena I wis was not absent,
Peanthesile with mannis hardyment,
Effygin, and Virgenius douchter fre,
With vther flouris of feminitie,
Baith of the new and the auld testament,
All on thay raid and left me in the tre.

In that desert dispers in sonder skatterit,
Were bewis bair quhome rane and wind on batterit,
The water stank, the feild was odious
Quhair dragouns, lessertis, askis, edders swatterit,
With mouthis gapand, forkit taillis tatterit,
With mony a stang and spoutis vennemous,
Corrupting air be rewme contagious,
Maist gros and vile, enpoysonit cludis clatterit,
Reikand like hellis smoke sulfurious.

My daisit heid fordullit disselie,
I raisit vp half in ane litargie,
As dois ane catiue ydrunkin in sleip,
And sa appeirit to my fantasie,
A schynand licht out of the north eist sky,
The quhilk with cure to heir I did tak keip,
Proportion sounding dulcest, hard I peip,
In musick number full of harmonie
Distant on far was caryit be the deip.

Farther, by water, folk may soundis heir
Than be the eirth, the quhilk with poris seir
Vp drinkis air that mouit is be sound.

Quhilk in compact water of ane riueir,
May nocht enter, bot rinnis thair and heir,
Quhill it at last be caryit on the ground.
And thocht throw din be experience is found.
The fische ar causit within the riuer steir,
Inwith the water the noyis dois not abound.

Violent din the air brekis and deiris,
Sine greit motioun of air the water steiris.
The water steirit, fisches for feirdnes fleis,
Bot out of dout na fische in water heiris,
For as we se, richt few of thame hes eiris.
And eik forsuith, bot gif wise clerkis leis.
Thair is na air inwith waters nor seis,
But quhilk na thing may heir (as wise men leiris)
Like as but licht thair is na thing that seis.

Aneuch of this, I not quhat it may mene,
I will returne till declair all bedene,
My dreidfull dreame with grislie fantasyis
I schew befoir quhat I had hard or sene,
Particularlie sum of my panefull tene.
Bot now, God wait, quhat feirdnes on me lyis,
Langer (I said) and now this time is twyis,
Ane sound I hard of angellis as it had bene.
With harmonie fordinnand all the skyis.

Sa dulce, sa sweit, and sa melodious,
That euerie wicht thairwith micht be joyous.
Bot I and catiues dullit in dispair,
A sorowful harte can not be mery.
For quhen a man is wraith or furious,
Melancholik for wo, or tedious,

Than is all plesance till him maist contrair,
And semblablie than sa did with me fair;
This melodie intonit heuinlie thus,
For profound wo constranit me mak cair.

And murnand thus, as ane maist wofull wicht,
Of the maist plesant court I had a sicht,
In warld adoun sen Adam was creat.
Quhat sang? Quhat joy? Quhat harmonie? Quhat licht? *Heuinlye harmonye.*
Quhat mirthfull solace plesance all at richt?
Quhat fresche bewtie? Quhat excelland estait?
Quhat sweit vocis? Quhat wordis suggurait?
Quhat fair debaitis? Quhat luifsum ladyis bricht?
Quhat lustie gallandis did on thair seruice wait?

Quhat gudlie pastance? and quhat menstralie?
Quhat game thay maid? in faith not tell can I,
Thocht I had profound wit angelicall.
The heuinlie soundis of thair harmonie,
Hes dynnit sa my drerie fantasie,
Baith wit and ressoun half is loist of all.
ȝit (as I knaw) als lichtlie say I sall,
That angellike and godlie companie
Till se, me thocht a thing celestiall.

Proceidand furth was draw ane chariote, *Goodly apparell.*
Be coursouris twelf, trappit in grene veluote,
Of fine gold wer junctures and harnasingis,
The lymnaris wer of birneist gold, God wote,
Baith aixtre and quheillis of gold I hote.
Of goldin cord wer lyamis, and the stringis

Festinnit coniunct in massie goldin ringis,
Euyr hamis conuenient for sic note,
And raw silk brechamis ouir thair halsis hingis.

The bodie of the cairt of euir bone,
With crisolitis and mony precious stone
Was all ouirfret in dew proportioun,
Like sternis in the firmament quhilks schone.
Reparrellit was that godlike plesand wone
Tyldit abone, and to the eirth adoun,
In richest claith of gold of purpure broun
But fas, nor vther frenȝeis, had it none,
Saif claith of gold anamallit all fassioun.

Quhairfra dependant hang thir megir bellis,
Sum round, sum thraw, in sound the quhilks excellis,
All wer of gold of Araby maist fine,
Quhilks with the wind concordandlie sa knellis
That to be glaid thair sound all wicht compellis,
The harmonie was sa melodious fine,
In mannis voice and instrument diuine,
Quhair sa thay went it semit nathing ellis
Bot ierarchyes of angellis ordours nine.

Venus and hyr court.

Amid the chair fulfillit of plesance,
Ane lady sat, at quhais obeysance
Was all that rout, and wonder is to heir
Of hir excelland lustie countenance,
Hir hie bewtie quhilk maist is to auance
Precellis all, thair may be na compeir;
For like Phebus in hiest of his spheir,

Hir bewtie schane castand sa greit ane glance,
All fairheid it opprest baith far and neir.

Scho was peirles of schap and portrature,
In hir had nature finischit hir cure,
As for gude hauingis thair was nane bot scho,
And hir array was sa fine and sa pure,
That quhairof was hir rob I am not sure,
For nocht bot perle and stanis micht I se,
Of quhome the brightnes of hir hie bewtie,
For to behald my sicht micht not indure,
Mair nor the bricht sone may the bakkis ee.

Hir hair as gold or topasis was hewit,
Quha hir beheld, hir bewtie ay renewit.
On heid scho had a crest of dyamantis.
Thair was na wicht that gat a sicht eschewit,
War he neuer sa constant or weill thewit,
Na he was woundit, and him hir seruant grantis.
That heuinlie wicht, hir cristall ene sa dantis,
For blenkis sweit nane passit vnpersewit,
Bot gif he wer preseruit as thir sanctis.

I wondert sair and fast in mind did stair,
Quhat creature that micht be was sa fair,
Of sa peirles excellent womanheid.
And farlyand thus I saw within the chair
Quhair that a man was set with lymmis squair
His bodie weill entailȝeit euerie steid. Blynd Cupyd.
He bair a bow with dartis haw as leid,
His cleithing was als grene as ane huntair,
Bot he forsuith had na eine in his heid.

I vnderstude be signes persauabill,
That was Cupyd the god maist dissauabill,
The lady Venus his mother a goddes,
I knew that was the court sa variabill
Of eirdly lufe, quhilk sendill standis stabill.
Bot ʒit thair mirth and solace neuertheles
In musick tone and menstralie expres
Sa craftelie with curage aggreabill,
Hard neuer wicht sic melodie I ges.

Accompanyit lustie ʒonkeirs with all,
Fresche ladyis sang in voice virgineall
Musyke. Concordis sweit, diuers entoned reportis,
Proportionis fine with sound celestiall,
Duplat, triplat, diatesseriall,
Sesqui altera, and decupla resortis,
Diapason of mony sindrie sortis,
War soung and playit be seir cunning menstrall
On lufe ballatis with mony fair disportis.

In modulatioun hard I play and sing
Faburdoun, pricksang, discant, countering,
Cant organe, figuratioun, and gemmell,
On croud, lute, harp, with mony gudlie spring,
Schalmes, clariounis, portatiues, hard I ring,
Monycord, organe, tympane, and cymbell.
Sytholl, psalttrie, and voices sweit as bell,
Soft releschingis in dulce delinering,
Fractionis diuide, at rest, or clois compell.

Not Pan of Archaid sa plesandlie playis,
Nor king David quhais playing as men sayis,

Coniurit the spreit the quhilk Saul confoundit,
Nor Amphion with mony subtell layis,
Quhilk Thebes wallit with harping in his dayis,
Nor he that first the subtell craftis foundit,
Was not in musick half sa weill igroundit,
Nor knew thair measure tent daill be na wayis,
At thair resort baith heuin and eird resoundit.

Na mair I vnderstude thir numbers fine,
Be God, than dois a gekgo or a swine,
Saif that me think sweit soundis gude to heir.
Na mair heiron my laubour will I tine,
Na mair I will thir verbillis sweit define,
How that thair musick tones war mair cleir
And dulcer than the mouing of the spheir,
Or Orpheus harp of Thrace with sound diuine,
Glaskeriane maid na noyis compeir.

Thay condiscend sa weill in ane accord,
That by na joint thair soundis bene discord,
In euerie key thay werren sa expert,
Of thair array gif I suld mak record,
Lustie springaldis and mony gudlie lord,
Tender ȝounglingis with pieteous virgin hart,
Elder ladyis knew mair of lustis art,
Diuers vthers quhilks me not list remord,
Quhais lakkest weid was silkis ouirbrouderit.

In vestures quent of mony sindrie gyse,
I saw all claith of gold men micht deuise,
Purpour colour, punik and skarlote hewis,

Veluot robbis maid with the grand assyse,
Dames, satyne, begaryit mony wise,
Cramessie satine, veluot enbroude in diuers rewis,
Satine figures champit with flouris and bewis,
Damesflure, tere pyle, quhairon thair lyis
Peirle, orphany, quhilk euerie stait renewis.

Thair riche entire, maist peirles to behald,
My wit can not discriue howbeit I wald,
Mony entrappit steid with silkis seir,
Mony pattrell neruit with gold I tald,
Full mony new gilt harnasing not ald,
On mony palfray luifsum ladyis cleir,
Mars. And nixt the chair I saw formest appeir,
Vpon a bardit curser stout and bald,
Mars, god of strife enarmit in birneist geir.

Euerie inuasibill wapon on him he bair,
His luik was grym, his bodie large and squair,
His lymmis weill entailȝeit to be strang,
His nek was greit, a span lenth weill or mair,
His visage braid with crisp broun curland hair,
Of stature not ouir greit, nor ȝit ouir lang.
Behaldand Venus, O ȝe my lufe (he sang).
And scho agane with dalyance sa fair
Hir knicht him cleipis, quhair sa he ryde or gang.

Thair was Arcyte, and Palemon aswa
Louers. Accompanyit with fair Aemilia,
The Quene Dido with hir fals lufe Enee,
Trew Troilus, vnfaithfull Cressida,

The fair Paris, and plesand Helena,
Constant Lucrece, and traist Penelope,
Kinde Piramus, and wobegone Thysbe,
Dolorous Progne, trist Philomena,
King Dauids lufe thair saw I Barsabe.

Thair was Ceix with the kind Alcyon,
And Achilles wroth with Agamemnon
For Brissida his lady fra him tane,
Wofull Phillis, and hir lufe Demophoon,
Subtell Medea, and hir knicht Jason.
Of France I saw thair Paris and Veane,
Thair was Phedra, Theseus and Adriane,
The secreit wise hardie Ipomedon,
Assueir, Hester, irrepreuabill Susane.

Thair was the fals vnhappy Dalida,
Cruell wickit and curst Deianira,
Waryit Biblis, and the fair Absolon,
Ypsyphile, abhominabill Sylla,
Tristram, Yside, Helcana and Anna,
Cleopatra and worthie Mark Anthone,
Jole, Hercules, Alcest, Ixion.
The onlie patient wife Gressillida,
Narcisus that his heid brak on ane stone.

Thair was Jacob with fair Rachel his maik,
The quhilk become till Laban for hir saik
Fourtene ȝeir bound, with hart immutabill,
Thair bene bot few sic now I vndertaik.
Thir fair ladyis in silk and claith of laik,

Thus lang sall not all foundin be sa stabill,
This Venus court, quhilk was in lufe maist abil,
For till discriue my cunning is to waik,
Ane multitude thay war innumerabill.

Of gudlie folke in euerie kinde and age,
With blenkis sweit, fresche lustie grene curage,
And daliance thay ryding furth in feir,
Sum leuis in hope, and sum in greit thirlage,
Sum in dispair, sum findis his panis swage,
Garlandis of flouris and rois chaipletis seir
Thay bair on heid, and samin sang sa cleir,
Quhill that thair mirth commouit my curage,
Till sing this lay quhilk followand ȝe may heir.

A ballet of inconstant loue.

Constranit hart belappit in distres,
Groundit in wo, and full of heuines,
Complene thy panefull cairis infinite,
Bewaill this warldis frail vnsteidfastnes,
Hauand regrait, sen gane is thy glaidnes,
And all thy solace returnit in dispite.
O catiue thrall inuolupit in syte,
Confes thy fatall wofull wretchitnes,
Deuide in twane and furth diffound all tyte
Aggreuance greit in miserabill indyte.

My cruell fait subiectit to pennance
Predestinate, sa void of all plesance,
Hes euerie greif amid mine hart ingraue,
The slide inconstant destenie or chance,
Vnequallie dois hing in thair ballance.

My demerites and greit dolour I haue,
This purgatorie redoublis all the laue.
Ilk wicht hes sum weilfair at obeysance
Saif me bysning, that may na grace ressaue,
Deid the addres, and do me to my graue.

Wo worth sic strang misfortoun anoyous,
Quhilk hes opprest my spreitis maist joyous,
Wo worth this warldis frenche felicitie,
Wo worth my feruent discis dolorous,
Wo worth the wicht that is not pieteous,
Quhair the trespassour penitent thay se.
Wo worth this deid that daylie dois me die,
Wo worth Cupyd, and wo worth fals Venus,
Wo worth thame baith, ay waryit mot thay be,
Wo worth thair court and cursit destenie.

He curseth the worlds felycite, fortune and al his pleasure.

Loude as I mocht in dolour all destrenȝeit,
This lay I sang, and not ane letter fenȝeit,
Tho saw I Venus on hir lip did bite,
And all the court in haist thair horsis renȝeit,
Proclamand loude, quhair is ȝone poid that plenȝeit,
Quhilk deith deseruis committand sic dispite,
Fra tre to tre thay seirching but respite.
Quhil ane me fand, quhilk said, and greit disdenȝeit,
Auant veillane, thow reclus imperfite.

All in ane feuir out of my muskane bowr,
On kneis I crap, and law for feir did lowre,
Than all the court on me thair heidis schuik, [28
Sum glowmand grim, sum girnand with visage sowre,

Sum in the nek gaue me feil dyntis dowre.
Pluk at the craw, thay cryit, deplome the ruik,
Pulland my hair, with blek my face they bruik,
Skrymmorie fery gaue me mony a clowre,
For Chyppynutie ful oft my chaftis quuik.

With pane, torment, thus in thair teneful play,
Till Venus bound thay led me furth the way,
Quhilk than was set amid a goldin chair;
And sa confoundit into that fell affray,
As that I micht considder thair array.
Me thocht the feild ouirspred with carpettis fair,
(Quhilk was tofoir brint, barrane, vile, and bair)
Wox maist plesand, bot all (the suith to say)
Micht nocht ameis my greuous pane full sair.

Enthronit sat Mars, Cupyd, and Venus,
Tho rais ane clerk was cleipit Varius,
The auctor accused.
Me till accusen of a deidlie crime,
And he begouth and red ane dittay thus.
Thou wickit catiue, wod and furious,
Presumpteouslie now at this present time
My Lady heir blasphemit in thy rime,
Hir sone, hir self, and hir court amorous,
For till betrais awaitit heir sen prime.

Now God thow wait, me thocht my fortune fey,
With quaikand voce and hart cald as a key,
On kneis I kneillit and mercie culd imploir.
Submittand me but ony langer pley,
Venus mandate and plesure to obey.

Grace was denyit and my trauell forloir,
For scho gaue charges to proceid as befoir.
Than Varius spak richt stoutlie me to fley
Inioynand silence till ask grace ony moir.

He demandit my answer, quhat I said,
Than as I mocht with curage all mismaid,
Fra time I vnderstude na mair supplie, Answer.
Sair abaisit, beliue I thus out braid;
Set of thir pointis of crime now on me laid,
I may be quite guiltles in veritie,
ȝit first agane, the judge quhilk heir I se,
This inordinate court, and proces quaid,
I will obiect for causis twa or thre.

Inclynand law (quod I) with peteous face,
I me defend, Madame, pleis it ȝour grace. Appellationem.
Say on (quod scho) than said I thus but mair;
Madame ȝe may not sit into this cace,
For ladyis may be judges in na place;
And mairatouir I am na seculair,
A spirituall man (thocht I be void of lair)
Cleipit I am, and aucht my liues space
To be remit till my judge ordinair.

I ȝow beseik Madame with bissie cure
Till giue ane gratious interlocuture,
On thir exceptiounis now proponit lait.
Than suddanelie Venus (I ȝow assure)
Deliuerit sone and with a voice sa sture,
Answerit thus, thow subtell smy, God wait,

A thretnyng. Quhat, wenis thow to degraid my hie estait,
Me to decline as judge, curst creature?
It beis not sa, the game gais vther gait.

As we the find, thow sall thoill judgement,
Not of a clerk we se the represent,
Saif onlie falset and dissaitfull taillis,
First quhen thow come with hart and haill intent,
Thow the submittit to my commandement.
Now now thairof methink to sone thow faillis,
I wene na thing bot folie that the aillis,
ȝit clerkis bene in subtell wordis quent,
And in the deid als schairp as ony snaillis.

ȝe bene the men bewrayis my commandis,
ȝe bene the men disturbis my seruandis,
ȝe bene the men with wickit wordis feill,
Quhilk blasphemis fresche lustie ȝoung gallandis,
That in my seruice and retinew standis,
ȝe bene the men that cleipis ȝow sa leill,
With fals behest quhill ȝe ȝour purpois steill,
Sine ȝe forsweir baith bodie, treuth, and handis,
ȝe bene sa fals ȝe can na word conceill.

Haue done (quod scho) Schir Varius alswyith
Do write the sentence, lat this catiue kyith
Gif our power may deming his misdeid.
Than, God thow wait, gif that my spreit was blyith,
The fewerous hew intill my face did myith
All my male eis, for swa the horribill dreid
Haill me ouirset; I micht not say my creid,

For feir and wo within my skin I wryith,
I micht not pray, forsuith thocht I had neid.

ȝit of my deith I set not half ane fle,
For greit effeir me thocht na pane to die,
Bot sair I dred me for sum vther jaip,
That Venus suld throw her subtillitie,
In till sum bysning beist transfigurat me,
As in a beir, a bair, ane oule, ane aip,
I traistit sa for till haue bene mischaip,
That oft I wald my hand behald to se
Gif it alterit, and oft my visage graip.

Tho I reuoluit in my minde anone,
How that Diane transformit Acteone,
And Juno eik as for a kow gart keip
The fair Yo, that lang was wobegone,
Argus her ȝimmit that ene had mony one,
Quhome at the last Mercurius gart sleip,
And hir deliuerit of that danger deip;
I rememberit also how in a stone,
The wife of Loth ichangit sair did weip.

I vmbethocht how Joue and auld Saturne,
Intill ane wolf thay did Lycaon turne,
And how the michtie Nabuchodonosor
In beistlie forme did on the feild soiurne,
And for his gilt was maid to weip and murne.
Thir feirfull wonders gart me dreid full soir,
For by exempilis oft I hard tofoir.

He suld bewar that seis his fellow spurne,
Mischance of ane, suld be ane vtheris loir.

And rolland thus in diuers fantaseis
Terribill thochtis oft my hart did gryis,
For all remeid was alterit in dispair.
Thair was na hope of mercie till deuyis,
Thair was na wicht my freind be na kin wyis,
All haillelie the court was me contrair.
Than was almaist writtin the sentence sair,
My febill minde seand this greit suppryis,
Was than of wit and euerie blis full bair.

THE SECVND PART.

LO thus amid this hard perplexitie,
Awaitand euer quhat moment I suld die,
Or than sum new transfiguratioun ;
He that quhilk is eternall veritie.
The glorious Lord, ringand in persounis thre, Consolation.
Prouydit hes for my saluatioun,
Be sum gude spreitis reuelatioun,
Quhilk intercessioun maid (I traist) for me,
I forȝet all imaginatioun.

All haill my dreid I tho forȝet in hy,
And all my wo, bot ȝit I wist not quhy,
Saue that I had sum hope till be releuit,
I raisit than my visage haistelie,
And with a blenk anone I did espy,
A lusty sicht quhilk nocht my hart engreuit,
Ane heuinlie rout out throw the wod escheuit,
Of quhome the bountie, gif I not deny,
Vneith may be intill ane scripture brewit.

With lawreir crownit in robbis side all new,
Of a fassoun and all of steidfast hew,
Arrayit weill ane court I saw cum neir,
Of wise degest eloquent fathers trew,
And plesand ladyis quhilks fresch bewtie schew, Poetis.
Singand softlie full sweit on their maneir
On poet wise, all diuers versis seir,

Historyis greit in Latine toung and Grew,
With fresche indite and soundis gude to heir.

And sum of thame *ad lyram* playit and sang
Sa plesand verse, quhill all the roches rang,
Metir saphik, and also elygie.
Thair instrumentis all maist war fidillis lang,
But with a string quhilk neuer a wreist ȝeid wrang,
Sum had ane harp, and sum a fair psaltrie,
[On lutis sum thair accentis subtelle]
Deuydit weill, and held the measure lang,
In soundis sweit of plesand melodie.

The ladyis sang in voices dulcorait
Facund epistillis quhilks quhylum Ouid wrait,
As Phillis quene send till duke Demophoon,
And of Penelope the greit regrait,
Send to hir lord scho douting his estait,
That he at Troy suld loisit be or tone.
How Acontius till Cydippe anone
Wrait his complaint, thair hard I weill, God wait,
With vther lustie missiues mony one.

I had greit wonder of thay ladyis seir,
Quhilks in that airt micht haue na way compeir,
Of castis quent, rethorik colouris fine,
Sa poeit like in subtell fair maneir,
And eloquent firme cadence regulair.
Thair veyage furth contenand richt as line,
With sang and play (as said is) sa deuine,
Thay fast approching to the place weill neir,
Quhair I was torment into my greit pine.

And as that heuinlie sort new nominait,
Remouit furth on gudlie wise thair gait,
Toward the court quhilk was tofoir expremit,
My curage grew, for quhat cause I nocht wait,
Saif that I held me payit of thair estait;
And thay war folk of knawledge as it semit,
Als into Venus court full fast thay demit;
Sayand, ȝone lustie court will stop or meit,
To justifie this bysning quhilk blasphemit.

Ʒone is (quod thay) the court rethoricall,
Of polit termis, sang poeticall,
And constand ground of famous storeis sweit,
Ʒone is the facound well celestiall,
Ʒone is the fontane and originall,
Quhairfra the well of Helicon dois fleit,
Ʒone are the folk that comfortis euerie spreit,
Be fine delite and dite angelicall,
Causand gros leid all of maist gudnes gleit.

Ʒone is the court of plesand steidfastnes,
Ʒone is the court of constant merines,
Ʒone is the court of joyous discipline,
Quhilk causis folk thair purpois to expres
In ornate wise, prouokand with glaidnes
All gentill hartis to thair lair incline.
Euerie famous poeit men may diuine
Is in ȝone rout, lo ȝonder thair princes
Thespis, the mother of the musis nine.

And nixt hir sine, hir dochter first byget
Lady Cleo, quhilk craftelie dois set .

The nyne Muses.

Historyis auld, like as thay war present;
Euterpe eik, quhilk daylie dois hir det
In dulce blastis of pypis sweit but let;
The third sister, Thalia, diligent
In wantoun writ, and chronikill dois imprent;
The feird endytis oft with cheikis wet
Sair tragedeis, Melpomene the gent.

Terpsichore the fyft with humbill soun,
Makis on psalteris modulatioun;
The sext Erato, like thir louers wilde,
Will sing, daunce, and leip baith vp and doun.
Polymnia, the seuint muse of renoun,
Dytis thir sweit rethorick colouris milde,
Quhilks are sa plesand baith to man and childe;
Vrania, the aucht sister with croun,
Writes the heuin and starnis all bedene.

The nynt, quhome to nane vther is compeir,
Calliope the lustie lady cleir,
Of quhome the bewtie and the worthines
Hir vertewis greit schynis baith far and neir,
For scho of nobill fatis hes the steir,
To write thair worschip, victorie and prowes
In kinglie stile, quhilk dois thair fame incres,
Cleipit in Latine heroicus, but weir,
Chief of all write like as scho is maistres.

Thir musis nine lo ȝonder may ȝe se,
With fresche nymphes of water and of sey,
And fair ladyis of thir tempillis auld,

Pyerides, Dryades and Saturee,
Nereides, Aones, Napee,
Of quhome the bounteis neidis not be tauld.
Thus demit the court of Venus monyfauld;
Quhilk speiche refreschit my perplexitie,
Reioysand weill, my spreit befoir was cauld.

The suddane sicht of that firme court foirsaid,
Recomfort weill my hew befoir was faid,
Amid my spreit the joyous heit redoundit,
Behalding how the lustie musis raid,
And all thair court quhilk was sa blyith and glaid,
Quhais merines all heuines confoundit;
Thair saw I weill in poetrie ygroundit,
The greit Homeir, quhilk in Greik language said Homer.
Maist eloquentlie, in quhome all wit ybowndit.

Thair was the greit Latine Virgilius, Virgil and other Latin poetis.
The famous father poeit Ouidius,
Dictes, Dares, and eik the trew Lucane,
Thair was Plautus, Poggius, and Persius,
Thair was Terence, Donate, and Seruius,
Francis Petrarche, Flaccus Valeriane,
Thair was Esope, Cato, and Allane,
Thair was Gaulteir and Boetius,
Thair was also the greit Quintiliane.

Thair was the satir poet Juuenall,
Thair was the mixt and subtell Martiall.
Of Thebes brute thair was the poet Stace,
Thair was Faustus, and Laurence of the Vale,

Pomponius, quhais fame of late sans faill,
Is blawin wide throw euerie realme and place.
Thair was the morall wise poet Horace,
With mony vther clerk of greit auaill,
Thair was Brunell, Claudius, and Bocchas.

Sa greit ane preis of pepill drew vs neir,
The hundreth part thair names ar not heir,
Ȝit saw I thair of Brutus Albyon,
Geffray Chauceir, as *a per se* sans peir
In his vulgare, and morall Johne Goweir.
Lydgait the monk raid musing him allone,
Of this natioun I knew also anone,
Greit Kennedie, and Dunbar ȝit vndeid,
And Quintine with ane huttok on his heid.

Chauser and other Englyshe and Scottishe poetis.

Howbeit I culd declair and weill indite,
The bounteis of that court dewlie to write
War ouir prolixt, transcending mine ingine,
Tuiching the proces of my panefull site.
Beliue I saw thir lustie musis quhite,
With all thair rout towart Venus decline,
Quhair Cupide sat with hir in throne deuine,
I standand bundin in ane sorie plite,
Bydand thair grace, or than my deidlie pine.

Straicht to thair quene thir samin musis raid,
Maist eloquentlie thair salutatiounis maid,
Venus again ȝald thame thair salusing
Richt reuerentlie, and on hir feit vpbraid,
Beseikand thame to licht, nay, nay, thay said,

We may not heir mak na lang tarying.
Calliope maist facound and bening,
Inquirit Venus quhat wicht had hir mismaid,
Or quhat was cause of hir thair soiourning.

Venus complaint

Sister (said scho) behald ȝone bysning schrew,
A subtell smy, considder weill his hew,
Standis thair bound, and bekinnit hir to me,
Ȝone catiue had blasphemit me of new,
For to degraid, and do my fame adew,
A laithlie ryme dispitefull and subtelle
Compylit hes, reheirsand loud and hie
Sclander, dispite, sorrow and velanie,
To me, my sone, and eik our court for ay.

He hes deseruit deith, he sall be deid,
And we remaine forsuith into this steid,
To justifie that rebald rennigait.
Quod Calliope, sister away all feid,
Quhy suld he die, quhy suld he lois his heid.
To slay him for sa small ane cryme, God wait,
Greitar degrading war to ȝour estait,
To sic as he to mak conter pleid,
How may ane fule ȝour hie honour chekmait ?

Quhat of his lak, sa wide ȝour fame is blaw,
Ȝour excellence maist peirles is sa knaw,
Na wretchis word may depair ȝour hie name.
Giue me his life, and modifie the law,
For on my heid he standis now sic aw,
That he sall efter deserue neuer mair blame,

Nocht of his deith ȝe may report bot schame,
In recompence for his missettand saw,
He sall ȝour hest in euerie part proclame.

Than, Lord, how glaid becam my febil goist,
My curage grew the whilk befoir was loist,
Seand I had sa greit ane aduocait,
That expertlie but prayer, price or coist,
Obtenit had my friwoll actioun almoist,
Quhilk was befoir perischit and desolait;
This quhile Venus stude in ane studie strait,
Bot finallie scho schew till all the oist
Scho wald do grace, and not be obstinait.

Mercy becumys all men and specily gentyl-wemen.

I will (said scho) haue mercie and pietie,
Do slaik my wraith, and let all rancour be.
Quhair is mair vice than to be ouir cruell?
And speciallie in wemen sic as me,
A lady, fy, that usis tyrannie,
Ane vennome is rather and a serpent fell.
A vennemous dragoun or ane deuill of hell
Is na compair to the iniquitie
Of bald wemen, as thir wise clerkis tell.

Greit God defend I suld be one of tho,
Quhilk of thair feid and malice neuer ho,
Out on sic gram I will haue na repreif.
Calliope sister said to Venus tho,
At ȝour requeist this wretche sall frelie go;
Heir I remit his trespas, and all greif
Sall be forȝet, sa he will say sum breif

Or schort ballat, in contrair pane and wo,
Tuitching my laude, and his plesand releif.

And secundlie, the nixt ressonabill command,
Quhilk I him charge, se that he nocht ganestand,
On thir conditiounis sister at ȝour requeist,
He sall gang fre; quod Calliope inclinand,
Grant mercie sister, I obleis be my hand,
He sall obserue in all pointis ȝour behest.
Than Venus bade do slaik sone my arreist.
Beliue I was releuit of euerie band,
Vprais the court, and all the parlour ceist.

Tho sat I doun lawlie vpon my kne,
At command of prudent Calliope,
ȝeildand Venus thankis ane thousand syith,
For sa hie freindship, and mercifull pietie,
Excelland grace, and greit humanitie,
The quhilk to me trespassour did scho kyith.
I the forgiue, (quod scho) than was I blyith.
Doun on ane stock I set me suddanelie
At hir command, and wrait this lay alswyith.

A ballat for Venus pleasour.

Vnwemmit wit deliuerit of dangair,
Maist happelie deliuerit fra the snair,
Releuit fre of seruice and bondage,
Expell dolour, expell diseisis sair,
Auoid displesure, womenting and cair,
Ressaue plesance, and do thy sorrow swage.
Behald thy glaid fresche lustie grene curage,
Reioyce amid thir louers but dispair,

Prouide ane place to plant thy tender age,
In lestand blis to remane and repair.

Quha is in welth? Quha is weill fortunait?
Quha is in pietie disscuerit fra debait?
Quha leuis in hope? Wha leuis in esperance?
Quha standis in grace? Quha standis in firme estait?
Quha is content, reioycit air or lait?
Or quha is he that fortoun dois auance?
Bot thow that is replenischit of plesance.
Thow hes comfort, all weilfair delicait,
Thou hes glaidnes, thow hes the happie chance,
Thow hes thy will, thow be nocht desolait.

Incres in mirthfull consolatioun,
In joyous sweit imaginatioun,
Abound in lufe of perfite amouris,
With diligent trew deliberatioun,
Rander louingis for thy saluatioun
Till Venus, and vnder her guerdoun all houris
Rest at all eis, but sair or sitefull schouris,
Abide in quiet, maist constant weilfair,
[Be glaid and lycht now in thy lusty flouris]
Vnwemmit wit deliuerit of dangeir.

This lay was red in oppin audience
Of the musis and in Venus presence.
I stand content; thou art obedient,
Quod Calliope, my companioun and defence.
Venus said eik it was sum recompence
For my trespas, I was sa penitent,

And with that word all suddanelie scho went,
In ane instant scho and hir court was hence,
ȝit still abaid thir musis on the bent.

Inclinand than, I said, Calliope,
My protectour, my help and my supplie,
My souerane lady, my redemptioun,
My mediatour, quhen I was dampnit to die,
I sall beseik the godlie maiestie,
Infinite thankis, laude, and benisoun
ȝow till acquite, according ȝour renoun;
It langis nocht my possibilitie,
Till recompence ten part of this guerdoun.

Gloir, honour, laude, and reuerence conding,
Quha may forȝeild ȝow of sa hie ane thing,
And in that part ȝour mercie I imploir,
Submitting me my lifetime induring,
ȝour plesure and mandate till obeysing.
Silence (said scho) I haue aneuch heirfoir,
I will thow wend and vesie wonderis moir.
Than scho me hes betaucht in keiping
Of ane sweit nimphe maist faithfull and decoir.

Thankes gyuyng.

Ane hors I gat maist richelie besene,
Was harneist all with wodbind leuis grene,
Of the same sute the trappours law doun hang,
Ouir him I straid at command of the quene,
Tho samin furth we ryding all bedene,
Als swift as thocht with mony a merie sang.
My nimphe alwayis conuoyit me of thrang,

Amid the musis to se quhat thay wald mene,
Quhilks sang and playit bot neuer a wreist ȝeid wrang.

Throw countreis seir, holtis and roches hie,
The auctours vyage. Ouir vailis, planis, woddis, wallie sey,
Ouir fludis fair, and mony strait montane,
We war caryit in twinkling of ane eye.
Our horsis flaw, and raid nocht, as thocht me,
Now out of France tursit in Tuskane,
Now out of Flanders heich vp in Almane,
Now into Egypt, now into Italie,
Now in the realme of Trace, and now in Spane.

The hie montanes we passit of Germanie,
Ouir Appennynus deuydand Italie,
Ouir Ryne, the Pow, and Tiber fludes fair,
Ouir Alpheus, by Pyes the riche cietie,
Vnder the eirth, that enteris in the see,
Ouir Rone, ouir Sane, ouir France, and eik ouir Lair,
And ouir Tagus the goldin sandit riuair,
In Thessalie we passit the mont Octhe,
And Hercules in sepulture fand thair.

Thair went we ouir the riuer Peneyus,
In Sicill eik we passit the mont Tmolus,
Pleneist with saiffron, honie, and with wyne,
The twa toppit famous Pernasus,
In Trace we went out ouir the mont Emus,
Quhair Orpheus leirit his harmonie maist fyne,
Ouir Carmelus quhair twa prophetis deuyne

Remanit, Helias and Heliseus,
Fra quhome the ordour of Carmelites come syne.

And nixt vnto the land of Amaȝon,
In haist we past the flude Termodyon,
And ouir the hudge hill that hecht Mynas,
We raid the hill of Bacchus Citheron,
And Olympus the mont of Macedon,
Quhilk semis heich vp in the heuin to pas,
In that countrie we raid the flude Melas,
Quhais water makis quhite scheip blak anone,
In Europe eik we raid the flude Thanas.

We raid the swift riuer Sparthiades,
The flude of Surry Achicorontes,
The hill sa full of wellis cleipit Yda,
Armenie hillis, and flude Euphrates,
The flude of Nyle the precious flude Ganges,
The hill of Sicill ay birnand Ethna,
And ouir the mont of Phrigie Dindama,
Hallowit in honour of the mother goddes,
Cauld Caucasus we past in Sythia.

We past the fludis of Tigris and Phison,
Of Thrace the riuers Hebrun and Strymon,
The mont of Modan and the flude Jordane,
The facund well and hill of Helicon,
The mont Erix, the well of Acheron,
Baith dedicate to Venus in certane,
We past the hill and desert of Libane,
Ouir mont Cinthus quhair god Appollo schone,
Straicht to the musis caballine fontane.

Beside that cristall well sweit and degest,
Thame to repois, thair hors refresche and rest,
Alichtit doun thir musis cleir of hew.
The companie all haillelie leist and best,
Thrang to the well to drink quhilk ran southwest,
Throw out ane meid quhair alkin flouris grew,
Amang the laif ful fast I did persew
To drink, bot sa the greit preis me opprest,
That of the water I micht not taste a drew.

Our horsis pasturit in ane plesand plane,
Law at the fute of ane fair grene montane,
Amid ane meid schaddowit with ceder treis,
Saif fra all heit, thair micht we weill remane.
All kinde of herbis, flouris, frute, and grane,
With euerie growand tre thair men micht cheis,
The beriall stremis rinnand ouir stanerie greis
Made sober noyis, the schaw dinnit agane
For birdis sang, and sounding of the beis.

The ladyis fair on diuers instrumentis,
Went playand, singand, dansand ouir the bentis,
Full angellike and heuinlie was thair soun.
Quhat creature amid his hart imprentis,
The fresche bewtie, the gudelie representis,
The merie speiche, fair hauingis, hie renoun
Of thame, wald set a wise man half in swoun,
Thair womanlines wryithit the elementis,
Stoneist the heuin, and all the eirth adoun.

The warld may not considder nor discriue
The heuinlie joy, the blis I saw beliue,

Sa ineffabill, abone my wit sa hie;
I will na mair thairon my foirheid riue,
Bot breiflie furth my febill proces driue.
Law in the meid ane pal3eoun picht I se,
Maist gudliest, and richest that micht be;
My gouernour ofter than times fiue,
Vnto that hald to pas commandit me.

Swa finallie straicht to that royall steid,
In fellowschip with my leidar I 3eid;
We enterit sone, the portar was not thra,
Thair was na stopping lang demand nor pleid, *The gate.*
I kneillit law, and vnheildit my heid,
And tho I saw our ladyis twa and twa,
Sittand on deissis, familiars to and fra
Seruand thame fast with ypocras and meid,
Delicait meitis, dainteis seir alswa.

Greit was the preis, the feist royall to sene,
At eis thay eit with interludis betwene,
Gaue problewmis seir, and mony fair demandis,
Inquyrand quha best in their times had bene,
Quha traist louers in lustie 3eiris grene,
Sum said this way, and sum thairto ganestandis,
Than Calliope, Ouide to appeir commandis,
My clerk (quod scho) of register bedene,
Declair quha war maist worthie of thair handis.

With lawrere crownit at hir commandement, *Valiant knightis.*
Vpstude this poeit digest and eloquent,
And schew the fatis of Hercules the strang,

How he the grislie hellis hounds out rent,
Slew lyounis, monsturis, and mony fell serpent.
And to the deith feil michtie gyantis dang.
Of Theseus eik, he schew the weiris lang
Agane the quene Ypolita the sweit,
And how he slew the Minotaur in Creit.

Of Perseus he tauld the knichtlie deidis,
Quhilk vinquischit, as men in Ouide reidis,
Cruell tyrantis and monstures mony one,
Of Dianis bair, in Callidon the dreidis,
How throw ane ladyis schot his sydis bleidis,
The bretheris deith, and sine the sisters mone.
He schew how king Priamus sone Yssacone,
Efter his deith, bodie and all his weidis,
Intill ane skarth transformit was anone.

He schew at Troy quhat wise the Greikis lands,
How feirs Achilles stranglit with his handis
The vailȝeant Cygnus, Neptunus sone maist deir,
Quhilk at Greikis arriuall on the strandis,
A thousand slew that day vpon the sandis,
Faucht with Achill and bluntit all his speir,
Na wapin was that micht him wound or deir,
Quhill Achilles brist of his helme the bandis,
And wirryit him be force for all his feir.

He schew full mony transmutatiounis,
And wonderfull new figuratiounis,
Be hundrethis mo than I haue heir expremit,
He tauld of lufis meditatiounis,

The craft of lufe and the saluatiounis,
How that the furie lustis suld be flemet.
Of diuers vther maters als he demit,
And be his prudent schairp relatiounis,
He was expert of all thing as it semit.

Vprais the greit Virgilius anone,
And playit the sportis of Daphnis and Corydone;
Sine Terence come, and playit the comedy Poetes.
Of Parmeno, Thrason, and wise Gnatone;
Juuenall like ane mowar him allone,
Stude scornand euerie man as thay ȝeid by;
Martiall was cuik till roist, seith, farce and fry,
And Poggius stude with mony girne and grone,
On Laurence Valla spittand and cryand fy.

With mirthis thus, and meitis delicait,
Thir ladyis feistit according thair estait,
Vprais at last, commandand till tranoynt.
Retreit was blawin loude, and than, God wait,
Men micht haue sene swift horsis haldin hait,
Schynand for sweit, as thay had bene anoynt.
Of all that rout was neuer a prik disioynt,
For all our tary, and I furth with my mait
Mountit on hors, raid samin in gude point.

Ouir mony gudelie plane we raid bedene,
The vaill of Hebron, the camp Damascene,
Throw Josaphat, and throw the lustic vaill,
Ouir waters wan, throw worthie woddis grene;
And swa at last in lifting vp our ene,

We se the finall end of our trauaill,
Amid ane plane a plesand roche to waill,
And euerie wicht fra we that sicht had sene,
Thankand greit God, their heidis law deuaill.

With singing, lauching, merines and play,
Vnto this roche we ryden furth the way,
Now mair to write for feir trimblis my pen,
The hart may not think nor mannis toung say.
The eir nocht heir, nor ȝit the eye se may,
It may not be imaginit with men,
The heuinlie blis, the perfite joy to ken,
Quhilk now I saw, the hundreth part all day
I micht not schaw, thocht I had toungis ten.

Thocht all my members toungis war on raw,
I war not abill the thousand fauld to schaw,
Quhairfoir I feir ocht farther mair to write,
For quhidder I this in saull or bodie saw,
That wait I nocht, bot he that all dois knaw,
The greit God wait, in euerie thing perfite,
Eik gif I wald this auisioun indite,
Janglaris suld it bakbite, and stand nane aw,
Cry out on dremis quhilks are not worth ane mite.

Senthis till me all veritie be kend,
I repute better thus to mak ane end,
Than ocht to say that suld heiraris engreif;
On vther side thocht thay me vilipend,
I considder prudent folk will commend
The veritie, and sic jangling repreif,

With quhais correctioun, support and releif.
Furth to proceid, this proces I pretend,
Traistand in God my purpois to escheif.

Howbeit I may not euerie circumstance
Reduce perfitelie in remembrance,
Myne ignorance ȝit sum part sall deuise,
Tuitching this sicht of heuinlie sweit plesance.
Now emptie pen write furth thy lustie chance,
Schaw wonderis feill, suppois thow be not wise,
Be diligent and ripelie the auise,
Be quick and schairp voidit of variance,
Be sweit, and caus not gentill hartis grise.

THE THIRD PART.

YE musis nine be in my adiutorie,
That maid me se this blis and perfite glorie,
Teiche me ȝour facund castis eloquent,
Len me a recent schairp fresche memorie,
Inuocation. And caus me dewlie till indite this storie,
Sum gratious sweitnes in my breist imprent,
Till mak the heirars bowsum and attent,
Reidand my writ, illuminate with ȝour loir,
Infinite thankis randerand ȝow thairfoir.

Now breiflie to my purpois for till gone,
About the hill lay wayis mony one,
And to the hicht bot ane passage ingraue,
Hewin in the roche of slid hard marbell stone,
Agane the sone like to the glas it schone,
The ascence was hie, and strait for till consaue.
ȝit than thir musis gudelie and suaue,
Alichtit doun and clam the roche in hie,
With all the rout, outtane my nimphe and I.

Still at the hillis fute we twa abaid,
Than suddanelie my keipar to me said,
Ascend galland; than for feir I quoik.
Be not affrayit, scho said, be not dismaid.
And with that word vp the strait rod abraid,
I followit fast, scho be the hand me tuik,
ȝit durst I neuer for dreid behind me luik,

With mekill pane thus clam I neir the hicht,
Quhair suddanelie I saw ane grislie sicht.

As we approchit neir the hillis heid,
Ane terribill sewch birnand in flammis reid,
Abhominabill, and how as hell to see,
All full of brintstane, pick, and bulling leid,
Quhair mony wretchit creature lay deid,
And miserabill catiues ȝelland loud on hie,
I saw, quhilk den micht weill compairit be
Till Xanthus the flude of Troy sa schill,
Birnand at Venus hest contrair Achill.

Amid our passage lay this vglie sicht,
Nocht braid but sa horribill to euerie wicht,
That all the warld to pas it suld haue dreid.
Weil I considderit na vppermair I micht,
And to discend sa hiddeous was the hicht,
I durst not auenture for this eird on breid,
Trimbland I stude with teith chatterand gude speid,
My nymphe beheld my cheir, and said let be,
Thow sall nocht aill, and lo the cause (quod sche).

To me thow art commit, I sall the keip,
Thir pieteous pepill amid this laithlie deip,
War wretchis quhilks in lustie ȝeiris fair,
Pretendit thame till hie honour to creip,
Bot suddanelie thay fell on sleuthfull sleip, Idyll people punyshed
Followand plesance drownit in this loch of cair.
And with that word scho hint me be the hair,
Caryit me till the hillis heid anone,
As Abacuk was brocht in Babylone.

As we bene on the hie hill situait,
Luik doun (quod scho) consaue in quhat estait,
Thy wretchit warld thow may considder now.
At hir command with meikill dreid, God wait,
Out ouir the hill sa hiddeous hie and strait,
I blent adoun, and felt my bodie grow,
This brukill eird sa litill till allow,
Me thocht I saw birne in ane fyrie rage,
Of stormie sey quhilk might na maner swage.

That terribill tempest, hiddeous wallis huge,
War maist grislie for to behald or judge,
Quhair nouther rest nor quiet micht appeir,
Thair was ane perrellous place folk for to ludge,
Thair was na help support nor ȝit refuge,
Innumerabill folk I saw flotterand in feir,
Quhilk pereist on the walterand wallis weir.
And secundlie I saw ane lustie barge,
Ouirset with seyis, and mony stormie charge.

This gudelie carwell taiklit traist on raw,
With blanschite saill milk quhite as ony snaw,
Richt souer, ticht, and wonder stranglie beildit,
Was on the bairdin wallis quite ouirthraw,
Contrariouslie the busteous wind did blaw
In bubbis thik, that na schipis sail micht weild it.
Now sank scho law, now hie to heuin vpheildit.
At euerie part swa sey and windis draif,
Quhill on ane sand the schip did brist and claif.

It was ane pieteous thing, alaik, alaik,
To heir the dulefull cry, quhen that scho straik,

Maist lamentabill the pereist folk to se,
Sa fameist, drowkit, mait, forwrocht and waik,
Sum on an plank of fir tre, and sum of aik,
Sum hang vpon a takill, sum on ane tre,
Sum fra thair grip sone weschin with the see,
Part drownit, part to the roche fleit or swam,
On raipis or burdis, sine vp the hill thay clam.

Tho at my nimphe breiflie I did inquire,
Quhat signifyit that feirfull wonders seir.
Ȝone multitude (said scho) of pepill drownit,
Ar faithles folk, quhilks quhill thay ar heir,
Misknawis God and followis thair pleseir,
Quhairfoir thay sall in endles fire be brint.
Ȝone lustie schip thow seis pereist and tint,
In quhome ȝone pepill maid ane perrellous race,
Scho hecht the Carwell of the State of Grace.

Faythles peopill.

Ȝe bene all borne the sonnis of ire, I ges,
Sine throw baptisme gettis grace and faithfulnes,
Than in ȝone carwell surelie ȝe remane,
Oft stormested with this warldis brukilnes,
Quhill that ȝe fall in sin and wretchitnes,
Than schip brokin sall ȝe drown in endles pane,
Except be faith ȝe find the plank agane
Be Christ, wirking gude warkis I vnderstand,
Remane thairwith, thir sall ȝow bring to land.

This may suffice, (said scho) tuitchand this part;
Returne thy heid behald this vther art,
Considder wonders and be vigilant,

That thow may better endyten efterwart,
Things quhilkis I sall the schaw or we depart,
Thow sall haue fouth of sentence and not scant,
Thair is na welth nor weilfair thow sall want,
The greit Palice of Honour thow sall se,
Lift vp thy heid, behald that sicht (quod sche).

At hir command I raisit hie on hicht,
My visage till behald that heuinlie sicht,
Bot to discriue this mater in effek,
Impossibill war till ony eirdlie wicht,
It transcendis far abone my micht
That I with ink may do bot paper blek,
I mon draw furth the ȝok lyis on my nek,
As of the place to say my leude auise,
Pleneist with plesance like to paradice.

I saw ane plane of peirles pulchritude,
Quhairin aboundit alkin thingis gude
Spyce, wine, corne, oyle, tre, frute, flour, herbis grene,
All foullis, beistis, birdis, and alkin fude.
All maner fisches baith of sey and flude
War keipit in pondis of poleist siluer schene,
With purifyit water as of the cristall clene,
To noy the small, the greit beistis had na will,
Nor rauenous foulis the lytill volatill.

Still in the sessoun all things remanit thair,
Perpetuallie but outher noy or sair,
Ay rypit war baith herbis, frute and flouris.
Of euerie thing the names to declair

Vnto my febill wit vnpossibill wair,
Amid the meid repleit with sweit odouris,
A palice stude with mony royall towris,
Quhair kyrnellis quent, feil turettis men micht find,
And goldin fanis waifand with the wind.

The descrip-tion of the Palace.

Pinnakillis, fyellis, turnpekkis mony one,
Gilt birneist torris, quhilk like to Phebus schone,
Skarsment, reprise, corbell, and battellingis,
Fulȝery, bordouris of mony precious stone,
Subtile muldrie wrocht mony day agone,
On buttereis, jalme, pillaris and plesand springis,
Quick imagerie with mony lustie singis,
Thair micht be sene, and mony worthie wichtis,
Befoir the ȝet arrayit all at richtis.

Furth past my nimphe, I followit subsequent,
Straicht throw the plane to the first waird we went
Of the palice, and enterit at the port,
Thair saw we mony staitlie tornament,
Lancis brokin, knichtis laid on the bent,
Plesand pastance, and mony lustie sport,
Thair saw we als, and sum time battell mort.
All thir (quod scho) on Venus seruice vaikis,
In deidis of armis for thair ladyis saikis.

Vesyand I stude the principall place but peir,
That heuinlie Palice all of cristall cleir,
Wrocht as me thocht of poleist beriall stone.
Bosiliall nor Oliab, but weir,
Quhilk *sancta sanctorum* maid maist riche and deir,

Nor he that wrocht the tempill of Salomon,
Nor he that beildit the royall Ylion,
Nor he that forgit Darius sepulture,
Culd not performe sa craftelie ane cure.

Studiand heiron my nimphe vnto me spak,
Thus in a stair, quhy standis thow stupifak,
Gouand all day, and nathing hes vesite.
Thow art prolixt, in haist returne thy bak,
Ga efter me and gude attendance tak,
Quhat now thow seis, luik efterwart thow write,
Thow sall behald all Venus blis perfite.
Thairwith scho till ane garth did me conuoy,
Quhair that I saw aneuch of perfite joy.

Amid ane throne with stanis riche ouirfret
And claith of gold Lady Venus was set,
By hir, hir sone Cupide quhilk nathing seis,
Quhair Mars enterit na knawledge micht I get,
Bot straicht befoir Venus visage but let,
Stude emerant stages twelf, grene precious greis,
Quhairon thair grew thre curious goldin treis,
Vpstandand weill the goddes face beforne,
Venus mirour. Ane fair mirrour be thame quentlie vpborne.

Quhairof it makit was I haue na feill,
Of beriall, cristall, glas or birneist steill,
Of diamant, or of the carbunkill gem,
Quhat thing it was, define may I not weill,
Bot all the bordour circulair euerie deill,
Was plait of gold, cais, stok, and vtter hem.

With verteous stanis picht that blude wald stem.
For quha that woundit was in the tornament,
Wox haill fra he vpon the mirrour blent.

This royall relick sa riche and radious,
Sa poleist, plesand, purifyit and precious,
Quhais bounteis half to write I not presume,
Thairon to se was sa delitious,
And sa excelland schaddowis gracious,
Surmounting far in brichtnes to my dome,
The coistlie subtell spectakill of Rome,
Or ȝit the mirrour send to Canace,
Quhairin men micht mony wonders se.

In that mirrour I micht se at ane sicht,
The deidis and fatis of euerie eirdlie wicht,
All thingis gone like as thay war present,
All the creatiounis of the angellis bricht,
Of Lucifer the fall for all his micht,
Adam first maid and in the eirth ysent,
And Noyes flude thair saw I subsequent,
Babylon beild, that towre of sic renoun,
Of Sodomes the feill subuersioun.

Abraham, Isaac, Jacob, Joseph I saw,
Hornit Moyses with his auld Hebrew law,
Ten plaiges in Egypt send for thair trespas,
In the Reid sey with all his court on raw
King Pharao drownit, that God wald neuer knaw,
I saw quhat wise the sey deuydit was,
And all the Hebrewis dry fute ouir it pas,

A lang cathaloge of nobyll men and wemen both of scriptur and gentyll stories.

Sine in desert I saw thame fourtie ȝeiris,
Of Josue I saw the worthie weiris.

Of Judicum the battellis strang anone,
I saw of Jephte, and of Gedeone,
Of Amalech the cruell homicide,
The wonderfull workis of douchtie duke Samsone,
Quhilk slew a thousand with ane asses bone,
Rent tempillis down and ȝettis in his pride,
Of quhais strenth merwellis this warld sa wide,
I saw duke Sangor thair with mony a knok,
Sex hundreth men slew with ane pleuchis sok.

The prophet Samuel saw I in that glas,
Anoyntit king Saull, quhais sone Jonathas,
I saw vincus ane greit oist him allane,
Ȝoung Dauid sla the grislie Golyas,
Quhais speir heid wecht thre hundreth vnces was,
Jesbedonab the gyant mekill of mane,
Lay be the handis of michtie Dauid slane,
With fingers sex on ather hand but weir,
Dauid I saw slay baith lyoun and beir.

This Dauid eik at ane onset a stound,
Aucht hundreth men I saw him bring to ground,
With him I saw Banayas the strang,
Quhilk twa lyounis of Moab did confound,
And gaue the stalwart Ethiop deidis wound,
With his awin speir that of his hand he thrang.
Vnabasitlie this campioun saw I gang,
In a deip cisterne, and thair a lyoun sleuch,
Quhilk in ane storme of snaw did harme aneuch.

Of Salomon the wisdome and estait, Salomon.
Thair saw I, and his riche tempill, God wait,
His son Roboam quhilk throw his helie pride,
Tint all his leigis hartis be his fait,
He was to thame sa outrageous ingrait,
Of twelf tribes ten did fra him diuide.
I saw the angell sla be nichtis tide
Four scoir thousandis of Sennacheribs oist,
Quhilk come to weir on Jowry with greit boist.

I saw the life of the king Eȝechy
Prolongit xv. ȝeir, and the prophet Hely
Amid a fyrie chair to paradice went.
The storyis of Esras and of Neemy,
And Daniell in the lyounis caue saw I,
For he the dragoun slew, Bel brak and schent,
The children thre amid the fornace sent,
I saw the transmigratioun in Babylon,
And baith the buikis of Paralipomenon.

I saw the halie archangell Raphaell,
Marie Sara the douchter of Raguell
On Thobias for his just fathers saik,
And bind the cruell deuill that was sa fell,
Quhilk slew hir seuin first husbands as thay tell;
And how Judith Holiphernes heid of straik,
By nichtis tyde, and fred hir toun fra wraik.
Jonas in the quhaillis wombe dayis thre,
And schot furth sine I saw at Niniue.

Of Job I saw the patience maist degest.
Of Alexander I saw the greit conquest,

Quhilk in twelf ȝeirs wan neir this warld on breid.
And of Anthiocus the greit vnrest,
How tyranlie he Jowrie all opprest,
Of Machabeus full mony ane knichtlie deid,
That gart all Grece and Egypt stand in dreid,
In quiet brocht his realme throw his prowes.
I saw his brether Symon and Jonathas,

Quhilks war maist worthie quhil thair dayis rang.
Of Thebes eik I saw the weiris lang,
Quhair Tydeus allone slew fiftie knichtis;
How finallie of Grece the campiounis strang,
All haill the flour of knichtheid in that thrang
Destroyit was, quhill Theseus with his michtis,
The toun and Creon wan for all his slichtis.
Thair saw I how, as Statius dois tell,
Amphiorax the bischop sank to hell.

The faithful ladyis of Grece I micht considder,
In claithis black all bairfute pas togidder,
Till Thebes sege fra thair lordis war slain;
Faythfull and constent women.
Behald ȝe men that callis ladyis lidder,
And licht of laitis, quhat kindnes brocht them hidder,
Quhat treuth and lufe did in thair breists remane,
I traist ȝe sall reid in na writ agane
In ane realme sa mony of sic constance.
Persaue thairby wemen ar till auance.

Of duke Pirithous the sponsage in that tide,
Quhair the Centauris reft away the bride,
Thair saw I, and thair battell hudge to se.

And Hercules quhais renoun walkis wide,
For Ixiona law by Troyis side,
Faucht and ouircome a monstour in the sey,
For quhilk, (quhen his rewaird denyit was) he
Maid the first seige and the destructioun
Of michtie Troy, quhylum that royall toun.

To win the fleis of gold tho saw I sent
Of Grece the nobillis with Jason consequent,
Haill thair conqueist, and all Medeas slichtis,
How for Jason Ypsiphile was schent,
And how at Troy as thay to Colchos went,
Greikis tholit of king Laomedon greit vnrichtis,
Quhairfoir Troy destroyit was be thair michtis,
Ixiona reuist and Laomedon slane,
Bot Priamus restorit the toun agane.

The judgement of Paris saw I sine,
That gaue the apill as poetis can define
Till Venus, as goddes maist gudlie,
And how in Grece he reuischit quene Helene,
Quhairfoir the Greikis with thair greit nauie,
Full mony thousand knichtis hastelie,
Thame till reuenge saillit towart Troy in hy,
I saw how be Vlixes with greit joy,
Quhatwise Achill was found and brocht to Troy.

The cruell battellis, and the dintis strang,
The greit debait, and eik the weiris lang
At Troyis seige, the mirrour to me schew,
Sustenit ten ȝeiris Greikis Troianis amang,

And ather partie set full oft in thrang,
Quhair that Hector did douchtie deidis anew,
Quhill feirce Achil baith him and Troylus slew,
The greit hors maid I saw, and Troy sine tint,
And fair Ylion all in flambis brint.

Sine out of Troy, I saw the fugitiues,
How that Eneas as Virgill weill discriues,
In countreis seir was be the seyis rage
Bewauit oft, and how that he arriues
With all his flote but danger of thair liues,
And how thay war resset baith man and page
Be quene Dido remanand in Carthage;
And how Eneas sine, as that thay tell,
Went for to seik his father doun in hell.

Ouir Stix the flude I saw Eneas fair,
Quhair Charon was the busteous ferriar,
The fludes four of hell thair micht I se,
The folk in pane, the wayis circulair,
The welterand stone wirk Sisipho mich cair,
And all the plesance of the camp Elise,
Quhair auld Anchises did commoun with Enee,
And schew be line all his successioun,
This ilk Eneas maist famous of renoun.

I saw to goddes mak the sacrifice,
Quhairof the ordour and maner to deuise
War ouir prolixt, and how Eneas syne,
Went to the schip, and eik I saw quhat wise,
All his nauie greit hounger did supprise,

How he in Italie finallie with greit pyne,
Arryuit at the strandis of Lauyne,
And how he faucht weill baith on landis and seyis,
And Turnus slew the king of Rutileis.

Rome saw I beildit first be Romulus,
And eik how lang as writes Liuius,
The Romane kingis abone the pepill rang,
And how the wickit proud Tarquinius,
With wife and barnis be Brutus Junius
War exylit Rome for thair insufferabill wrang,
Bot all the proces for to schaw war lang,
How chaist Lucrece the gudliest and best
Be Sextus Tarquine was cruellie opprest.

Chast Lucretia.

The Punik battellis in that mirrour cleir,
Betwene Carthage and Romanis mony ȝeir
I saw, becaus Eneas pieteous
Fled fra Dido be admonitiounis seir,
Betwene thir pepill rais ane langsum weir;
I saw how worthie Marcus Regulus,
Maist vailȝeand, prudent, and victorious,
Howbeit he micht at libertie gone fre,
For commoun profite cheisit for to die.

The constancye of Marcus Regulus.

Tullus Seruilius douchtie in his daw,
And Marcus Curtius eik in the mirrour I saw,
Quhilk throw his stoutnes in the fyrie gap
For commoun profite of Rome himself did thraw,
Richt vnabaisitlie hauand na dreid nor aw,
Mountit on hors, vnarmit thairin lap;

And Hánniball I saw be fatall hap,
Win contrair Romanis mony fair victorie,
Quhill Scipio eclipsit all his glorie.

This worthie Scipio cleipit Aphricane,
I saw vincus this Hanniball in plane,
And Carthage bring vnto finall ruine,
And sine to Rome conquerit the realme of Spane.
How king Iugurtha hes his brether slane,
Thair saw I eik, and of his weir the fine.
Richt weill I saw the battellis intestine
Of Catilina and of Lentulus,
And betwene Pompey and Cesar Julius.

And breiflie euerie famous douchtie deid,
That men in storie may se, or chronikill reid,
I micht behald in that mirrour expres;
The miserie, the crueltie, the dreid,
Pane, sorrow, wo, baith wretchitnes and neid,
The greit inuy, couetous dowbilnes,
Tuitchand warldlie vnfaithfull brukilnes.
I saw the feind fast folkis to vices tyst,
And all the cumming of the Antechrist.

Plesand debaitmentis quha sa richt reportis,
Thair micht be sene, and all maner disportis,
The falconnis for the riuer at thair gait,
Newand the foullis *in periculo mortis*,
Layand thame in be companeis and sortis.
And at the plunge part saw I handillit hait.
The werie hunter besie air and lait,

With questing houndis seirching to and fra,
To hunt the hart, the bair, the da, the ra.

I saw Raf Coilȝear with his thrawin brow,
Craibit Johne the Reif, and auld Cowkewyis sow;
And how the wran came out of Ailssay;
And Peirs Plewman that maid his workmen fow;
Greit Gowmakmorne and Fyn Makcoul, and how
Thay suld be goddis in Ireland as they say;
Thair saw I Maitland vpon auld Beird Gray;
Robene Hude, and Gilbert with the quhite hand,
How Hay of Nauchtoun flew in Madin land.

The nigromansie thair saw I eik anone,
Of Benytas, Bongo, and Freir Bacone,
With mony subtill point of juglary;
Of Flanders peis maid mony precious stone,
Ane greit laid sadill of a siching bone,
Of ane nutemug they maid a monk in hy,
Ane paroche kirk of ane penny py;
And Benytas of ane mussill maid ane aip,
With mony vther subtill mow and jaip.

Nigramansye.

And schortlie to declair the veritie,
All plesand pastance and gammis that micht be,
In that mirrour war present to my sicht;
And as I wonderit on that greit farlie,
Venus at last, in turning of her eye,
Knew weill my face, and said, be Goddis micht,
ȝe bene welcum my presonar to this hicht,
How passit thow (quod scho) this hiddeous deip?
Madame (quod I) I not mair than ane scheip.

Na force thairof (said scho) sen thow art heir,
How plesis the our pastance and effeir?
Glaidlie (quod I) madame, be God of heuin.
Rememberis thow (said scho) withouttin weir,
On thy promit quhen of thy greit dangeir
I the deliuerit? As now is not to neuin.
Than answerit I agane with sober steuin,
Madame ȝour precept quhat sa be ȝour will,
Heir I remane all reddy to fulfill.

Weill, weill, (said scho) thy will is sufficent,
Of thy bowsum answer I stand content.
Then suddanelie in hand ane buik scho hint,
The quhilk to me betaucht scho or I went,
Commandand me to be obedient,
And put in ryme that proces than quite tint,
I promisit hir forsuith or scho wald stint,
The buik ressauand, thairon my cure to preif,
Inclynand sine, lawlie I tuik my leif.

By thys boke he menis Virgil.

Tuitchand this buik perauenture ȝe sall heir,
Sum time efter, quhen I haue mair laseir.
My nimphe in haist scho hint me be the hand,
And as we samyn walkit furth in feir,
I the declair (quod scho) ȝone mirrour cleir,

The Auctors conclution of Venus merour.

The quhilk thow saw befoir Dame Venus stand,
Signifyis na thing ellis to vnderstand,
Bot the greit bewtie of thir ladyis facis,
Quhairin louers thinks thay behald all graces.

Scho me conuoyit finallie to tell,
With greit plesance straicht to the riche castell,

Quhair mony saw I preis to get ingres.
Thair saw I Sinon and Achitophell,
Preissand to clim the wallis, and how they fell.
Lucius Catiline saw I thair expres,
In at an windo preis till haue entres,
Bot suddanelie Tullius come with ane buik,
And straik him doun quhill all his chaftis quoik.

The Palice of Honour is patent for honest vertuus men an not for vicius fals and craftye pepyll.

Fast climmand vp thay lustie wallis of stone,
I saw Jugurtha and tressonabill Tryphone,
Bot thay na grippis thair micht hald for slidder.
Preissand to clim stude thousandis mony one,
And to the ground thay fallin euerie one.
Than on the wall ane garitour I considder,
Proclamand loud that did thair hartis swidder;
Out on all falsheid the mother of euerie vice,
Away inuy and birnand couetice.

Falsched the moder of al vice.

That garitour tho, my nimphe vnto me tald,
Was cleipit Lawtie, keipar of that hald
Of hie honour, and thay pepill outschet,
Swa preissand thame to clim quhylum war bald,
Richt verteous ȝoung, bot fra time thai wox ald,
Fra honour haill on vice thair minde is set.
Now sall thow go (quod scho) straicht to the ȝet
Of this Palice, and enter but offence,
For the portar is cleipit Patience.

Patience.

The michtie prince, the greitest empreour,
Of ȝone Palice (quod scho) hecht hie Honour,
Quhome to dois serue mony traist officiair.

The discription of the Prince of hie Honore wyth his palys and count, Charity, Constance, Liberalite, Innocens, Deuotyon.

For Cheritie of gudlines the flour,
Is maister houshald in ȝone cristall towr,
Firme Constance is the kingis secretair,
And Liberalitie hecht his thesaurair,
Innocence and Deuotioun as effeiris,
Bene clerkis of closet and cubiculairis.

Discrecion. Humanite, Trew relation, Peace, Temperance.

His comptrollar is cleipit Discretioun,
Humanitie and trew Relatioun
Bene ischaris of his chalmer morne and ewin,
Peice, quiet Rest, oft walkis vp and doun,
In till his hall as marschellis of renoun,
Temperance is cuik his meit to taist and preif,

Humilite, Discyplinc, Mercye.

Humilitie carwer, that na wicht list to greif,
His maister sewar hecht Verteous discipline,
Mercie is copper and mixis weill his wine.

His chancelair is cleipit Conscience,
Quhilk for na meid will pronounce fals sentence.

Conscience, Justyce, Prudence, Diligens, Clene lyuyng.

With him ar assessouris four of ane assent,
Science, Prudence, Justice, Sapience,
Quhilks to na wicht list in commit offence ;
The chekker rollis and the kingis rent
As auditouris thay ouirse quhat is spent.
Lauborous diligence, Gude warkis, Clene leuing,
Bene outstewartis and catouris to ȝone king.

Gude hope remains euer amang ȝone sort,
Ane fine menstraill with mony mow and sport,

Hope. Piety, Fortitud, Weryte.

And Pietie is the kingis almoseir,
Sine Fortitude, the richt quha list report,

Is Lieutenand all wretchis to comfort.
The kingis minȝeoun roundand in his eir.
Hecht Veritie, did neuer leill man deir,
And schortlie euerie vertew and plesance,
Is subiect to ȝone kingis obeysance.

Cum on (said scho) this ordinance to vesite.
Than past we to that cristall palice quhite,
Quhair I abaid the entrie to behold,
I bad na mair of plesance nor delite,
Of lustie sicht, of joy and blis perfite,
Nor mair weilfair to haue aboue the mold,
Than for to se that ȝet of birneist gold,
Quhairon thair was maist curiouslie ingraue,
All naturall thingis men may in eird consaue.

Thair was the eirth enuironit with the sey,
Quhairon the schippis sailland micht I se,
The air, the fire, all the four elementis,
The spheiris seuin, and *primum mobile*,
The signes twelf perfitelie euerie gre, Astronomi.
The Zodiak haill as buikis representis,
The Pole Antartick that euer himself absentis,
The Pole Artick and eik the Vrsis twane,
The seuin starnis, Phaton and the Charlewane.

Thair was ingraue how that Ganamedes
Was reft till heuin, as men in Ouide reidis,
And vnto Juppiter maid his cheif butlair.
The douchteris fair into thair lustie weidis
Of Driada, amid the sey but dreidis

Swymmand, and part war figurit thair,
Vpon ane craig dryand thair ȝallow hair,
With facis not vnlike, for quha thame seing
Micht weill considder that thay all sisters being.

Of planeitis all the coniunctiounis,
Thair episciclis and oppositiounis
War portrait thair, and how thair coursis swagis.
Thair naturall and daylie motiounis,
Eclipsis, aspectis and digressiounis
Thair saw I, and mony gudlie personages,
Quhilks semit all lustie quick images,
The warkmanschip exceding mony fold -
The precious mater, thocht it was fynest gold.

Wonderand heiron agane my will, but let,
My nimphe in greif schot me in at the ȝet.
Quhat deuill (said scho) hes thow nocht ellis ado,
Bot all thy wit and fantasie to set
On sic doting? and tho for feir I swet
Of hir langage; bot than anone (said scho),
List thow se farleis, behald thame ȝonder lo,
ȝit studie nocht ouir mekill a dreid thow varie,
For I persaue the halflingis in ane farie.

Within that Palice sone I gat ane sicht,
Quhair walkand went full mony worthie wicht
Amid the clois, with all mirthis to waill.
For like Phebus with fyrie bemis bricht,
The wallis schane castand sa greit ane licht,
It semit like the heuin imperiall;

And as the ceder surmountis the rammall
In perfite hicht, sa of that court a glance
Exceidis far all eirdlie vane plesance.

For lois of sicht considder micht I nocht
How perfitelie the riche wallis war wrocht;
Swa the reflex of christall stanis schone,
For brichtnes scarslie bleuk thairon I mocht;
The purifyit siluer surelie as me thocht,
Insteid of symont was ouir all that wone,
ȝit round about full mony ane beriall stone,
And thame coniunctlie jonit fast and quemit,
The clois was pathit with siluer as it semit.

The durris and the windois all war breddit
With massic gold, quhairof the fynes scheddit.
With birneist euir baith Palace and towris
War theikit weill, maist craftelie that cled it,
For sa the quhitlie blanschit bone ouirspred it,
Midlit with gold anamalit all colouris,
Importurait of birdis and sweit flouris,
Curious knottis, and mony hie deuise,
Quhilks to behald war perfite paradise.

And to proceid my nymphe and I furth went,
Straicht to the hall throwout the Palice gent,
And ten stages of topas did ascend.
Schute was the dure, in at a boir I blent,
Quhair I beheld the glaidest represent
That euer in eirth a wretchit catiue kend.
Breiflie this proces to conclude and end,

Me thocht the flure was all of amatist,
Bot quhairof war the wallis I not wist.

The multitude of precious stainis seir
Thairon sa schane, my febill sicht but weir
Micht not behald thair verteous gudlines.
For all the ruif as did to me appeir,
Hang full of plesand lowpit sapheiris cleir,
Of dyamontis and rubeis as I ges.
War all the buirdis maid of maist riches,
Of sardanis, of jasp, and smaragdane,
Traistis, formis, and benkis war polcist plane.

Baith to and fro amid the hall thay went,
Royall princes in plait and armouris quent,
Of birneist gold couchit with precious stanis.
Enthronit sat ane God omnipotent,
On quhais glorious visage as I blent
In extasie, be his brichtnes atanis
He smote me doun, and brissit all my banis;
Thair lay I still in swoun with colour blaucht,
Quhill at the last my nymphe vp hes me caucht.

Sine with greit pane, with womenting and cair,
In hir armis scho bair me doun the stair,
And in the clois full softlie laid me doun,
Vpheld my heid to tak the hailsum air,
For of my life scho stude in greit despair.
Me till awalk ay was that lady boun,
Quhill finallie out of that deidlie swoun,
I swyith ouircome, and vp mine ene did cast.
Be merie man (quod scho) the worst is past.

Get vp (scho said) for schame be na cowart,
My heid in wed thow hes ane wyifes hart,
That for a plesand sicht was sa mismaid.
Than all in anger vpon my feit I start;
And for hir wordis war sa apirsmart,
Vnto the nimphe I maid a busteous braid.
Carling (quod I) quhat was ȝone that thow said?
Soft ȝow (said scho) thay are not wyse that stryifis,
For kirkmen war ay gentill to thair wyifis.

I am richt glaid thow art worthin sa wicht,
Langeir me thocht ȝow had nouther force nor micht,
Curage nor will for to haue greuit ane fla.
Quhat aillit the to fall? (quod I) the sicht
Of ȝone goddes grim fyrie visage bricht
Ouirset my wit, and all my spreitis swa,
I micht not stand; bot was that suith, ȝa, ȝa.
Than said the nimphe richt merilie and leuch,
Now I considder thy mad hart weill aneuch.

I will na mair (quod scho) the thus assay
With sic plesance, quhilk may thy spreit affray,
ȝit sall thow se surelie, sen thow art heir,
My ladyis court in thair gudlie array;
For to behald thair mirth cum on thy way.
Than hand in hand swyith went we furth in feir,
At a posterne towart the fair herbeir.
In that passage full fast at her I franit,
Quhat folk thay war within that hall remanit.

ȝone war (said scho) quha sa the richt discriues,
Maist vailȝeand folk and verteous in thair liues,

Now in the court of Honour thay remane
Verteouslie, and in all pleasance thriues.
For thay with speir, with swordis, and with kniues,
In just battell war fundin maist of mane,
In thair promittis thay stude euer firme and plane,
In thame aboundit worschip and lawtie,
Illuminat with liberalitie.

Honour (quod scho) to this heuinlie ring
Differris richt far fra warldlie gouerning,
Quhilk is bot pompe of eirdlie dignitie,
Geuin for estait of blude, micht, or sic thing;
And in this countrie prince, prelate, or king,
Allanerlie sall for vertew honourit be.
For eirdlie gloir is nocht bot vanitie,
That as we se sa suddanelie will wend,
Bot verteous honour neuer mair sall end.

Behald (said scho) and se this warldis glorie,
Maist inconstant, maist slid and transitorie.
Al warldly glorye is bot a dreame.
Prosperitie in eird is bot a dreme,
Or like as man war steppand ouir ane scoir,
Now is he law that was sa hie befoir,
And he quhylum was borne pure of his deme,
Now his estait schynis like the sone beme.
Baith vp and doun, baith to and fra, we se
This warld walteris, as dois the wallie sey.

To papis, bischoppis, prelatis and primaitis,
Empreouris, kingis, princes, potestatis
Deith settis the terme and end of all thair hicht;

Fra thay be gane, let se quha on thame waitis!
Nathing remanis bot fame of thair estaitis,
And nocht ellis bot verteous warkis richt
Sall with thame wend; nouther thair pompe nor micht.
Ay vertew ringis in lestand honour cleir,
Remember than that vertew hes na peir.

For vertew is a thing sa precious,
Quhairof the end is sa delicious,
The warld can not considder quhat it is.
It makis folk perfite and glorious,
It makis sanctis of pepill vitious,
It causis folk ay liue in lestand blis,
It is the way to hie honour I wis,
It dantis deith, and euerie vice throw micht;
Without vertew, fy on all eirldlie wicht.

A comendation of vertue quhilk is the way to honour, and not riches or hie blud.

Vertew is eik the perfite sicker way,
And nocht ellis, till lestand honour ay.
For mony hes sene vitious pepill vphieit,
And efter sone thair glore vanische away,
Quhairof exampillis we se this euerie day.
His eirdlie pompe is gone quhen that he deit,
Than is he with na eirdlie freind suppleit
Saifand vertew; weill is him hes sic a feir!
Now wil I schaw (quod scho) what folk bene heir.

The strangest Sampsoun is into ȝone hald,
The forcie puissant Hercules sa bald,
The feirs Achill, and all the nobillis nyne,
Scipio Affricane, Pompeius the ald,

Exemplis of vertuus men and women.

Vther mony quhais namis befoir ar tald,
With thousandis ma than I may heir defyne,
And lustic ladyis amid thay lordis syne,
Semiramis, Thamar, Hippolita,
Penthessilea, Medea, Zenobia.

Of thy regioun ȝonder bene honourit part,
The kingis Gregour, Kenneth, and king Robart,
With vther ma that beis not heir reheirsit.
Waryit (quod scho) ay be thy megir hart,
Thow suld have sene had thow biddin in ȝone art,
Quhat wise ȝone heuinlie companie conuersit.

Wicious people punyshed. Inuye, Pryde.

Wa worth thy febill brane sa sone was persit,
Thow micht haue sene remanand quhair thow was,
Ane hudge pepill puneist for thair trespas,

Quhilks be wilfull manifest arrogance,
Inuyous pride, pretendit ignorance,

Ignorance. Disseyt.

Foull dowbilnes and dissait vnamendit,
Enforcis thame thairselfis to auance
Be sle falsheid, but lawtie or constance,
With subtelnes and slichtis now commendit.
Betraisand folk that neuer to thame offendit,
And vpheis thameself throw fraudeful lipps,
Thocht God caus oft thair eirdlie gloir eclipps.

Dissait, craftynes ar haldyn wisdome now a day, as verite and iustice is callyt

And nobillis cummin of honorabill ancestry,
Thair verteous nobilitie settis nocht by,
For dishonest vnlefull warldlie wayis,
And throw corruptit couetous inuy,
Bot he that can be dowbill, nane is set by.

Dissait is wisdome; lawtie, honour away is,
Richt few or nane takis tent thairto thir dayis,
And thair greit wrangis to reforme, but let,
In judgement ȝone God was ȝonder set.

simplycitye and folyshnes.

Remanand ȝonder thow micht haue hard beliue,
Pronouncit the greit sentence diffinitiue,
Tuitchand this actioun, and the dreidfull pane
Execute on trespassouris ȝit on liue,
Swa that thair malice sall na mair prescriue.
Madame (quod I) for Goddis sake turne agane,
My spreit desyris to se thair torment fane.
(Quod scho) richt now thair sall thow be reioisit,
Quhen thow hes tane the air and better appoisit.

Bot first thow sall considder commoditeis
Of our garding, so full of lustie treis,
All hie cypres of flewer maist fragrant.
Our ladyis ȝonder bissie as the beis,
The sweit flureist flouris of rethoreis
Gadderis full fast, mony grene tender plant,
And with all plesance pleneist is ȝone hant,
Quhair precious stanis on treis dois abound,
In steid of frute chargeit with peirlis round.

Vnto that gudlie garth thus we proceid,
Quhilk with a large fowsie far on breid
Inueronit was, quhair fisches war anew,
All water foullis war swemand thair gude speid;
Als out of growand treis thair saw I breid
Foullis that hingand be thair nebbis grew.

Out ouir the stank of mony diuers hew
Was laid ane tre, ouir quhilk behouit vs pas,
Bot I can not declair quhairof it was.

My nimphe went ouir, chargeand me follow fast,
Hir till obey my spreitis wox agast,
Sa perrellous was the passage till espy.
Away scho went and fra tiine scho was past,
Vpon the brig I enterit at the last,
Bot sa my harnis trimblit besily,
Quhill I fell ouir, and baith my feit slaid by,
Out ouir the heid into the stank adoun,
Quhair as me thocht I was in point to droun.

The aucthour returnes frome his dreame to him self agane.

Quhat throw the birdis sang, and this affray,
Out of my swoun I walknit quhair I lay,
In the garding quhair I first doun fell.
About I blent, for richt cleir was the day,
Bot all this lustie plesance was away.
Me thocht that fair herbrie maist like to hell,
In till compair of this ȝe hard me tell.
Allace, allace, I thocht me than in pane,
And langit sair for to haue swemit agane.

The birdis sang, nor ȝit the merie flouris,
Micht not ameis my greuous greit dolouris,
All eirdlie thing me thocht barrane and vile.
Thus I remanit into the garth twa houris,
Cursand the feildis with all the fair colouris,
That I awolk oft wariand the quhile,
Alwayis my minde was on the lustie ile,

I purpoisit euer till haue dwelt in that art,
Of rethorik cullouris till haue found sum part.

And maist of all my curage was aggreuit,
Becaus sa sone I of my dreme escheuit,
Not seand how thay wretchis war torment,
That honour mankit and honestie mischeuit.
Glaidlie I wald amid this writ haue breuit,
Had I it sene how thay war slane or schent.
Bot fra I saw all this weilfair was went,
Till mak an end, sittand vnder a tre,
In laude of honour I wrait thir versis thre.

A ballade in the commendation of honour and verteu.

O hie honour, sweit heuinlie flour degest,
Gem verteous, maist precious, gudliest.
For hie renoun thow art guerdoun conding,
Of worschip kend the glorious end and rest,
But quhome in richt na worthie wicht may lest.
Thy greit puissance may maist auance all thing,
And pouerall to mekill auaill sone bring.
I the require sen thow but peir art best,
That efter this in thy hie blis we ring.

Of grace thy face in euerie place sa schynis,
That sweit all spreit baith heid and feit inclynis,
Thy gloir afoir for till imploir remeid.
He docht richt nocht, quhilk out of thocht the tynis;
Thy name but blame, and royal fame diuine is;
Thow port at schort of our comfort and reid,
Till bring all thing till glaiding efter deid,

All wicht but sicht of thy greit micht ay crynis,
O schene I mene, nane may sustene thy feid.

Haill rois maist chois till clois thy fois greit micht,
Haill stone quhilk schone vpon the throne of licht,
Vertew, quhais trew sweit dew ouirthrew al vice,
Was ay ilk day gar say the way of licht;
Amend, offend, and send our end ay richt.
Thow stant, ordant as sanct, of grant maist wise,
Till be supplie, and the hie gre of price.
Delite the tite me quite of site to dicht,
For I apply schortlie to thy deuise.

The Author directis his Buik to the Richt Nobill and Illuster Prince IAMES *the Feird, King of Scottis.*

Trivmphovs laud with palme of victorie,
The lawrer crowne of infinite glorie,
Maist gracious Prince, our souerane James the Feird,
Thy Maiestie mot haue eternallie
Supreme honour, renoun of cheualrie,
Felicitie perdurand in this eird,
With eterne blis in heuin by fatall weird ;
Ressaue this roustic rurall rebaldrie,
Laikand cunning, fra thy pure leige vnleird,

Quhilk, in the sicht of thy magnificence,
Confidand in sa greit beneuolence,
Proponis thus my vulgair ignorance
Maist humbillie with dew obedience,
Beseikand oft thy michtie excellence,
Be grace to pardoun all sic variance
With sum bening respect of firme constance ;
Remittand my pretendit negligence,
Thow, quhais micht may humbill thing auance.

Breif buriall quair of eloquence all quite,
With russet weid and sentence imperfite,
Till cum in plane se that thow not pretend the.
Thy barrant termis, and thy vile indite
Sall not be mine, I will not haue the wite,
For as for me I quit clame that I kend the :
Thow are bot stouth, thift louis, licht-but lite,
Not worth ane mite, pray ilk man til amend the.
Fair on with site, and on this wise I end the.

FINIS.

VERITAS VINCET TANDEM
VERBVM DEI

KING HART.

CONSCIENCE.

KING HART.

[Canto the First.]

KING HART, into his cumlie castell strang
Closit about with craft and meikill vre,
So semlie wes he set his folk amang,
That he no dout had of misaventure:
So proudlie wes he polist, plane and pure,
With ȝouthheid and his lustie levis grene;
So fair, so fresche, so liklie to endure,
And als so blyth as bird in symmer schene.

Cor in corpore hominis. Hart in body of man.

For wes he never ȝit with schouris schot,
Nor ȝit ourrun with rouk, or ony rayne;
In all his lusty lecam nocht ane spot,
Na never had experience into payne,
Bot alway into lyking, nocht to layne;
Onlie to love, and verrie gentilnes,
He wes inclynit cleinlie to remane,
And wonn vnder the wyng of wantownnes.

3

Ȝit was this wourthy wicht King vnder warde ;
For wes he nocht at fredom vtterlie.
Nature had lymmit folk, for thair rewarde,
This gudlie king to governe and to gy ;
For so thai kest thair tyme to occupy.
In welthis for to wyne for thay him teichit,
All lustis for to laue, and vnderly ;
So prevelie thai preis him and him preichit.

Juventus et quot nomina habet. Ȝouthheid and quhat names.

First [war thair] Strenth, [and Rage,] and Wantownnes,
Grein Lust, Disport, Jelosy, and Invy ;
Freschnes, New Gate, Waist-gude, and Wilfulnes,
Delyuernes, Fulehardenes thairby :
Gentrice, Fredome, Petie-previe I espy,
Want-wyt, Vanegloir, Prodigalitie,
Vnrest, Nicht-walk, and felon Glutony,
Vnricht, Dyme sicht, with Slicht, and Subtiltie.

Thir war the inwarde ythand seruitouris,
Quhilk gouernouris war to this nobil King,
And kepit him inclynit to thair curis ;
So wes thair nocht in erde that ever micht bring
Ane of thir folk away fra his duelling.
Thus to thair terme thai serve for thair rewarde :
Dansing, disport, singing, revelling,
With Bissines all blyth to pleis the lairde.

Desideria cordis iuuenture. The desyris of Hart in ȝouth.

Thir folk, with all the femell thai micht fang,
Quhilk numerit ane milȝon and weill mo,
That wer vpbred as seruitouris of lang,
And with this King wald wonn, in weill and wo,

For favour, nor for ferd, wald found him fro ;
Vnto the tyme thair dait be run and past :
That gold, nor gude, micht gar thame fro him go,
No greif, nor grame, suld grayth thame so agast.

7

Fyve Seruitouris this King he had without,
That teichit war ay tressoun to espy.
Thai watchit ay the wallis round about,
Fo[r] innemeis that of hapning ay come by.
Ane for the day, quhilk jugeit certanly,
With cure to ken the colour of all hew,
Ane for the nicht, that harknit bissely
Out of quhat airt that ever the wyndis blew.

Syne wes thair ane to taist all nutriment
That to this King wes servit at the deiss ;
Ane wther wes [of] all fovellis for sent,
Of licour, or of ony lustie meiss :
The fyft thair wes quhilk culd all [ken,] but leiss,
The heit, the cauld, the harde, and eik the soft ;
Ane ganand servand bayth for weir and peice.
ȝit hes thir folk thair king betrasit oft.

Honour persewit to the Kingis ȝet
Thir folk said all thai wald not lat him in ;
Becaus thai said thair lord to feist wes set,
With all his lustie seruandis more and myn.
Bot he ane port had enterit with ane gyn,
And vp he can in haist to the grit toure :
And said he suld it parall all with fyn
And fresche delyt with mony florist floure.

So strang this King him thocht his castell stude.
With mony towre and turat crownit hie:
About the wall thair ran ane water void,
Blak, stinkand, sowr, and salt as is the sey,
That on the wallis wiskit, gre by gre,
Boldning to ryis the castell to confound;
Bot thai within maid sa grit melody,
That for thair reird thay micht nocht heir the sound.

With feistis fell, and full of jolitee,
This cumlie court thair King thai kast to keip,
That noy hes none bot newlie novaltee,
And ar nocht wonnt for wo to woun and weip,
Full sendill sad, or soundlie set to sleip,
No wandreth wait, ay wenis welth endure;
Behaldis nocht, nor luikis nocht, the deip,
As thame to keip fra all misaventure.

Richt as the rose vpspringis fro the rute,
In ruby colour reid most ryck of hew;
Nor waindis nocht the levis to outschute,
For schyning of the sone that dois renew
Thir vther flouris greyne, quhyte, and blew,
Quhilk hes na craft to knaw the wynter weit,
Suppois that sommer schane dois thame reskew,
That dois thame quhile ourhaill with snaw and sleit.

Dame Plesance had ane pretty place besyd,
With fresche effeir, and mony folk in feir;
The quhilk wes parald all about with pryde,
So precious that it prysit wes but peir

With bulwerkis braid, and mony bitter beir.
Syn wes ane brig, that hegeit was, and strang;
And all that couth attene the castell neir,
It made thame for to mer amiss, and mang.

With touris grit, and strang for to behold,
So craftlie with kirnellis kervin hie;
The fitchand chaynis floreist all of gold.
The grundin dairtis scharp, and bricht to se,
Wald mak ane hart of flint to fald and fle
For terrour, gif thai wald the castell saill;
So kervin cleir that micht na cruelte
It for to wyn in all this warld avale.

Servit this Quene Dame Plesance, all at richt,
First Hie Apporte, Bewtie, and Humilnes;
With mony vtheris madinis, fair and bricht,
Reuth, and Gud Fame, Fredome, and Gentilnes;
Constance, Patience, Raddour, and Meiknes,
Conning, Kyndnes, Heyndnes, and Honestie,
Mirth, Lustheid, Lyking, and Nobilnes,
Bliss and Blythnes, [Gudenes] and pure Pietie.

This war the staitis worthyest and ding,
With mony mo, that servit to this Quene.
Ane legioun liell war [ay] at hir leding,
Quhen [that] hir court leist semble fair and clein.
In thair effeir Fayr Seruice micht be sene;
For wes thair nocht that semit be avyse,
That no man micht the poynting of ane prene
Repreve; nor pece, but payntit at devyse.

7

Hapnit this wourthy Quene, vpon ane day,
With hir fresche court arrayit weill at richt,
Hunting to ryd, hir to disport and play,
With mony ane lustie ladie fair and bricht.
Hir baner schene displayit, and on hicht
Wes sene abone thair heidis quhair thai rayd;
The grene ground wes illuminyt of the lycht;
Fresche Bewtie had the vangarde and wes gyde.

Ane legioun of thir lustie ladeis schene
Folowit this Quene, (trewlie this is no nay;)
Harde by this castell of this King so kene
This wourthy folk hes walit thame a way;
Quhilk did the dayis watcheis to effray,
For seildin had thai sene sic folkis befoir,
So mirrelie thai muster, and thai play,
Withoutin outher brag, or bost, or schore.

The watcheis of the sicht wes sa effrayit,
Thai ran and tauld the King of their intent:
Lat nocht this mater, schir, be lang delayit;
It war speidfull sum folk ȝe outwarde sent,
That culd reherss quhat thing ȝone peple ment;
Syne ȝow agane thairof to certifie.
For battell byd thai bauldlie on ȝon bent;
It war bot schame to feinȝe cowartlie.

Ȝouthheid vpstart, and cleikit on his cloik,
Was browdin all with lustie levis grene;
Ryse, fresch Delyte, lat nocht this mater soke;
We will go se quhat may this muster mene;

So weill we sall ws it copé betwene,
Thair sall nothing pas away vnspyit.
Syn sall we tell the king as we haue sene,
And thar sall nothing trewlie be denyit.

ȝouthheid furth past, and raid on Innocence,
Ane mylk quhyt steid that ambilit as the wynd;
And fresche Delyt raid on Benevolence,
Throw out the meid that wald nocht byd behind.
The beymes bricht almost had maid thame blind,
That fra fresche Bewtie spred vnder the cloude;
To hir thai socht, and sone thai culd her find,
No saw thai nane never wes half sa proude.

The bernis both wes basit of the sicht,
And out of mesour marrit in thair mude;
As spreitles folkis on blonkis hvffit on hicht,
Both in ane studie starand still thai stude.
Fayr Calling freschlie on hir wayis ȝuid,
And both thair reynȝeis cleikit in hir handis;
Syn to hir castell raid, as scho war woude,
And festnit vp thir folkis in Venus bandis.

Becaus thair come no bodwarde sone agane,
The King outsent New Gate, and Wantownnes,
Grene Luif, Disport, Waistgude that nocht can lane,
And with thame freschlie feir Fule-hardynes:
He bad thame spy the cais quhow that it wes,
And bring bodwart, or [he] himself outpast.
Thai said thai suld; and sone thai can thame dres,
Full glaid thai glyde as gromés vnagaist.

On grund no greif quhill thai the grit ost se,
Wald thai nocht rest, the rinkis so thay ryde.
Bot fra thay saw thair sute, and thair semblie,
It culd thame bre, and biggit thame to byde.
Dreid of Disdane on fute ran thame besyde,
Said thame, bewar, sen Wisdome is away;
For and ȝe prik amang thir folk of pryde,
A pane ȝe sal be restit be the way.

Full-hardynes full freschlie furth he flang,
A fure leynth fer befoir his feiris fyve;
And Wantones, suppois he had the wrang,
Him followit on als fast as he micht dryve.
So thai wer lyke amang thameself to stryve:
The fouresum baid, and huvit on the grene,
Fresche Bewtie with ane wysk come [vp] belyve,
And thame all reistit war thai never so kene.

With that the fouresum fayn thay wald haue fled
Agane vnto thair castell, and thair King.
Thai gave ane schout, and sone thai hane thame sched,
And besselie thay kan thame bundin bring
Agane vnto thair Quene; and bandis thring
About thair handis and [thair] feit so fast,
Quhill that thai maid thame with thair tormenting
Haly of thair lyvis half agast.

The watchis on the kingis wallis hes sene
The chassing of the folk, and thair suppryse.
Vpstart King Hart in propir yre and tein,
And baldlie bad his folk all with him ryse.

I sall nocht sit, he said, and se thame thryse
Discomfit clein my men, and put at vnder;
Na, we sall wrik ws on ane vther wyse,
Set we be few to thame be fifty hounder.

Than out thai raid all to a randoun richt,
This courtlie King, and all his cumlie ost,
His buirtlie bainer brathit vp on hicht;
And out thay blew with brag and mekle bost,
That lady and hir lynnage suld be lost.
Thai cryit on hicht thair seinȝe wounder lowde:
Thus come they keynlie carpand one the cost;
Thai preik, thai prance, as princis that war woude.

Dame Plesance hes hir folk arrayit weill,
Fra that scho saw thai wald battell abyde,
So Bewte with hir wangarde gane to reill,
The greitest of thair ost scho can ourryd.
Syne fresche Apport come on the tother syd;
So bisselie scho wes to battell boune,
That all that ever scho micht ourtak that tyde,
Horsis and men with brount scho straik all doune.

Richt thair King Hart scho hes in handis tane,
And puirlie wes he present to the Quene;
And scho had fairlie with ane fedderit flayne
Woundit the King richt wonderful to wene.
Delyuerit him Dame Bewtie vnto sene
His wound to wesche, in sobering of his sair;
Bot alwayis as scho castis it to clene,
His malady incressis mair and mair.

Woundit he wes, and quhair ʒit he na wait;
And mony of his folk hes tane the flicht.
He said, I yeild me now to ʒour estait,
Fair Quene! sen to resist I haue no micht.
Quhat will ʒe saye me now for quhat[en] plycht?
For that I wait I did ʒou never offence.
And gif I haue done ocht that is vnrycht,
I offer me to ʒour beneuolence.

Be this battell wes neir vincust all;
The kingis men ar tane, and mony slane.
Dame Plesance [than] can on fresche Bewtie call,
Bad hir command the folk to presoun plaine.
King Hart sair woundit was, bot he wes fayne,
For weill he traistit that he suld recure.
The Lady and her ost went hame agane,
And mony presoner takin vnder hir cure.

King Hart his castell levit hes full waist,
And Hevenes maid capitane it to keip.
Radour ran hame full fleyit and forchaist,
Him for to hyde crap in the dungeoun deip.
Langour he lay vpon the wallis but sleip,
But meit, or drink; the watché horne he blew;
Ire wes the portour, that full sayr can weip,
And Jelousy ran out; he wes never trew.

He said he suld be spy, and bodwart bring,
Bayth nicht and day, how that his maister fure.
He folowit fast on fute eftir the King
Vnto the castell of Dame Plesance pure.

In the presoun fand he mony creature ;
Sum fetterit fast, and [vthers] fre and large
Quhair ever thame list within the wallis fure.
Sone Jelousy him hid vnder ane targe.

Thair saw he Lust by law [ly] vnder lok,
In streinȝe strong fast fetterit fute and hand ;
Grene Luif lay bund[in] with ane felloun blok
About the crag was claspit with ane band ;
Ȝouthheid wes lous, and ay about waverand ;
Desyre lay stokkit by ane dungeoun dure ;
Ȝit Honestie [culd] keip him fayr farrand,
And Waistgude followand him quhair euer he fure.

Discretioun wes as than bot ȝoung of age,
He sleipit with Lust quhair euer he micht him find ;
And he agane wes crabbit at the page.
Ane ladill full of luif, stude him behind,
He swakit in his ene, and maid him blinde,
Sua [that] fra that tyme furth he micht nocht se :
Speik thow ane wourde thy four feet sall I bind,
Syn swak the our the wallis in the se.

Bissines, New Gate, Freschnes, and syn Disporte,
Fredome, Gentrice, Cuning, and Fair Maner,
All thir war lous daylie, and ȝeid ouerthort
To clois befoir the dungeoun windo neir,
Quhair wynnit fair Dame Plesance, that wes cleir,
Quhilk hes espyit richt weill thair gouernance ;
And, lauchan he, commandit tymés seir
Thame to await vpone thair observance.

This lustic Quene, within hir dungeoun strang,
Coud dysyde ay hir ladeis hir about.
And as scho list scho leirit thame to mang,
That wald be in all folk that wer without.
For Hie Apport scho is hir capitane stout;
Bewtie hir baner beris hir beforne;
Dame Chaistetie hir chalmarere but dout;
And Strangenes hir portare can weill scorne.

Fayr Calling is grit garitour on hicht,
That watchis ay the wallis hie abone,
And Sweit Semblance is marschale in hir sicht;
As scho commandis so swyth all is done.
Sa is thair [lakt] nocht mvsik nor of tvne;
The ladeis sweit thai mak sic melodie,
Quhat wicht, that micht it heir, suld juge [it] sone
To angell song, and hewinlie armony.

King Hart intill ane previe closet crappe,
Was neir the dungeoun wall, neirby the ground;
Swas he micht heir and se, sic wes his happe,
The meikle mirth, the melodie, and sound,
Quhilk fra the wallis sweitlie can redound
In at his eir, and sink vnto his hart;
And thairin wirkis mony previe wound,
That dois oftsys him strang with stoundis smart.

Ay seik he is, and ever he hes his heill
In battale strang, and hes both pece and rest;
The scharpe, and als the soft, can with him deill;
The sweit, the sour, both rewle, and als vnrest;

Dame Danger hes of dolour to him drest
Ane pallioun that na proudnes hes without,
With teiris weit ar rottin, may nocht lest,
Fast brikand by the bordouris all about.

Bot ȝouthheid had him maid ane courtlie cote,
Als grene as gerss, with goldin stremis bricht
Broudin about, fast bukkillit to his throte:
A wourthy weid, weill closand, and full licht.
Ane wysar, that wes payntit for the sicht,
As ruby reid, and pairt of quhyt amang;
Off coulours micht thair nane be frescher dicht,
Bot Hevines had fassonit it all wrang.

This wourthy King in presoun thus culd ly,
With all his folk, and culd thair nane out brek.
Full oft thai kan vpone dame Pietie cry:
Fair thing! cum doun a quhyle, and with ws speik.
Cum: farar way ȝe micht ȝour harmes wreik,
Than thus to murdour ws that ȝoldin ar.
Wald ȝe ws rew, quhair euir we micht our reik,
We suld men be to ȝow for euirmare.

Than answert Danger, and said, That wer grete doute,
A madin sweit amang sa mony men
To cum alane, but folk war hir about;
That is ane craft myself culd never ken.
With that scho ran vnto the Lady kene:
Kneland, Madame, scho said, keip Pietie fast.
Sythen scho ask, no licence to her len;
May scho wyn out, scho will play ȝow a cast.

Than Danger to the dure tuik gude keip,
Both nicht and day, that Pietie suld nocht pass;
Quhill all fordwart, in [the] defalt of sleip,
Scho bisselie as for-travalit scho was,
Fair Calling gaif hir drink into ane glas:
Sone efter that to sleip scho went anone.
Pietie was war that ilk [wes] prettie cass,
And privelie out at the dure is gone.

The dure on chare it stude; all wes on sleip;
And Pietie doun the stair full sone is past.
This Bissines hes sene, and gave gud keip:
Dame Pietie hes he hint in armeis fast.
He callit on Lust, and he come at the last,
His bandis gart he birst in peces smale:
Dame Pietie wes gritlie feirit and agast.
Be that wes Confort croppin in our the wall.

Sone come Delyte, and he begouth to dance;
Grene Love vpstart, and can his spreitis ta.
Full weill is me, said Disport, of this chance,
For now I traist gret melody to ma.
All in ane rout vnto the dure thay ga;
And Pietie put thairin first thame befoir.
Quhat was thair mair, Out! Harro! Taik, and slay!
The hous is wone withoutin brag or schoir.

The courtinis all of gold about the bed
Weill stentit was quhair fair Dame Plesance lay:
Than new Desyr, als gredie as ane glede,
Come rinnand in, and maid ane grit deray.

The Quene is walknit with ane felloun fray,
Vp glifnit, and beheld scho wes betraysit;
ȝeild ȝow, madame, on hicht can Schir Lust say:
A wourde scho culd nocht speik scho wes so abasit.

ȝeild ȝow, madame; grene Lust culd say all sone;
And fairlie sall we governe ȝow and ȝouris.
Our lord King Hartis will most now be done,
That ȝit is law amang the nether bowris;
Our lang, madame, ȝe keipit thir hie towris;
Now thank we none bot Pietie ws suppleit.
Dame Danger [than] into ane nuk scho kowris;
And quakand thair the quene scho lay for dreid.

Than Busteousnes come with brag and bost,
All that ganestude he straik deid in the flure.
Dame Plesance said, Sall we thus-gate be lost?
Bring vp the King, lat him in at the dure;
In his gentrice richt weill I dar assure.
Thairfor sweit Confort cryit vpone the King:
Than Bissines, that cunning creature,
To serve Dame Plesance sone thar can him bring.

So sweit ane swell as straik vnto his hart
Quhen that he saw Dame Plesance at his will.
I ȝeild me, schir, and do me nocht to smart,
(The fayr Quene said vpone this wyss him till)
I sauf ȝouris, suppois it be no skill.
All that I haue, and all that myne may be,
With all my hairt I offer heir ȝow till,
And askis nocht bot ȝe be trew till me.

Till that [quhilk] Loue, Desyre, and Lust devysit,
Thus fair Dame Plesance sweitlie can assent.
Than suddandlie Schir Hart him now disgysit,
On gat his amouris clok or euer he stent.
Freschlie to feist thir amouris folk ar went.
Blythnes wes first brocht bodwarde to the hall;
Dame Chastite, that selie innocent,
For wo ȝeid wode, and flaw out our the wall.

The lustie Quene scho sat in middes the deiss;
Befoir hir stude the nobill wourthy King.
Servit thai war of mony dyuerss meis,
Full sawris sweit and swyth thai culd thame bring.
Thus thai maid ane [richt] mirrie marschalling:
Bewtie and Loue ane hait burde hes begun;
In wirschip of that lustie feist so ding,
Dame Plesance has gart perce Dame Venus tun.

[End of Canto the First.]

[Canto the Second.]

QUHA is at eis, quhen bayth ar now in blis,
Bot fresche King Hart that cleirlie is aboue;
And wantis nocht in warld, that he wald wis,
And traistis nocht that euir he sall remoue.
Sewin ȝeir, and moir, Schir Lyking, and Schir Loue,
Off him thai haue the cure and gouernance,
Quhill at the last befell, and sua behuif,
Ane changeing new that grevit Dame Plesance.

A[t] morrowing tyde, quhen at the sone so schene
Out raschit had his bemis frome the sky,
Ane auld gude man befoir the ȝet was sene,
Apone ane steid that raid full easalie.
He rappit at the ȝet, but courtaslie,
ȝit at the straik the grit dungeoun can din;
Syne at the last he schowted fellonlie,
And bad thame rys, and said he wald cum in.

Sone Wantownnes come to the wall abone,
And cryit our, Quhat folk ar ȝe thair out?
My name is Age, said he agane full sone;
May thow nocht heir? Langar how I culd schout!
What war ȝour will? I will cum in, but dout.
Now God forbid! In fayth ȝe cum nocht heir;
Rin on thy way, [or] thow sall heir ane route:
And say, the portar he is wonder sweir.

Sone Wantownnes he went vnto the King,
And tald him all the caiss quhow that it stude.
That taill, [quoth he,] I traist be na leising;
He wes to cum. That wist I, be the rude.
It dois me noy, be God, in bane and blude,
That he suld cum sa sone! Quhat haist had he?
The Quene said [than], To hald him out war gude.
That wald I fayne war done, and it micht be.

Ȝouthheid vpstart and knelit befoir the King:
Lord, with your leif, I may na langar byde.
My warisoun, (I wald that with me bring)
Lord, pay to me, and gif me leif to ryde.
For micht I langer resyde ȝow besyde,
Full fayne I wald, no war my felloun fa.
For dout of Age, Schir King, ȝe latt me slyde;
For and I byde in fayth he will me sla.

Sen thow man pas, fair Ȝouthheid, wa is me!
Thow wes my freynd, and maid me gude seruice.
Fra thow be went never so blyth to be,
I mak ane vow, [all]thocht that it be nyce.
Off all blythnes thy bodie beiris the pryce.
To warisoun I gif the, or thow ga,
This fresche visar, wes payntit at devyce.
My lust alway with the se that thow ta.

For saik of the I will no colour reid,
Nor lusty quhyte, vpone my bodie beir,
Bot blak and gray; alway quhill I be deid,
I will none vther wantoun wedis weir.

Fayr weill my freynd! Thow did me never deir!
Vnwelcum Age, thow come agane my will!
I lat the wit I micht the weill forbeir.
Thy warisoun suld be [richt] small, but skill.

Than ȝouthheid said, Disport and Wantounnes,
My brether both, dispone ȝow with me ryde.
Vpstart on fute lyflie Delyverance;
Said, Schirris, I pray ȝow tak me for ȝour gyde.
Trow ȝe that I sall lye heirin to hyde
This wourthy craft that Nature to me gaif?
Na! Na! This cowartnes sall nocht betyde!
Fair on! I sal be formest of the laif.

Out at ane previe postrome all thai past;
And wald nocht byd all-out to tak thair leif.
Than fresche Delyte come rynnand wonder fast,
And with ane pull gat ȝouthheid be the sleif:
Abyd! Abyd! Gud fallow, the nocht greif;
Len me thy cloke, to gys me for ane quhyle;
Want I that weid in fayth I will mischeif.
Bot I sall follow the within ane myle.

Delyte come in, and all that saw his bak
Thay wenit it had bein ȝouthheid bundin still.
Bot eftirwart, quhen that thai with him spak,
Thay knew it wes ane feinȝe made thame till.
Sone quhen he had disportit him his fill,
His courtlie cloke begouth to fayd of hew;
Thriftles, threid bair, and reddy for to spill,
Lyk failȝeit blak, quhilk wes befoir tyme blew.

ȝit wald he nocht away allutterlie,
Bot of retinew feit he him as than;
And, or he wist, he spendit spedellie
The flour of all the substance that he wan:
So wourde he pure and powrit to the pan.
ȝit Appetyt, his sone, he bad duell still.
Bot, wit ȝe weill, he wes ane sory man;
For falt of gude he wantit all his will.

Be that wes Age enterit, and ȝit first
His branchis braid out bayr he mony bore.
Vnwylcum was the noy, quhen that thai wist,
For followand him thair come fyve hunder score
Off hairis that King Hart had neuer befoir.
And quhen that fayr Dame Plesance had thame sene,
Scho grevit, and scho angerit weill moir;
Her face scho wryit about for propir teyne.

Scantlie had Age restit him thair ane quhyle,
Quhen Conscience come cryand our the wall:
How lang think ȝe to hald me in exile?
Now, on my saule, ȝe ar bot lurdanis all!
And sum of ȝow, be God, shall haue ane fall,
May I him meit fra presence of the king.
All fals tratours I may ȝow full weill call,
That seruit weill be draw both heid and hing.

Fra Age [had] harde that Conscience was comeing,
Full sone he rais belyve, and leit him in.
Sadnes he had, ane cloik fra meture mvming
He had vpon, and wes of Ageis kin:

It war richt harde thay tua in sunder twin,
Thairfoir aftir his bak he ran anone.
In mid the clois thair Conscience met with Syn,
Ane felloun rout he layde on his rig-bone.

Conscience to Syn gave sic ane [angrie] dunt,
Quhill to the erde he flaw and lay at vnder;
ȝit Conscience his breist hurt with the dynt:
Bot Sadnes hes to put this tua in sunder.
Folie and Vyce into thair wit thay wounder
Quhow sic ane maister-man so sone suld rys,
In mid the clois, on luikand neir fyve hunder,
The kingis folk to ding and to suppryse.

Thai war adred, and sone hes tane the flicht;
Syne in an hirne to hyde sone can thame hy.
Than Conscience cum to the kingis sicht;
Out at ane dore ran Falset, and Invy,
Gredie Desyr, and gamsome Glutony,
Vant, and Vaneglоir, with new grene Appetyte;
For Conscience luikit sa fellounlie,
They ran away out of his presens quyte.

God blis the lord; thus Conscience can say,
This quhyle bygane thow hes bene all to glaid.
ȝa, Conscience; and ȝit fayne wald I play;
Bot now my hart [it] waxis wounder sad.
Thai haue bene wickit counsalouris thow had,
Wist thow the suth, as thow sall eftir heir;
For, wit thow weill, thair burding [ay] wes bad;
The rute is bitter, scharp as ony breir.

Thy tresour haue thay falsle fra the tane,
Thir wickit folk thow wenit had bene trew;
And stowin away fra the ane and ane.
For think, thay never cum the for to glew.
Quhair is thy garment grene and gudlie hew?
And thy fresche face, that ȝouthheid to the maid?
Thow bird think schame, and of thy riot rew,
Saw thow thyself into thy colour sad.

Now mervale nocht, suppois I with the chyde;
For, wit thow weill, my hairt is wounder wa.
Ane vther day, quhan thow may nathing hyde,
I man accuse the as thy propir fa.
Off thy vane werk first witnes thow me ta,
Quhen all thy jolitie beis justifeit;
It grevis me that thow suld gracceles ga
To waist thy weilfair, and thy welth so wyde.

As Conscience wes chydand thus on hicht,
Reassoun, and Wit, richt at the ȝet thai rang,
With rappis lowd, for it drew neir the nicht;
Bad lat thame in, for thai had standing lang.
Said Conscience, In gude fayth this is wrang!
Gif me the key, I sall be portar now.
So come thai in, ilkane throw vther, thrang,
Syn with ane wysk almost I wait nocht how.

Ressoun ran on quhair at Discretioun lay,
Into ane nuke, quhar na man culd him find;
And with his kniyf he schure the flesche away
That bred vpone his ene, and maid him blind.

Syne gaif he him the thuide ewin behind;
Now may thow se. Get vp! No langar ly;
And scouner nocht to ryd in rane and wynd.
Quhair euir I be, se that thow be neirby.

The King begouth to speik vpone this wyse:
Fayr Conscience, ȝe ar to crabbit now.
Ȝour souerane and ȝour lord for to suppryse
Thar is no man of gude will ȝow allow.
Quhat haue I done that thus hes crabbit ȝow?
I followit counsale alway for the best;
And gif thai war vntrew, I dar avow,
Nature did miss sic folk vpon me cast.

Nature me bred ane beist into my nest,
And gaif to me Ȝouthheid first seruitour;
That I no fut micht find, be eist nor west,
Bot euir in warde, in tutourschip and cure;
And Wantownnes quha wes to me more sure:
Sic Nature to me brocht, and first devysit
Me for to keip fra all misaventure.
Quhat blame serve I, this way to be supprysit?

Ȝe did greit miss, fayr Conscience, be ȝour leif,
Gif that ȝe war of kyn and blude to me,
That sleuthfullie suld lat ȝour tyme our sleif,
And come thus lait. How suld ȝe ask your fe?
The steid is stollin, steik the dure; lat se
Quhat may avale; God wait! the stall is tume!
And gif [that] ȝe be ane counsalour sle,
Quhy suld ȝe sleuthfullie your tyme forsume?

Off [all] my harme and drerie indigence,
Giff thair be ocht amys, me think, perdé,
That ȝe ar caus verray of my offence,
And suld sustene the bettir part for me.
Mak answer now. Quhat can ye say? Lat se!
Ȝourself excuse and mak ȝow foule or clene.
Ressoun, cum heir, ȝe sall our juge [now] be,
And in this caus gif sentence ws betwene.

Schir, be ȝour leif, into my propir caus
Suppois I speik, ȝe suld nocht be displesit.
Said Conscience, This is ane villaneis caus,
Gif I suld be the caus ȝe ar disesit.
Na, ȝoung counsale in ȝow sa lang was seisit,
That hes ȝour tressour and ȝour gude distroyit.
Richt fayne wald I with mesour it war meisit,
For of ȝour harme God wait gif I be noyit.

Ȝe put grit wyt that I so lang abaid,
Gif that I culd with counsale ȝow avale;
Schir, traist [ȝe] weill ane verrie caus I had,
Or ellis war no ressoun in my taile.
My terme wes set by ordour naturale,
To quhat work alway I most obey;
No dar I nocht be no way mak travale,
Bot quhair I se my maister get a swey.

For stand he on his feit, and stakkir nocht,
Thir hundreth ȝeir sall cum into his hald.
Bot nevirtheles, schir, all thing ȝe haue wrocht
With help of Wisdome, and his willis wald,

I sall reforme it blythlie. Be ȝe bald,
And Ȝouthheid sall haue wyt of ȝour misdeid.
Thairfoir requyr ȝe Ressoun mony fald,
That he his rollis raithlie to ȝow reid.

Ressoun rais vp, and in his rollis he brocht.
Gif I sall say, the sentence sall be plane;
Do never the thing that ever may scayth the ocht;
Keip mesour and trouth, for thairin lyes na trayne.
Discretioun suld ay with King Hart remane;
Thir vthir ȝoung folk-seruandis ar bot fulis.
Experience mais Knawlege now agane,
And barnis ȝoung suld lerne at auld mennis sculis.

Quha gustis sweit, and feld nevir of the sowre,
Quhat can [he] say? How may he seasoun juge?
Quha sittis hate, and feld nevir cauld ane hour,
Quhat wedder is thairout vnder the luge
How suld he wit? That war ane mervale huge!
To by richt blew, that nevir ane hew had sene!
Ane servand be, that nevir had sene ane fuge!
Suppois it ryme it accordis nocht all clene.

To wiss the richt, and to disvse the wrang,
That is my scule to all that list to leyr.
Bot Wisdome, gif ȝe suld duell vs amang,
Me think ȝe duell our lang; put doun ȝour speir;
Ȝe micht weill mak ane end of all this weir,
Wald ȝe furth schaw ȝour wourthy document.
For is thair none that [ever] can forbeyr
The work of Vice, withoutin ȝour assente.

Wit said, Schir King be war, or ȝe be wa,
For Foirsicht hes now full lang bein flemit
Vnto knaw thy freynd forbe thy fa,
Giff thow will haue thy cuntre all weill ȝemit.
And be thow weill, to hald the so it semit;
[Neir weinand aucht to do that war amis:]
Eftir thy deith thy deidis man be demit,
Be thy desert outher to baill or blis.

Honour he raid the castell round about
Vpon ane steid that wes als quhyte as milk.
Is Eis thairin? cryit he [ay] with ane schout.
Dame Plesance spak, hir face hid with ane silk:
He is ane gouernour of ouris that ilk.
Wit said, Cum in! Full welcum to thir wanis!
I compt not all your werkis wirth ane wilk;
Ȝe sall nocht herbere me and Eis at anis.

Wirschip of Weir come on the tother syde,
Vpon ane steid rampand wes reid as blude.
He cryit on Strenth, Cum out man! Be my gyde;
I can nocht ryde out-our this water woude.
Dame Plesance harde, and on hir wayis scho ȝeid
Richt to the King, and bad him Strenth arreist;
I wald not, schir, for mekle warldlie gude
Want Strenth ane hour quhen euir we go to feist.

In all disport he may ws gritlie vaill;
Gif him na leif, bot hald him quhill ȝe may.
The King full weill had harde Dame Plesance taill,
And Strenth he hes arreistit be the way.

Abyde! he said: we sall ane vther day
Seik Wirschip at our will and ws avance.
I dreid me sair, Schir Strenth, of that delay;
For armes hes both happie tyme and chance.

Strenth said: Now I am grene, and in my flouris,
Fayne wald I follow Wirschip, and I micht;
For, gif I byde, in fayth the falt is ȝouris,
I man obey to ȝow sen that is richt.
Now se I weill, Dame Plesance, hes grit slicht;
And fy on Eis that haldis Honour out.
He is the man micht bring ws all to hicht;
Lo quhair he rydis bakwart with his route!

With this Bewtie come in the Kingis sicht;
Full reverendlie scho knelit in his presence:
Dame Plesance sayis, schir, that ȝe do vnricht.
Durst I it say vnto ȝour hie reuerence,
ȝe haue displesit hir hie magnificence,
That suld lat Conscience in hir castell cum;
He is hir fo, and dois hir grit offence,
And oft tymes can her seruitouris ouercome.

Thairwith the King vpstart, and turnit abak
On Conscience, and all his court in feir;
And to the Quene the richt way can he tak,
Full suddanlie in armis hint the cleir.
Scho wryit about, to kyss scho wes full sweir.
Than he agane full fayrlie to hir spak;
No! Be no wraith with me, my lady deir!
For as I may I sall ȝow mirrie mak.

Thocht Conscience and Wisdome me to keip
Be cunning both, I sall thame weill begyle;
For trewlie, quhan [that] thai ar gane to sleip,
I sal be heir within ane bonny quhyle;
My solace sall I sleylie thus oursyle.
Richt sall nocht rest me alway with his rewle;
Thocht I be quhylum bowsum as ane waile,
I sal be cruikit quhill I mak [him fule.]

Dame Plesance [said], My freyndis now ar flede;
The lusty folk that ȝe furth with ȝow brocht.
Methink thir carlis ar nocht courtlie clede!
Quhat joy haue I of thame? I compt thame nocht.
Ȝouthheid, and fresche Delyte, micht thai be brocht!
For with thair seruice I am richt weill kend.
Fayne wald I that ȝe send men and thame socht,
Allthocht it war vnto the warldis end.

The Quene wourde wrayth; the King wes sore addrede,
For hir disdane he culd nocht gudlie beir.
Thai sowpit sone, and syne thai bownit to bede;
Sadnes come in and rownit in his eir!
Dame Plesance hes persauit hir new feyr;
And airlie, affore the sone, scho gan to ryse
Out of the bed, and turst vp all hir geir.
The King wes sound on sleip, and still he lyis.

Horsis and harnes hint scho hes in haist;
With all [hir] folk scho can hir wayis fayr.
Be this it wes full neir myd-day almaist,
Than come Diseis in rydand with ane rair;

The Quene is went, allace, I wait nocht quhair!
The King began to walk, and harde the beir:
Than Jelosie come strekand vp the stair,
To serve the King, and drew him wounder neir.

Ressoun come [in]: Schir King, I reid ȝe ryse,
Thair is ane grit pairt of this fayr day run.
The sone was at the hicht, and dounwarde hyis.
Quhair is the thesaure now that ȝe have woun?
This drink wes sweit ȝe fand in Venus tun!
Sone eftir this it sal be staill and soure;
Thairfoir of it I reid no moir ȝe cun:
Lat it ly still and pleis ȝour paramour.

Than Wisdome sayis, Schape for sum governance,
Sen fayr Dame Plesance on hir wayis is went.
In ȝour last dayis ȝe may ȝourself avance,
Gif that ȝe wourde of the same indigent.
Go to ȝour place, and ȝow thairin present;
The castell ȝet is strang aneuche to hald.
Than Sadnes said, Schir King, ȝe man assent;
Quhat haue ȝe now ado in this waist fald?

The King hes harde thair counsale at the last,
And halelie assentit to thair saw.
Mak reddie sone, he sayis, and speid ȝow fast.
Full suddanlie thai can the clarioun blaw;
On hors thai lap, and raid then all on raw
To his awin castell, thairin he wes brede.
Langour the watche attour the kirnale flaw;
And Hevines to the grit dungeoun flede.

He cryit, Schir King, welcome to thy awin place!
I haue it keipit trewlie sen thow past.
Bot I haue meikill mervale of thy face,
That changeit is lyk [with] ane winter blast.
ȝe, Havines, the King said at the last,
Now haue I this with fer mo harmes hint,
Quhilk grevis me, quhen I my comptis kast,
How I fresche ȝouthheid and his fallowis tynt.

Strenth wes as than fast fadit of his flouris,
Bot still ȝit with the King he can abyde;
Quhill at the last in the hochis he cowris,
Than prevelie out at the ȝet can slyde.
He stall away, and went on wayis wyde,
And socht quhair ȝouthheid and his feiris wonnd:
Full suddanlie, suppois he had na gyde,
Behinde ane hill he hes his feiris funde.

Swa, on ane day, the dayis watchis tua
Come [in;] and said thai saw ane felloun mist.
ȝa, said Wisdome, I wist it wald be wa:
That is ane sing befoir ane hevie trist!
That is perell to cum, quha [that] it wist,
For, on sum syde, thair sall ws folk assaill.
The King sat still; to travaill he nocht list;
And herknit syn ane quhyle to Wit his taill.

Desyre wes dalie at the chalmer dure;
And Jelousie wes never of his presence;
Ire kepit ay the ȝet, with meikle cure;
And Wretchitnes wes hyde into the spence.

Sic folk as thir, he said, to mak defence,
With all thair familie fullie hundrethis fyve!
Schir Eis he was the gritest of renerence;
Best lovit with the King of leid on lyve.

Vnto the ȝet come rydand on ane day
Wirschip of Weir, quhilk sawis Honouris hie:
Go to the King, with sture voce can he say,
Speir gif ony office he hes for me;
For, and him list, I will him serve for fee.
Wysdome come to the wall, cryand our agane:
Man, seik thy fortoun with Aduersitie;
It is nocht heir sic thing as the suld gane.

Strenth is away, outstolling lyk anė theif,
Quhilk keipit ay the thesaure of estait;
Thair is na man suld cheris the sa leif,
Thir vther folk of wirschip ar full blait.
Wirschip of Weir agane with Wysdome flate;
Quhy wald ȝe nocht me se quhen Strenth ȝe had?
Thairwith come Eis; said, I sit warme and hait,
Quhen thai thairout sal be with stouris stade.

Wirschip sayis, Ware I wait ȝe haue at hand,
Quhilk sall assailȝe your wallis hie and strang.
Than Wysdome said, Dame Plesance, sueit sembland,
In ȝouthheid wald nocht thole ws Wirschip fang.
Adew, fayrweill! Wirschip sayis, now I gang
To seik my craft vnto the warldis end.
Wysdome sayis, Tak ȝow Diseis amang,
And wait on me als quhylum quhair ȝe wend,

For, do ȝe nocht, ȝe may nocht weill eft heif.
What is ȝour name? Wisdome for suyth I hecht.
All wrang, God wait! oft tymes, schir, be ȝour leif,
Myn aventure will schape out of ȝour sicht:
Bot nevirtheles may fall that ȝe haue richt.
Reuth have I none, outtak fortune and chance,
That man I ay persew both day and nicht;
Eis I defy so hingis in his ballance.

Richt as thir two ware talkand [fast] in feir,
Ane hiddous ost thai saw come our the myre;
Decrepitus, his baner schane nocht cleir,
Was at the hand, with mony chiftanis sture.
A crudge bak that cairfull cative bure,
And cruikit war his laythlie lymmis bayth.
But smirk, or smyle, bot rather for to smyre,
But scoup, or skift, his craft is all to scayth.

Within ane quhyle the castell all about
He seigit fast with mony sow and gyne:
And thai within gaif mony hiddowus schout,
For thai war wonder wa King Hart to tyne!
The grundin ganȝeis, and grit gunnis syne,
Thai schut without: within thai stanis cast.
King Hart sayis, Had the hous, for it is myne
Gif it nocht our als lang as we may lest.

Thus thai within had maid full grit defence,
Ay quhill thai micht the wallis [hie] haue ȝemit,
Quhill, at the last, thai wantit thame dispence,
Ewill purvayit folk, and sa weill stemit!

Thair tunnis, and thair tubbis, war all temit,
And failȝet was the flesche that wes thair fude:
And at the last Wisdome the best hes demit
[Comforte to byd thame kepe, that he ne ȝoude.]

And he be tynt, in perel put we all;
Thairfoir had wait and lat him nocht away.
Be this thai harde the meikle fore-tour fall,
Quhilk maid thame in the dungeoun to effray.
Than rais thair meikle dirdum and deray!
The barmekin birst, thai enterit in at large:
Heidwerk, Hoist, and Parlasy, maid grit pay,
And Murmouris mo with mony speir and targe.

Quhen that thai saw na bute wes to defend,
Than in thai leit Decrepitus full tyte.
He socht King Hart, for he full weill him kend,
And with ane swerde he can him smertlie smyte
His bak in twa, richt pertlie for dispyte;
And with the brand [syne] brak he both his schinnis.
He gaif ane cry, than Comfort fled out quyte;
And thus this bailfull bargane he begynnis.

Ressoun forfochtin [wes] and ewill drest;
And Wisdome wes ay wanderand to the dure:
Conscience lay [him] doun ane quhyle to rest,
Becaus he saw the King wourd waik and pure;
For so in dule he micht no langar dure.
Go send for Deid, thus said he verament;
Ȝit for I will dispone of my thesaure,
Vpon this wyse mak I my testament.

To fayr dame Plesance ay quhen scho list ryde
My prowde palfry, vnsteidfastnes, I leif,
With fikkilnes, hir sadill set on syde;
This aucht thair none of reassoun hir to reve.
To fresche Bewtie, becaus I culd hir heve,
Grein Appetyte hir servand for to be;
To crak and cry alway quhill he hir deve,
That I command him straitlie quhill he de.

Grein Lust, I leif to the at my last ende,
Of fantisie ane fostell fillit fow.
ȝonthheid, becaus that thow my barne-heid kend,
To Wantounnes ay will I that thow bow.
To Gluttony, that oft maid me our fow,
This meikle wambe, this rottin levir als,
Se that ȝe beir, and that command I ȝow;
And smertlie hing [thame] both abone his hals.

To Rere-Supper, be he amang that route,
ȝe me commend; he is ane fallow fyne!
This rottin stomak that I beir aboute,
ȝe rug it out, and reik it to him syne:
For he hes hinderit me of mony dyne,
And mony tyme the mess hes gart me sleip;
Myn wittis hes he waistit oft with wyne,
And maid my stomak with hait lustis leip.

Delinernes hes oft tymes done me gude,
Quhen I wes ȝoung, and stede in tendir age;
He gart me ryn full rakles, be the rude,
At ball and boull; thairfoir greit weill that page:

This brokin schyn, that swellis and will nocht swage,
ȝe beir to him ; he brak it at the ball :
And say to him that it sal be his wage ;
This breissit arme ȝe beir to him at all.

To Chaistite, that selie innocent,
Heir leif I now my conscience for to scour
Off all the wickit roust that throw it went,
Quhen scho for me the teiris doun culd powre.
That fayr sweit thing, bening in everie bour,
That never wist of vyce nor violence,
Bot euirmore is mareit with mesour,
And clene of lustis curst experience.

To Fredome sall ȝe found, and fairlie beir
This threid-bair cloik, sum-tyme wes thik of wow ;
And bid for my saik that he [sall] it weir,
Quhen he hes spendit of that he hes now.
Ay, quhen his purs of penneis is nocht fow,
Quhair is his fredome than ? Full far to seik !
A ! ȝon is he, wes quhylum till allow.
Quhat is he now ? No fallow wourth ane leik.

To Waistgude tak and beir neid that I lefe ;
To Covatice syn gif this bleis of fyre ;
To Vant and Voky ȝe beir this rowm slef ;
Bid thame thairin that thai tak thair hyre.
To Bissines, that nevir wes wont to tyre,
Beir him this stule, and bid him now sit doun,
For he hes left his maister in the myre,
And wald nocht draw him out thocht he suld droun.

Fulehardines, beir him this brokin brow,
And bid him bawldlie bind it with ane clout;
For he hes gottin morsellis on the mow,
And brocht his maister oft in meikle dout.
Syn sall ye eftir faire Dame Dangere schout,
And say, becaus scho had me ay at feid,
This brokin speir, sum-tyme wes stiff and stout,
To hir I leif, bot se it want the heid.

QUOD MAISTER GAVVIN DOUGLAS,
BISHOP OF DUNKELD.

CONSCIENCE.

QUHEN halie Kirk first flurist in ȝouthheid,
Prelatis wer chosin of all perfectioun ;
For Conscience than the brydill had to leid,
And Conscience maid the hale electioun,
Syne eftir that come schrewit correctioun,
And thocht that Conscience had our large ane weid,
And of his habite out cuttit thay ane skreid.

And fra Conscience the Con thay clip away,
And maid of Conscience Science and na mair ;
Bot ȝit the Kirk stude weill, full mony day,
For it wes rewlit be mene of wit and layre ;
Syn eftir that Sciens began to payr,
And thocht at Sciens was our lang ane jaip,
The Sci away fast can thay rub and scraip ;

And fra Sci of Science wes adew,
Than left thai nocht bot this sillab Ens,
Quhilk in our language singnifies that schrew
Riches and geir, that gart all grace go hens ;

For Sciens baith and faythfull Consciens
Sa corruptit ar with this warldis gude,
That falset joukis in everie clerkis hude.

O hungrie Ens! cursit with cairis calde,
All kynd of folk constrenis thow to wirk;
For thé that thief Judas his Maister sald;
For thé Symon infectit Halie Kirk;
To poysoun Justice thow dois nevir irk;
Thow fals Ens, go hens, thou monsture peralous,
God send Defens with Conscience in till ws!

FINIS QUOD BISCHOP DOUGLAS
OF DUNKELDE, &C.

NOTES

AND VARIOUS READINGS.

NOTES AND VARIOUS READINGS.

THE PALICE OF HONOUR.

[In the following notes, L. Ed. refers to the London Edition of 1553; Edin. Ed. to that of Edinburgh, 1579. References are frequently made to Dr. Jamieson's Dictionary of the Scottish Language, to Dr Irving's "History of Scotish Poetry," to Pinkerton's edition of the Palice of Honour, in his "Scotish Poems, reprinted from scarce Editions," published in 1792, and edition of King Hart, in his "Ancient Scotish Poems," published in 1786.]

Page clxx., *line* 15.—The "argument" or synopsis of the Palice of Honour, in imitation of the old Scottish language, prefixed by Pinkerton to his edition of 1792, is as follows:

Part I. "The poet gangs into a gardyne—Falls in a swoun—Is transportit to a desert—Complaint agan Fortoun—Court of Minerva apperis—Wise men hir attendants—Gangand till the Palace of Honour—Court of Diana—Court of Venus—Hir attendants—The poet complains agan her, and is bound and broht befoir hir court—His defens and hir reply—He is condemnit.

Part II. The Court of the Muses apperis—Famous poets thair attendants—Calliope inquiris Venus quhat the poet had done—He is reprevit, and singis in praise of Venus—Calliope gives him till a nymph with quham he travellis our monie countries, and restis on Parnassus—A festival, at quhilk Ovid and uther poets appeir—Proceiding with the nymph, the poet cumis to a plesand rock in a plane.

Part III. The poet ascendis the rock—Hell of idlenes—Shipwreck of the carvel of the State of Grace—First sight of the Palace of Honour—Descriptioun of it—Venus thar, and her mirrour quhilk reflectis al the gret acts of auld tymes—Account of sacred and profane historie—Plesand debaitments, mock heroes as Fingal, &c., and enchaunters alsua sene—Allegoricall descriptioun of King Honour and his court—The persouns thar—The poet wishing to pas intil the gardyne of flouris of rethoric, supposis he droppis from a brig, and wakis—Address to King James IV.

P. 1, *l.* 3, *the heuinly;* L. Ed. *be heuinlye.* *L.* 17. *alars yet.* "This may signify," says Jamieson, "the *yet* or gate overspread with the branches of the *alder*, or the gate made of this tree: A. S. *alr;* Su. G. *al;* Alem. elira, id.; Su. G. *alar*, of or belonging to the alder-tree. I suspect, however, that it is not the *alder*, but the elder that is meant. For as the elder or bore-tree is still by the superstitious supposed to defend from witchcraft, it was formerly a common custom to plant it in gardens. In many it is preserved to this day. It is probable, therefore, that the allusion is to this tree; and that for greater security, the trunk of it might be used for supporting the garden-gate, if this itself was not also made of the wood. Belg. *holler*, id. I dare not assert, however, that *alars* may not here signify *common* or *general*, q., the gate which opened into the whole garden. In this case, it would be the same with *allaris*." That the word *alars* means alder-trees is thus simply a guess. The Rev. Mr Skeat thinks it is *allures*, alleys, a well-known English word, from Lat. *alura*, or rather from Fr. *aller*. It has been suggested that *alars* may have been originally written *altars*, in which case the meaning of the line would be—which [dewdrops] the branches of verdure poured over the altars, reflecting the mists with smoky incense.

P. 2, *l.* 5, *echo;* L. Ed. *eccon.* *L.* 10, *Eous*, the morning star, Lucifer. *L.* 19, *reserue;* L. Ed. *preserue.*

P. 3, *l.* 9, *stone* ; L. Ed. *stane.*

P. 4, *l.* 23, *pulsis;* L. Ed. *punsys.* *L.* 25, *desie;* L. Ed. *dasyt.*

P. 5, l. 7, *heiring naturall;* L. Ed. *hetis naturale.* *L.* 17, *swevven;* L. Ed. *stewen.* *L.* 22. *visioun;* L. Ed. *avision.*

P. 6. The woodcut here inserted is that of the Royal Arms of Scotland of the period, and is taken from the L. Ed.

P. 7, *l.* 3, *badnystie.* Jamieson, s. v., explains this word as *silly stuff*, Fr. badinage; but the true reading seems to be *bad nystie*—bad ignorance. *Nystie*, from A.S. *nitan* (*ne*, not, and *witan*, to know), p. *ic nyste.* *L.* 6, *rymis;* L. Ed. *ranys.*

P. 8, *l.* 4, *swappis;* L. Ed. *skauppis.* *L.* 17, *rock;* L. Ed. *royk.* *L.* 26. The quaint side-notes or summaries, of which the first is here given, are taken from the L. Ed. They are wanting in the Edin. Ed.

P. 9, *l.* 19, *ye;* L. Ed. *ya.* *L.* 27, *plague Septentrionall*, the north zone.

P. 10, *l.* 1, *affrayit;* L. Ed. *afferit.* *L.* 10, *faitis;* L. Ed. *feitis.* *L.* 17, *haiknayis all;* L. Ed. *haiknays four.*

P. 11, *l.* 20. *Cassandra*, daughter of Priam, who foretold the destruction of Troy by the gift of prophecy conferred upon her by Apollo. *Delbora*—Deborah. The introduction of *l* is curious. Old MSS. often have *lk* for *kk*, and *lb* for *bb*. These get copied as *lk* and *lb.* *Circes*—Circe, daughter of Helios, the sun, a sorceress.

P. 12, *l.* 1. *Permenydus*—Parmenides, a philosopher of Elea, contemporary with Socrates, who wrote a didactic poem entitled "Nature." *L.* 2. *Melysses*—Melissus of Samos, a disciple of Parmenides, who belonged to the Eleatic school. *L.* 3. *Sidrach*—Shadrach, who was conversant with all the learning of the Chaldeans. He was miraculously delivered from the fiery furnace (Daniel i. 3). *Secundus*, a distinguished tragic poet in the reigns of Tiberius, Caligula, and Claudius. *Solenyus*, probably C. Julius Solinus, author of a geographical compendium in fifty-seven books, still extant. He flourished about A.D. 238. *L.* 4. *Ipocras*—Hippocrates, born at Cos about B.C. 460, the most celebrated physician of antiquity. *L.* 5. *Neptenabus.* There were two Egyptian kings of the name of Nectanebis or Nectanabis. In the old romances, Nectanebis was made the progenitor of Alexander the Great.

P. 13, *l.* 2. *Synon.* See the story of Sinon told in Douglas' Virgil, vol. ii. p. 71. Dante punishes Sinon with an eternal sweating sickness—*Inferno* xxx. *L.* 15, *haue na tume.* The Edinr. Ed. reads *haur na tume*, which seems a misprint of *haue.* *L.* 22. *Imagining;* L. Ed. *imaginand.*

P. 14, *l.* 10, *befoir;* L. Ed. *tofore.* *L.* 12. *Acteon;* L. Ed. *Action.* *L.* 18, *at them batit;* L. Ed. *at thaym batit*—Pink. *at him batit.*

P. 15, *l.* 2. *Polixena*, daughter of Priam, beloved by Achilles, and sacrificed by the Greeks to his shade. *L.* 3. *Peanthesile*—Penthesilea, Queen of the Amazons. In the Trojan war she assisted the Trojans, but at last was killed by Achilles. *L.* 4. *Effygin.* The Ed. ed. reads *Effyoin.* Iphigenia, daughter of Agamemnon and Clytemnestra, the story of whose sacrifice by her father, in propitiation of Artemis, is well known. *L.* 4. *Virgenius douchter*—Virginia, daughter of L. Virginius, a brave centurion, the attempt made upon whose chastity by Appius Claudius was the immediate cause of the downfall of the Roman Decemvirs, B.C. 449. *L.* 21, *north eist;* L. Ed. *northest.* *L.* 23, *sounding;* L. Ed. *soundis.*

P. 16, *l.* 6, *inwith;* L. Ed. *inoth.*

P. 18, *l.* 11. *But;* L. Ed. *Bot.* *L.* 12, *claith;* L. Ed. *plate.*

P. 20, *l.* 6, *bot yit;* L. Ed. *bot yf.* *L.* 17, *war soung and playit;* L. Ed. *war songin and plait.* *L.* 20, *countering;* L. Ed. *conturing.*

P. 21, *l.* 1. *Saul;* L. Ed. *kyng Saul.* *L.* 2. *Amphion*, son of Zeus and Antiope, to whom Apollo gave a lyre. He henceforth practised song and music so successfully, that when he played, the stones moved of their own accord and formed the wall of Thebes. *L.* 5, *igroundit;* L. Ed. *groundit.* *L.* 9. *Be God than dois a gekgo or a swine.* The Edin. Ed. reads, *than dois a Greik or a swine.* The word *gekgo*, a cuckoo, is supplied from the L. Ed. Dr Irving remarks that "Bishop Douglas, who certainly did not fall below the common standard of clerical decorum, has not scrupled to bedeck his compositions with abundance of oaths, which are generally introduced with as much significance as the frequent ejaculations of the ancient classics." He quotes Lord Hailes, who states as follows: "I have never been able to discover from what cause our ancestors became so monstrously addicted to profane swearing. I remember Tom Brown somewhere uses 'swear like a Scotsman' as a proverbial expression." *Hist. of Scot. Poetry*, p. 249: The Rev. Mr Scott, in his notes to the Perth Ed., thought that by a slight alteration better sense would be made of this line; and in his Ed. he reads, *than dois of Greik a swine*, and in this he has been followed by Pinkerton. Mr Scott also adds, "the good Bishop's word might have been taken for his ignorance in music, without the solemnity of his oath. There is little doubt, however, of the reading, and that Douglas has taken the idea, oath and all, from Chaucer—Knight's Tale, 952:

> "She wot no more of all this hot faire
> By God, than wot a cuckow or a hare."

L. 16. *Glaskeriane.* According to the old English ballad:

> "Glasgerion was a kinges owne sonne,
> And a harper he was goode."
> —*Percy's Reliques*, iii. p. 43; also *Percy's fol. MS.*, vol. i. p. 246.

L. 25, *ouirbrouderit;* L. Ed. *or brounvert.*

P. 22, *l.* 3, *veluot;* L. Ed. *veluos.* *L.* 25. *Arcite and Palemon.* For the story of these heroes see Chaucer's Knight's Tale. For *aswa* read *alswa.* *L.* 26. *Aemelia*, a vestal virgin, who, when the sacred fire was on one occasion extinguished, prayed for assistance, and miraculously rekindled it by throwing a piece of her garment upon the extinct embers. *L.* 28. *Troilus and Cressida*—Troilus, youngest son of Priam, King of Troy, and Cressida or Cryseyde, daughter of Calchas, priest of Apollo. The tale of their loves and tragic fate during the siege of Troy forms the subject of the Troylus and Crysyde of Chaucer, and the well-known Troilus and Cressida of Shakespeare.

P. 23, *l.* 1. *Paris and plesand Helena.*—Paris, the second son of Priam, famous for his abduction of Helena, wife of Menelaus, King of Sparta. *L.* 2. *Lucrece.*—Lucretia, wife of L. Tarquinius Collatinus, whose rape by Sex. Tarquinius led to the dethronement of Tarquinius Superbus and the establishment of the Roman Republic. *L.* 2. *Penelope*, wife of Ulysses, King of Ithaca, who, during the absence of her husband during the Trojan war, was so importuned by numerous suitors, that she deceived them by declaring that she must finish the weaving of a large robe for her aged father-in-law, Laertes, before she could make up her mind. *L.* 3. *Piramus and wobegone Thisbe.*—Thisbe, a beautiful Babylonian maiden, beloved by Pyramus, but whose parents would not sanction their marriage. They agreed to meet at the tomb of Minus. Thisbe arriving first, perceived a lioness tearing in pieces an ox, and took to flight. Pyramus following, found her garment covered with blood, and thinking she had been murdered, killed himself under a mulberry tree, the fruit of which henceforth was red as blood. Thisbe afterwards finding the body of her lover, likewise killed herself. *L.* 4. *Progne.* — Procne, a nymph changed into a swallow. *L.* 4. *Philomena.*—Probably Philomela is here referred to, a daughter of King Pandion in Attica, who, being dishonoured by her brother-in-law, Toreus, was metamorphosed into a nightingale. *L.* 6. *Ceix with the kind Alcyon.*—Ceyx, son of Lucifer; Alcyone, daughter of Æolus. Their story is told in Ovid, Metam. xi., 410. *L.* 9. *Phillis, and her lufe Demophoon.*—Phyllis, daughter of the Thracian king, Sithon, put an end to her life, thinking herself forgotten by Demophoon, son of Theseus and Phædra, who accompanied the Greeks against Troy.

L. 11. *Paris and Veane.*—The title of a celebrated mediæval romance, translated from the Provençal. One of the earliest French translations is entitled, "Histoire du tres vaillant Cheualier Paris et de la belle Vienne, fille du Dauphin, 1487." It was translated into English and printed by Caxton. *L.* 12. *Phedra*, daughter of Minos and wife of *Theseus*, King of Athens, celebrated for destroying robbers and monsters. *Ariadne*, daughter of Minos, King of Crete, who fell in love with Theseus, and gave him the means by which he found his way out of the Labyrinth. *L.* 13. *Ipomedon.*—Hippomedon, a Spartan. He was set aside from the crown of Sparta, and Lycurgus chosen in his stead. His life forms the subject of some of the old Romances. See *Weber's Metrical Romances*, vol. ii. *L.* 14. *Assueir.*—Ahasuerus, King of Persia, referred to in the Book of Esther. *Hester.*—Esther. *L.* 15. *Dalida.*—Delilah, who betrayed Samson. Chaucer also calls her Dalida. *L.* 16. *Deianeira*, wife of Hercules, who unwittingly caused his death, and afterwards hung herself. *L.* 17. *Biblis.*—Her story will be found in Ovid's Metamorph., B. 9. *L.* 18. *Ypsiphile.*—Hypsiphile, daughter of Thoas, King of Lemnos. She saved her father and concealed him, when the women of Lemnos killed all the men in the island. *L.* 19. *Tristram.*—A British legendary hero, son of Roland Rise, Lord of Ermonie, celebrated for his prowess and fatal passion for Ysonde, or Ysolt, an Irish princess, and wife of Mark, King of Cornwall. *Helcana.*—Elkanah, the father of the prophet Samuel. *Anna.*—Hannah, mother of the prophet Samuel. *L.* 21. *Iole*, daughter of Eurytus, King of Œchalia, in Thessaly. She was the last beloved of Hercules. To divert his affection from her, Deianeira sent him the white garment which she steeped in the preparation made from the blood of Nessus. This occasioned those sufferings which were ended by the translation of the hero to heaven. *Alcest.*—Alcestis or Alceste, the fairest of the daughters of Pelias, King of Iolcus. She was celebrated for having devoted herself to death to save the life of her husband, Admetus, King of Pheræ, in Thessaly. An extant drama of Euripides, "The Alcestis," is founded on this incident. *Ixion*, King of the Lapithæ, invited by Jupiter to his table, but afterwards chained by Hermes to a fiery wheel, which rolled perpetually in the air or in the lower world. *L.* 22. *Gressilida.*—Griselda, heroine of the 10th novel of the 10th day of Boccaccio. She was the daughter of a poor man, and was married to the Marquess of Saluzzo. After a long period of ill-treatment, which she bore with patience, she was at length restored to her husband's favour. *See* Chaucer's "Clerkes Tale." *L.* 23. *Narcisus.*—Pinkerton reads Hyacinthus, who was slain by a stone or quoit thrown by Apollo. *L.* 26, *with hart immutabill;* L. Ed., *with fyrm hart.*

P. 24, *l.* 14. The ballad that here begins has ten lines in the stanza, as has also the ballad beginning on *p.* 39, *l.* 21. *L.* 20, *involupit in syte;* L. Ed., *innolnit in dispyte.*

P. 25, *l.* 28, *girnand;* L. Ed., *grinand.*

P. 26, *l.* 4, *skrymmorie fery.*—The fairy called Skrymmorie. According to Jamieson, skrymmorie is a designation of Gothic origin. Sibbald renders it "frightful, filling with terror," viewing it as an adjective. But it seems rather, he thinks, an appellative, allied to Su. G., *skraem-a*, to frighten, and a variety of other terms. *Skrymma* is a verb, used to denote the appearance of spectres. Hence *skrymel* signifies both a spectre and an idol. It is probably from O. N. *Skumari*, a vapourer. *L.* 5. *Chyppynutie*, another mischievous spirit; probably one of those who fatally wounded the cattle that were believed to be elf-shot—Meso-Gothic, *kaupat-jan*, to strike, and *not*, *naut*, an ox. (Jam.) *L.* 16. *Varius.*—Q. Varius Hydrida, a tribune of the people, B.C. 90, who obtained considerable power by his eloquence. In his tribuneship he brought forward a law to punish all those who had assisted or advised the Socii to take up arms against the Roman people. He was condemned under his own law, and put to death. *L.* 25, *cald as a key.*—Key-cold occurs in Shakespeare, Rich. III., i. 2.

P. 27, *l.* 10, for *be*, read *me*. *L.* 15, *pleis it;* L. Ed., *plesyt.*

P. 28, *l.* 11, *yit;* L. Ed., *ye*. *L.* 14, *disturbis;* L. Ed., *distrublis.*

P. 29, *l.* 4, *to die;* L. Ed., *to be*. *L.* 13, *Acteon*, son of Aristæus and Autonoë, a daughter of Cadmus. After being trained to hunting by the centaur Chiron, he was torn in pieces by his own 50 hounds on Mount Cithaeron. *L.* 15. *Yo.*—Io, daughter of Inachus, loved by Jupiter, by whom she was metamorphosed into a white cow. *L.* 22. *Lycaon*, son of Pelasgus, and King of Arcadia, who, when sacrificing a child on the altar of Jupiter, was changed into a wolf. *L.* 24, *sojurne;* L. Ed., *sudiourn.*

P. 30, *l.* 2, is an old proverb; "Be warned in time by others' harm, and you shall do full well," is the form in which it appears in the "Ingoldsby Legends," *Misadventures at Margate.*

P. 31, *l.* 8, *intercessioun;* L. Ed., *intercion.*

P. 32, *l.* 9, omitted in Ed. Ed., supplied from L. Ed. *L.* 10, *held the measure;* L. Ed., *held measure*. *L.* 14. *Phillis.*—(*See* note to *p.* 23, *l.* 9.) *L.* 18. *Acontius*, a beautiful youth of the isle of Ceos. He fell in love with Cydippe, daughter of a noble Athenian, and at last married her through the interposition of Diana.—*Ovid, Heroid.* 20, 21. *L.* 21, *thay ladyis;* L. Ed., *thair layis.* *L.* 22, *na way compeir;* L. Ed., *na compeir.* *L.* 29, *into my greit pine;* L. Ed., *in my gastly pyne.*

P. 33, *l.* 2, *thair gait;* L. Ed., *the gate*. *L.* 6, *knawledge;* L. Ed., *knawledgis.* *L.* 8, *court;* L. Ed., *rout:* *or meit;* L. Ed., *our mate*. *L.* 12, *storeis;* L. Ed., *historyis.* *L.* 27, *Thespis.*—Dr Irving thinks Douglas wrote *Thespia.* *the mother of the musis nine;* L. Ed., *the morthyr of musis nyne.*

P. 34, *l.* 4, for *third*, read *thrid*. *L.* 15, *the aucht sister with croun;* L. Ed., *the aucht and sistir schene.* *L.* 20, *hir vertewis;* L. Ed., *the vertuys.* *L.* 28. *And fair ladyis;* L. Ed., *and Phance.*

P. 35, *l.* 1, *Saturee*—Satyrs. *L.* 2, *Aones*—Nymphs of the shore. *Napee*, ναπαῖαι, nymphs of forests, groves and glens. *L.* 9, *spreit;* L. Ed. *brest.* *L.* 10, *behalding;* L. Ed., *behaldand.* *L.* 14. *Greik;* L. Ed., *Grew.* *L.* 18. *Dictes and Dares.* Dictys Cretensis and Dares Phrygius, two authors whose works on the history of the Trojan war are usually printed together. *L.* 21. *Flaccus Valeriane*—Valerius Flaccus, author of the heroic poem in eight books on the Argonautic expedition. *L.* 22. *Allane*—probably Alanus de Insulis or of Lille, known also by the name of the Universal Doctor, a writer of much celebrity in the middle ages. He was for some time Prior of Canterbury, and died in the year 1202. *L.* 23. *Gaultier*—Philippe Gualtier de Chatillon, a native of Lille and a canon of Tournay, flourished about the year 1200. His principal work is a poem on the exploits of Alexander the Great, entitled "Alexandreidos libri decem," printed at Strasbourg in 1513. "Gualtier's poem," says Dr. Irving, written in hexameter verse, must be regarded as a very elegant relique of that barbarous age; and it had attained to such popularity in the course of the 13th century that it was read in the grammar schools, to the exclusion of more classical productions. The fifth book contains a verse which is frequently quoted, and which it is probable that few of those by whom it is quoted can refer to its proper author:—

"Incidis in Scyllam cupiens vitare Carybdin."

Hist. of Scottish Poetry, p. 271.

L. 27. *Stace*—Papinius Statius, a Latin poet. The Thebais alluded to in the text is by this author. *L.* 28. *Faustus*—an ecclesiastical writer who flourished during the latter part of the 5th century. *Laurence of the Vale*—Laurentius, or Lorenzo Valla, a distinguished scholar of the 15th century, who died at Rome in 1457.

P. 36, *l.* 1. *Pomponius*—probably Pomponius Laetus, who obtained a high reputation while he filled a Professor's chair at Rome, but who ended his days in an hospital. *L.* 5. *Brunell*—The Brunell here mentioned Dr Irving thinks not the name of a poet, but the title of a poem. Brunellus is the name of the ass which makes the principal figure in the satirical composition otherwise called *Speculum Stultorum.* The author was Nigellus Wireker, a monk and precentor of the Church of Canterbury, who flourished during the reigns of Henry the Second and Richard the First. The precentor's poem, which is written in elegiac verse, is by no means despicable for the age in which it was produced. Among other proofs of its popularity it is familiarly quoted by Chaucer :—

> I have wel red in Dan Burnel the asse
> Among his vers, how that ther was a cok,
> That, for a preostes sone yave him a knok
> Upon his leg while he was yonge and nice,
> He made him for to lese his benefice.
>
> *Cant. Tales,* v. 15,318.

Claudius—Claudius Claudianus. *Bocchas*—Giovanni Boccaccio, the celebrated author of the Decameron. His great work on mythology, called a Genealogy of the Gods, seems to have been carefully studied by Douglas, who refers to it in his Prologues to Virgil. *L.* 8. *Brutus Albyon*—Brutus or Brut, a legendary hero, the great grandson of Æneas the Trojan, and the son of Æneas Sylvius. Having accidentally killed his father, and in consequence left his native country, he, after many combats with the giants in Albion, or Britain, conquered the whole island. His adventures form the subject of an Anglo-Norman metrical chronicle, entitled Le Roman de Brut. *L.* 9. *Chauceir*—The works of Chaucer and Gower were familiar to old Scottish poets. James I. calls the former his dear Master, and Douglas, in the Prologue of the first Book of Virgil, calls him " principal poet but peir." *L.* 11. *Lydgate*—John

Lydgate, a monk of the Benedictine Abbey of Bury St Edmunds, an early English poet who flourished in the beginning of the 15th century. His most esteemed works are the histories of Thebes and Troy. *L.* 13. *Kennedie*—Walter Kennedy, a native of Carrick in Ayrshire, celebrated in the poem called "The flyting of Dunbar and Kennedy." He is described by Lyndsay, as well as Douglas, as one of the greatest poets of Scotland. With the exception, however, of his invectives against Dunbar, and two short poems, "The prais of Age" and one against "Mouth thankless," there are none of his works extant by which his merits as a poet can be estimated. *Dunbar*—the most eminent of the early Scottish poets, born about the middle of the 15th century, and one of Douglas' contemporaries. The time of his death is uncertain, but supposed to have been about 1530. *Quintine*—The poet here described with a velvet cap or *huttock* is Quintin Shaw, and is referred to by Lindsay as a man of eminence. Only one of his poems is known to be extant, "Advice to a courtier," and is printed from the Maitland MS. in Pinkerton's "Ancient Scottish Poems," vol. i., p. 133.

P. 37 *l.* 1, *may not heir;* L. Ed., *may as here.* *L.* 12, *relanie;* L. Ed., *wallaway.* *L.* 13, *our;* L. Ed., *my.* *L.* 16, *rebald;* L. Ed., *rebell.* *L.* 21, *To sic as he to mak conter pleid;* L. Ed., *All out than wes his sclander or sich plede.* *L.* 22, *honour;* L. Ed., *renoun.*

P. 38, *l.* 18, *ane vennome is rather and a serpent fell;* L. Ed., *wo woman is rather a serpent fell.* *L.* 25, *said to Venus tho.* Sic in Edin. Ed., but *to* should be omitted. Pink. reads—*said to hir Venus tho.*

P. 39, *l.* 10, *relenit;* L. Ed., *releschit.* *L.* 28, *but dispair;* L. Ed., *lait and air.*

P. 40, *l.* 2, *In lestand blis to remain and repair;* L. Ed., *Quhair thou in ioy and plesance may repair;* *L.* 15, *perfite amouris.* L. Ed., *purifyit.* *L.* 18, *guerdoun;* L. Ed., *guard.* *L.* 21, supplied from the L. Ed., omitted in Edin. Ed. *L.* 26, *companioun.* L. Ed., *campion.*

P. 41, *l.* 19, *wend;* L. Ed., *passe.*

P. 42, *l.* 9. *Almane*—Germany, Fr. *Allemagne.* *L.* 15, *Alpheus by Pyes.* Douglas here has fallen into some confusion, probably occasioned by Virgil giving the epithet of Alpheæ to the Etruscan city Pisæ, because it was said to have been founded by colonists from Pisae, in Elis. Alpheus is spoken of by Douglas as an Italian river, near Pyes or Pisa, whereas it is the chief river of the Peloponnesus, and falls into the Ionian sea.

P. 43, *l.* 1, *Heliseus*—The prophet Elijah. His connection with the Carmelites, to which reference is made in the text, arose from the dedication to the Virgin of a chapel on the spot from which Elijah saw the cloud (a type of the Virgin) rise out of the sea. Other legends trace the origin of the order to the prophet himself, as the head of a society of Anchorites, inhabiting Carmel. *L.* 3, *Amazon*—The Amazonian mountains mentioned by Pliny, are situated in Pontus, the modern Trebizond, and Siwas. These mountains are believed to be the modern Magon Dagh. *L.* 4, *Termodgon*—Thermodon, now Thermeh, a river of Pontus, having its source in the Amazonian mountains. *L.* 5, *Mynas*—Probably Maenalus (Μαίναλος) a mountain in Arcadia. *L.* 9. *Melas*—Probably a river of Phthiotis, in Thessaly; there were many rivers of this name. *L.* 11, *Thanas*—The river Tanais or Don, the boundary between Europe and Asia. *L.* 12, *Sparthiades*—Probably Spercheius, a river of Thessaly. *L.* 13, *Achicorontes*—The Orontes, the chief river of Syria. *L.* 23, *Modan*—Native city of the Maccabees; so lofty as to be conspicuous from the Mediterranean Sea. 1 Macc. ii. 1. *L.* 29, *Caballine*—Pinkerton here reads *Castaline.*

P. 44, line 16, *stanery;* L. Ed., *sterny; stanery greis*—gravelly steps, a pretty expression for a rough stream-bed. *L.* 13, *ladyis;* L. Ed., *musis.*

P. 45, *l.* 14, *deissis;* L. Ed., *deace.* *L.* 15, *ypocras*—a drink composed usually of red wine, but sometimes white, with the addition of sugar and spices. It is not improbable that it was so called from the circumstance of its being strained; the woollen bag used for that purpose being called by the apothecaries *Hippocrates's sleeve.* It was a very favourite beverage, and usually given at weddings.

P. 46, *l.* 4, *Theseus*—the great legendary hero of the Athenians, who conquered Hippolyte, Queen of the Amazons. He also slew the Minotaur and carried off Helen. *schew*; L. Ed., *tohl.* *L.* 7, *Perseus*—son of Zeus and Danaë, celebrated for his cutting off the head of the Gorgon Medusa. *L.* 13, *Yssacone*—Aesacus, a son of Priam, who for grief at the death of the nymph Hesperia threw himself from a precipice overlooking the sea, but before reaching the water was transformed into a cormorant. *L.* 18, *Cygnus*—a son of Poseidon or Neptune. He assisted the Trojans against the Greeks, but was slain by Achilles. As he could not be killed with iron, Achilles strangled him with a thong of his helmet.

P. 47, *l.* 7, *Daphnis and Corydone*—Daphnis, a Sicilian hero, to whom the invention of bucolic poetry is ascribed. He was the favourite of Apollo or Corydus. *L.* 9, *Parmeno, Thrason and wise Gnatone*—characters in the Eunuchus of Terence. *L.* 13, *Poggius*—Poggio Bracciolini born near Florence, about 1380, author of various works, of which the history of Florence is the most important. He died in 1459. His literary quarrel with Laurentius Valla was maintained on both sides with the utmost license of calumnious abuse.

P. 52, *l.* 13, *perrellous place*; L. Ed., *peralus palyce.* *L.* 16, *weir*; L. Ed., *were.*

P. 53, *l.* 9, *that*; L. Ed., *tha*, correctly.

P. 55, *l.* 21, *Battle mort*—battle to the death. Tournaments in jest often became in earnest, and terminated fatally. *L.* 27, *Bosiliall nor Oliab*—Bezaleel and Aholiab, artificers to whom were confided the design and execution of the works of art required for the tabernacle in the wilderness. Exodus xxx. 1-6.

P. 56, *l.* 3, *Darius sepulture*—Darius I., king of Persia, caused a celebrated tomb to be constructed for himself. He died 485 B.C. *L.* 19, L. Ed. reads, *Twelf amarant stagis stude, twelf grene precious greis.*

P. 57, *l.* 11. *Canace*—Daughter of Æolus, King of the winds. Ovid, Heroides, Ep. xi.

P. 58, *l.* 10, *duke Sangor*—Shamgar. see Judges iii. 31. *L.* 23, *Banayas*—See 2 Sam. xxxiii. 20.

P. 59, *l.* 19, *Raphael*—see Apocrypha, Tobit, chap. iii. *L.* 24. *Judith*—Apoc., Judith, chap. xiii.

P. 60, *l.* 3, *tyrantie he Jowrie all;* L. Ed., *tyrand lyk all Jowrye he.* *L.* 10, *Tydeus*—a notice of Tydeus is given in "The storie of Thebes," by John Lydgate, with which Douglas would no doubt be familiar. See Skeat's "Specimens of Early English," p. 30. *L.* 26, *Pirithous*—a son of Ixion, by Dia of Larissa, in Thessaly. He was one of the Lapithæ. When he was celebrating his marriage with Hippodameia, the intoxicated Centaur Eurytion carried her off, which occasioned the celebrated fight between the Centaurs and the Lapithæ.

P. 61. *l.* 2, *Ixiona*—for Hesione, a daughter of Laomedon, King of Troy, and sister of Priam. She was saved by Hercules from being devoured by a sea monster, and given by him as a slave to Telemon.

P. 63, *l.* 19, *Marcus Regulus*—the story of Regulus and his cruel death, inflicted by the Carthaginians, is one of the most celebrated events in the annals of Rome. *L.* 23, *Tullus Servilius*—probably Servius Tullus, the sixth king of Rome, celebrated for the new constitution which he gave to the Roman state. *L.* 24, *Marcus Curtius;* L. Ed., *Quincyus*—the hero of one of the Roman traditions, who, when the earth in the Forum gave way, and when the aruspices declared that the chasm could not be filled up except by throwing into it that on which Rome's greatness was to be based, came forward, and after stating that Rome possessed no greater treasure than a

Roman citizen in arms, offered himself as the victim demanded. He then leaped into the abyss, and the earth closed over him. *L. 28. enarmit* an error in both L. and Ed. editions for *enarmit.*

P. 64, l. 24. The falcounis for the reuere at thair gate— Hawking at the river was a favourite diversion in the ancient times. It is related of Edward the Third by Froissart, that "the kynge had a xxx. faukoners a horsback with haukes, and a lx. couple of houndes, and as

many greyhoundes; so that nere euery day ether they hunted or hauked at the ryuer, as it pleased hym" (vol. i. pp. 210). See also Doug. Works, vol. ii., p. 220. The woodcut here introduced is from "The Book of Hauking, huntyng, and fysshyng," printed by Copland about the same time as his edition of Douglas' Virgil, and gives a representation of a hawking party of the period.

L. 25, *Newand;* L. Ed., *Mewand*; *newand* probably, for *noyand*, annoying.

P. 65, *ll.* 2-11. The whole stanza is omitted in London Ed., probably, says Pinkerton, because the editor could make nothing of the strange names. *L.* 3, *Raf Coilyear*—an ancient poetical tale, the title of which is, "The taill of Rauf Coilyear, how he harbreit king Charlis." It and the tale of John the Reeve were very popular in Scotland at an early period, and are referred to in Dunbar's poems addressed to king James IV. A unique copy of the first of these tales exists in the Advocates' Library, and was reprinted in Laing's "Early Poetry of Scotland," in 1822. It is very amusing. *L.* 4, *Johne the Reif*—in his "Border Minstrelsy" Sir W. Scott states that "John the Reif is mentioned by Dunbar in one of his poems, where he styles mean persons,

Kyne of Rauf Colyard, and Johne the Reif.

They seem to have been robbers; Lord Hailes conjectures John the Reif to be the same with Johnie Armstrong; but surely not with his usual accuracy; for the 'Palice of Honour' was printed twenty-eight years before Johnie's execution. John the Reif is mentioned by Lindesay, in his tragedy of 'Cardinal Beatoun.'—

—— disagysit, like John the Raif, he geid."*

It is, however, the title of an ancient popular ballad, which, in 1868, was for the first time printed from Bishop Percy's folio MS. of Ballads and Romances, vol. ii., p. 550. It represents an incident that took place in the days of King Edward, how John the Reeve, a bondsman, entertained the King, (who had got separated from his suite) without being aware of the quality of his guest. *Cowkewyis sow*—A singular poem, composed after the time of Chaucer, of which the author's name is unknown.

* Vol. i. p. 20.

"A merry man," says Dr Irving, "named Colkelbie or Cockelbie had a black sow, which he sold for the reasonable sum of threepence; and a detail of the various effects connected with the disbursement of this sum constitute the substance of the poem. It throws much light on the manners and rustic festivities of the Scottish peasantry at the time it was composed." It is printed from the Bannatyne MS., in Laing's "Early Scottish Poetry," 1822. *L. 5, And how the wran came out of Ailssay*—"The wren," says Sir W. Scott (*Bord. Minstrelsy*, i., p. 20), "I know not why, is often celebrated in Scottish song. The testament of the wren is still sung by the children, beginning—

> The wren she lies in care's nest,
> Wi' meikle dole and pyne."

Ailsa, a rocky isle on the Ayrshire coast. It is about four miles in circumference, and one of the few places frequented by solan geese. The story of the wren that came out of Ailsa, says Dr Irving, was probably contained in some popular poem, in the form of an allegory. *L. 6, Piers Plewman*—the allusion here is to Langland describing Piers Plowman feeding his workmen, whom he does not seem to have overfed. Piers Pl., ed. Skeate, B text, VI. 280-303. *L. 7, Gowmacmorne and Fyn Makcoul*—Douglas here represents Gaul the son of Morni and Fingal, the Ossianic heroes, as of Irish origin. Boyce, a contemporary of Douglas, describes Fynmakcoule as a man seventeen cubits high. "It is said Fynmakcoule the sonne of Coelus, Scottisman, was in thir days ane man of huge statoure, of xvii cubitis of hicht. He was ane gret huntar, and richt terrible, for his huge quantite, to the pepill, of quhome ar mony vulgar fabillis among us nocht unlike to thir fabillis that ar rehersit of King Arthure." (*Boyce by Bellenden*, vol. i., p. 287). *L. 9, Maitland vpon auld Beird Grey* Sir W. Scott, in commenting on this line thinks that it is obviously corrupted; the true reading probably being "with his auld beird gray." In an old ballad the following lines occur:—

> "Of auld Sir Richard of that name,
> We have heard sing and say,
> Of his triumphant nobill fame,
> And of his auld baird gray."
> *Border Minstrelsy*, i. p. 23.

L. 10, *Gilbert with the quhite hand*—One of the companions of Robin Hood, and was likewise famous for his skill in archery. He is thrice mentioned in the "Lytell Jeste of Robin Hood,"—

> Thryes Robin shot about,
> And alway he slist the wand,
> And so dyde good Gylberte
> With the White Hand.

L. 11. *Hay of Nauchtane.* Sir William Hay of Nauchtane was one of the knights who followed the Earl of Mar in 1408, when he fought in Flanders. In Winton's Chronicle the following is one of many allusions to him:—

> Lord of the Nachtane, Schire William,
> Ane honest knycht, and of gud fame,
> A travalit knycht lang before than.
> *Vol. ii., p.* 433.

flew in Madin land—Sir W. Scott thinks this should be read *slew in Madin land;* and that perhaps Madin is a corruption for Maylin, or Milan land. *Bord. Minst.*, vol. i., p. 21. *Madin land*, however, probably means France—the land of Joan of Arc, whose successes against the English were much admired in Scotland. Boyce states that "Jane, the Madin of France, cloithit baith in mannis array and hardyment, came out of Lorine in France, send nocht but speciall favour of God; be quhais hardiment and happy victoryis King Charles recouirit his realme, and ejeckit Inglishmen out of all boundis thairof." *Boyce by Bellenden, vol. ii., p.* 495. *L.* 13, *Benytas, Bongo, and Freir Bacone*—Roger

Bacon, an English Franciscan Monk, was born in 1214. Through his wonderful scientific discoveries he was believed by the vulgar to be a necromancer, and a full account of the prodigious things he did, assisted by Friar Bungey, another conjurer, and the devil, will be found in a tract entitled, "The historie of Friar Bacon," printed in 1652, and reprinted in the "Miscellanea Antiqua Anglicana." 1816.

P. 68, *l.* 20, *list in commit offence*; L. Ed., *lyst committing.*

P. 69, 16, *The spheiris seuin and primum mobile*—The primum mobile was the ninth sphere, the eighth being the sphere of fixed stars. See Chaucer's Astrolabe, ed. Skeat, fig. 10. *L.* 22, *Ursis twane*—Great and little bear. *L.* 23, *The seuin stars*—Called also Charles' Wain, in the tail and back of Ursa Major. *L.* 24, *Ganamedes*—Placed in the Zodiac under the name of Aquarius. *L.* 28, *Driada*; L. Ed., *Dorida.*

P. 70, *l.* 6, *Episciclis*—See Chaucer's Astrolabe, ed. Skeat, p. 84. *L.* 28, *Imperiall*—For empyrean of the coelum empyreum, or fiery heaven. Milton uses the word empyreals, *Par. Lost*, ii. 1047.

P. 71, *l.* 8, *Surelie as me thocht*; L. Ed., *suithla as my thocht.* *L.* 27, *A wretchit*; Ed. Ed., *I wretchit.*

P. 73, *l.* 9, *Thair wyifis*; L. Ed., *ther wyngs.* *L.* 18, *mad hart*; L. Ed., *mait hart.*

P. 75, *l.* 1, *be gane*; L. Ed., *began.* *L.* 9, *can not*; L. Ed., *ma not.* *L.* 27, *nobillis nyne*—Lists of these nine worthies differ. See Shakespeare's *Love's Lab. Lost.*

P. 76, *l.* 8. Pinkerton here remarks that "this account of the persons seen in Honour's court, is far too short, but the poet had forestalled the names in describing other courts."

P. 77, *l.* 18, *flouris*; L. Ed. *colouris.* *L.* 27. Birds growing on trees—the famous story of the barnacles, fully explained in Müller's Lectures on the Science of Language, series 2. See also Mandeville's Description, quoted in Morris' "Specimens of Early English."

P. 79, *l.* 16, *quhome;* L. Ed., *quhan.* *L.* 21. This and the following stanza contain no less than three, and often four internal rimes in every line. Similar stanzas occur in Chaucer.

P. 82. The woodcut here given is from the Edin. Ed. of 1579.

KING HART.

P. clxxii., *l.* 8. Prefixed to Pinkerton's edition of King Hart, in his "Ancient Scotish Poems," there is given an Argument, or Synopsis of the poem, in imitation of the old Scottish language. It is as follows:—

Canto I.

"This Poeme is ane alegorycale representatioun of human lyfe. The hart of man, beand his maist nobil pairt, and the fontane of his lyfe, is heir put for Man in generale; and holdis the cheif place in the poeme, vnder the titel of King Hart. This mysticale king is first representit in the blume of youtheid, with his lustie attendaunts, the atributis or qualities of youthe; Nixt is pictured furthe the Palais of Plesour, neirby the castel of King Hart, with its luvelie habitants. Quene Plesance, with the helpe of hir ladyis assalis King Hart's castel, and takis him, and maist of his servitouris presoneris. Petie at last relessis thame, and thay assailye the Quene Plesance, and vinquus hir and hir ladyis in thair turne. King Hart than weddis Quene Plesance, and solacis himselfe lang in hir delycius castel, to end of this Canto.

Canto II.

So far is Man's dealing with plesour; but now quhan King Hart is past mydeild, cumis anither scene. For Age arryvand at the castel-yet of Quene Plesance, with quham King Hart duellit euir syne his maryage with hir, insistis on admissioun; quhilk he ganis. King Hart takis leif of Youtheid with meikil sorrow. Age is no sooner admittit, than Conscience cumis alsua to the castel, and forcis entraunce. Conscience beginnis to chyde the King, and Wit and Ressoun tak pairt in the communing. After this and uther aventuris, Quene Plesance suddanlie levis the King, and Ressoun and Wisdom persuad King Hart to return to his awin palais: that is quhan Plesour and the Passiounis leve man, Ressoun and Wisdome rendir him his awin maister. After sum uther materis, Decrepitude attakis and mortallie woundis the King quho dies, after making his testament.

P. 85, *l.* 13, *Nocht to layne*—an expression equivalent to "not to lie." It has been misread by Pinkerton.

P. 86, *l.* 9, *First* [*war thair*], &c.—"Among these personifications the reader will find some of a singular hue; such as New-Gate, or New-Way, for Novelty. Waste-good; Want-wit; Night-walk; Dim-sight. But in the course of the poem he will find others still more odd; such as Innocence and Benevolence personified as horses upon which Youthheid and Fresche Delyte ride, (*p.* 91, *l.* 5), and personifications with name and surname so to speak, as Dreid of Disdane; and Wirschip of Weir, or Honour of War; resembling the old surnames John of Dunbar, &c., afterwards shortened into John Dunbar, &c." (Pink.) The words within brackets in this stanza, and throughout the poem, are wanting in the original MS.

P. 87, *l.* 5, *Fiue Seruitouris*—The five senses, viz., seeing—*ane for the day*; hearing—*ane for the nicht*; tasting—*ane to taste*; smelling—*ane for sent*; and feeling—*ane to ken the heit*, &c. See Piers Plowman, B. Text, Passus ix. l. 19. "Of these descriptions," says Pinkerton, "the fourth, or that of smelling, is very ill chosen; as to smell meat is the meanest of all its offices, and by this it is too much confounded with tasting. It is also obscure; *sent*, is evidently *scent;* but *favellis*, or *savellis*, I can find in no glossary, and though the meaning may be guessed, I know not what to make of the word. The passage implies, I imagine, *all savours for to scent*." The word which puzzled Pinkerton is, however, *fovellis*, or as it is spelt in *Richard Coer de Lion*, 1471, *fowayle*, provisions, necessaries.

P. 88, *l.* 13, *or soundlie*—*or* often means ere, and probably may be so read here. *L.* 14, *no wandreth wait*—no danger expect.

P. 90, *l.* 5-7 have a general resemblance to the lines in Chaucer's Knight's Tale :—

> The rude statue of Mars with spere and targe
> So *schyneth* in his white *baner* large
> That all the feeldes glitteren up and down.

P. 91, *l.* 7, *Youthheid raid on Innocence*—See Piers Plowman, Passus, ii. *ll.* 161-190—where a number of allegorical characters are represented as mounting on horses.

P. 92, *l.* 8, *a pane*—Fr. a pèine, scarcely. *L.* 19. *thame sched*—dispersed themselves.

P. 93, *l.* 10, *seinye*—a war cry, "which," says Pinkerton, "was sometimes only the family name, at other times another word or sentence. Thus the war cry of Percy was *Percy!* or *Esperance!*; that of Douglas, *Douglas!* In the very curious and particular account given by Froissart of the Scottish expedition into England, in the beginning of Edward the Third's reign, when William, Earl of Douglas breaks into the English camp at midnight, he exclaims, "Douglas! vous y mourrez tous, larrons Anglois." Thus translated by Lord Berners :—" sodenly he brake into the Englysshe ooste, about mydnyght, criyng Duglas, Duglas, ye shall all dye theues of Inglande: and he slewe, or he seassed ccc. men; some in their beddis, and some skant redy: and he strake his horse with the spurres, and came to the Kyngis owne tent, always criyng Duglas, and strake ii. or iii. cordis of the kyngis tent, and so departed, and in the retret he lost some of his men." (Vol. i. p. 24, ed. 1812).

P. 94, *l.* 22, *The wache horn he blew*—"Horns were formerly used instead of trumpets, and the hero of metrical romances frequently blows his horn. Roland the champion of Charlemagne, blew his horn so loud, says Turpin (cap. 33) that Charles heard it at eight miles distance, though there was a mountain between them; 'sonum tamen Carolus trans montem ultra octo miliaria exaudiverit.' The Scots were particularly famous for their horns. Froissart, in describing the battle of Otterburn, between Percy and Douglas, which he says exceeded for mutual valour any battle that ever was fought in the world, gives a curious description of Scotish horns. He tells, that all the Scotishmen had their horns, which they blew in different notes to the great terror of their foes and encouragement of themselves. The minstrels (menestriers) of their chiefs first sounded, and were followed by all the others. This horrible noise was frequent in their camp all night; and seemed, says he, as if all the devils in hell had been let loose to display their skill in music. Is it from this that the enseinye or war cry is called a *slughorn* by Scottish writers?" (Pink.)

P. 95, *l.* 13, *Discretioun*—Here Discretion seems to answer to *Lyf* in Piers Plowman, B. Text Passus xx., *l.* 151, where Life takes Fortune for his "lemman." *L.* 14, *Lust*—The following is Pinkerton's characteristic note on this passage:—"Nothing so hurts an ancient writer as when a word, quite honest in his day, takes an unseemly meaning with posterity. *Lust* and *lusty* were formerly only *desire* and *desirable*. The *ladle full of love* in this stanza is a figure of speech, for which we will in vain explore Aristotle, Hermogenes, or Quintilian, nay, Apthonius himself. We say *personification*; is not this a *ladelification?* But critics will perhaps call it by the general name of *thingification*, for we find it again, *p.* 118, *l.* 10, *a vessel full of fancy*." *L.* 24, *dungeoun*—The word is used in two senses.

At p. 94, l. 20, it means what we now call a dungeon; but here, and most generally in ancient writers, it means the keep, or chief tower of a castle, where the lord resided. (Pink.) *L.* 27, *lauchan he*—laughing loudly. Pinkerton has altered he into she.

P. 96, *l.* 4, *That wald be in all folk that wer without*—"Does this imply," says Pinkerton, "the idea of some modern, that marriage is all a net; all the fishes that are out want to be in, and all that are in want to be out? The following personifications are very well managed, and such as might have been expected from the author of the admirable prologues to the Books of Virgil." *L.* 6, *Bewtie hir baner beris*—In Piers Plowman Pride bears Antichrist's banner.—Passus xx. *L.* 24, *strang*—Pink. misreads *stang.*

P. 97, *l.* 2, *Ane pallioun*—a cloak; Pink. misread *passion*, and consequently misunderstood the whole stanza. Pallioun, however, generally means a pavilion, but it occurs in Piers Plowman in the same sense as here, in an allusion to Law Sergeants:—

> "Shal no seriaunte for that seruyse wer a selk hone,
> Ne pelour in his *pauylon* for pleding at the barre."
> *Piers Ploughman, C. Text, Pass.* iv., *l.* 451.

P. 98, *l.* 3. *fordwart*—probably contracted from *fordouert*, weary, overworked; or *for-werd*, worn out, A.S. werian, to wear. *L.* 22, *put thairin first thame befoir*—this line has been misread by Pinkerton. *L.* 23. *Out! Harrow!* Chaucer has Out! Harrow and waileway: *Nonne Prest's Tale*, *l.* 559. In Lyndsay's Squire Meldrum the following line occurs—

> "There was nocht els but tak and slaye."

P. 99, *l.* 11. *kowris;* the MS. reads *lowris.*

P. 100, *l.* 9. *deiss*—"This Mr Tyrrwhit has well shewn to be the place at the head of a hall, where the floor was raised higher than the rest, and which was the honourable part; a canopy was frequently spread over it; but it is not the canopy, but the elevated floor that is meant by deis." (Pink.) The dais was originally the canopy, and although afterwards applied to an elevated platform, it was only properly so when that had a canopy superimposed. *L.* 14. *hait burde*—a hot tussle. Pink. thought it meant a warm feast.

P. 101. *l.* 18. *thair out*—out there. See p. 109, l. 16.

P. 104. *l.* 5. *powrit to the pan*—impoverished to the very skull. This passage is misread by Pinkerton. *L.* 10. *His branchis braid out bayr he mony bore.*—Pink. states that this line is unintelligible; the last word, however, is *bore*, not *loir*, as given in his text. *L.* 13. *hairis*—masters; "used by Shakespeare in the Merry Wives of Windsor. It is from the Isl. *here, herra*, dux; and is still used by the Dutch, *Heer, Myn, heer.*" (Pink.) *L.* 18. *Conscience come cryand*—Conscience is a character frequently introduced in Piers Plowman, see B. text xx., 302. *L.* 20. *lurdanis*—On this word Pink. remarks that "it is said to mean Lord Danes, but this may be doubted. Perhaps it is from the same root as lurk, lurch, and other ugly words of similar sound. It is used as an adjective sometimes." The word is of French origin, from *lourdin*—dull, blockish. *Ane lurdane spreit*, occurs in the Maitland 4to MS. *L.* 21. *sum of yow be God*—"The prophane swearing of Conscience is very ludicrous, especially in a poem written by a divine. But the lesser morals are full of fluctuation; Plato swears like a trooper." (Pink.) See note to p. 21, l. 9. *L.* 24, means—"that deserves well to be hanged, drawn and beheaded." "Hanged and to-drawe" is a similar solecism in old romances—"sware he should be hanged and to-drawe 'Launsal.'" (Pink.) *L.* 27. *Sadnes he had*—this line is not very plain in the MS. The meaning seems to be that Conscience had Sadness with him, who had on a cloak for better mumming or acting his part.

P. 105, *l.* 4. *rig-bone*—back-bone. The word is also used in the old English Romances. A knight commonly kills a dragon by cutting him through the rig-bone. (Pink.) *L.* 14. *in ane hirne to hyde*—to hide in a corner. So Piers Plowman, "*All fledden for fere, and flowen into hernes.*" B. ii., l. 233.

P. 106, *l.* 17. *Conscience*—This stanza, in which Conscience, Reason, and Wit now come to King Hart, is not unlike the passage in Piers Plowman, where the King sends Conscience for Reason, while Wisdom and Wit follow them. B. iv., ll. 1-28. *L.* 27. The allegory here, says Pink., shocks the imagination of the reader.

P. 107, *l.* 5, *The King*, &c.—"This conversation between Conscience and the King, in which the latter shews more conscience, I believe, than conscience himself, is highly naif and entertaining." (Pink.) *L.* 26, *the stall is tume*—misread by Pink. *L.* 28, *forsume*—also misread by Pink.

P. 108, *l.* 11. Altered by Pinkerton to, *Thir ar villanus laus*. *L.* 28. *willis wald*—power of will; A.S., *weald.*

P. 109, *l.* 16. *under the luge*—under the lodge, or arbour of leaves. See Isaiah i., 8. Pink. thought that luge here meant the firmament, at which conclusion he arrives in a very easy way—"the Celtic lug, log, is a *place*, whence the Lat. *locus*, and the Scot. *ludge.*" Here, he says, it implies the great place, or firmament.

P. 110, *l.* 6. This line is wanting in the Maitland MS., but has been supplied by Pink.

P. 111, *l.* 24. *the cleir*—the beautiful one; a fine figure very frequent in old English and Scottish poets. We still, remarks Pinkerton, say, *the fair;* but the old poets, *the sad, the good, the free, the hend,* &c.

P. 112, *l.* 2. *Be cunning*—Pink. misreads *Be cuming*. *L.* 8. *mak him fule*—the MS. here *mak reule*—which Pink. has altered.

P. 113, *l.* 11. *cun*—try A. S. *cunnian*.

P. 115, *l.* 12. *As the suld gane*—as should profit thee.

L. 21. *Ware*—this may either be beware! or war; the former is perhaps the best meaning.

P. 116, *l.* 13. *crudgebak*—Eng. crouchback. King Richard III. was from his bodily deformity called a "crocheback," or "crouchback." See Notes and Queries, v. iii., 1851, p. 300. *L.* 16, *But scoup or skift*—not understood by Pinkerton, probably may mean "without scope or shift." *Scoup* may mean escape, O. N. *skopa* to run. *L.* 18, *with mony sow and gyne*—with many a battering ram, and engine. "These," says Pinkerton, "give the whole ancient machinery for attacking fortified places. They shattered the walls with *sows* or battering rams, while they protected the men with *gynes* or engines; and also threw stones from them, as appears from the curious account of the taking of Carlaveroc Castle, in Galloway, by Edward I., in 1300, written in French, and preserved in the British Museum." *L.* 20, much misread by Pinkerton. *L.* 28. The MS. reads *ewill purvayit folk for weir, and* &c.

P. 117, *l.* 3. Not in MS., supplied by Pink. *L.* 6. *had wait*—hold watch. *L.* 10. *barmekin*—"In old English," says Pinkerton, "sometimes *barnekin;* and explained by the authors of a late History of Cumberland and Westmoreland, as 'the outermost fortification of a castle being that where the *barns*, stables, &c., were.' The reader must beware of supposing *barnkin* synonymous with *barbacan*; the latter being a detatched watch tower." The Rev. Mr Skeat thinks the word allied to German *brame*, a brim, or border, verbramen to border, and certainly unconnected with Eng. *barm*, a bosom. It is, however, interesting to remark that while we still hear of 'breast-works' the barmkin or ramparts close to the entrance of an ancient castle are occasionally, in outline, not unlike that of the female bosom. *L.* 11, *Heidwerk, hoist, and parlasy*—Of these three agreeable companions, *heidwerk*, is headach; *heidwerk sekenesse*—Cephalia; *heidwark sufferer, or he that suffryth heedwarke*

—Cephalicus. *Promp. parv. Hoist and parlasy*, cough and palsy. (Pink.) *L.* 28. *mak I my testament*—Pinkerton was of opinion that this testament should have been omitted, as unworthy of the poem, and remarks, in his usual style, that "Jehan de Meune having written his Testament and Codicil at the end of that mass of perfect stupidity 'Le Roman de la Rose,' testaments were written by poets without the help of a notary, down to the sixteenth century. There is a Testament of Creseide ascribed to Chaucer, but really written as Mr Tyrwhit shews, by Robert Henrysoun. Lindsay wrote the Papingo's Testament, which is much in the style of this; and Squire Meldrum's Testament, at the end of his *Historie*, which is the best of the Testaments, and seems truth mingled with fiction, ordering his heart to be carried to the temple of Mars, &c. For these two centuries poets have been modest enough to make no Testaments."

P. 118, *l.* 17, *Rere-Supper*—This word has been misread *Rere supper* by Pinkerton. It is a well known word, and signifies a second supper coming after the first. Pinkerton remarks that "the author seems to have had a singular aversion to this gentleman, who had formerly been called names by Horace. He indeed deserves total neglect and contempt as the enemy both of health and the muses. The legacy is a shocking one, but has a parallel in the complaint of the Papingo."

P. 119, *l.* 2. *the ball*—"The foot ball," says Pinkerton, "and shooting arrows at butts, seem to have been the chief if not the only games of diversion used in the open air by the Scottish gentry in former times. The foot-ball seems to have been played in ancient times with more vigour than now. In the (fol.) Maitland MS. there is this quatrain against it:

"Brissit brawnis, and brokin bains,
Stiff discorde and waistie wanis,

Cruikit in old, syn halt withall,
Thir are the bewteis of the fut-ball."

L. 9. *bening*—benign or gracious. This word, and the rest of the stanza have been much misread by Pinkerton. *L.* 23. *To Vant and Voky*—To Vaunting and Pride. Pinkerton misread *To servant Voky*; and remarks that in Scotland they say a man is *voggy* when he is proud; he does not, however, seem to have understood the line.

P. 120, *l.* 8, *want the heid*—Pinkerton remarks "this is a proper conclusion to this testament, which, to use a vulgarism, has neither head nor tail."

CONSCIENCE.

P. 121, *l.* 16, *this syllab Ens*—Ens in Latin signifies substance, house property, wealth. *L.* 17. means "which, when translated into Scottish, signifies mischievous riches and gear which caused all grace to go hence."

END OF VOLUME I.

TURNBULL AND SPEARS, PRINTERS, EDINBURGH.

www.ingramcontent.com/pod-product-compliance
Lightning Source LLC
Chambersburg PA
CBHW020312240426
43673CB00039B/779
* 9 7 8 3 7 4 3 3 7 3 5 1 8 *